# Cyber Wars

# Cyber Wars

Hacks that shocked
the business world

Charles Arthur

KoganPage

First published in Great Britain and the United States in 2018 by Kogan Page Limited

| | | |
|---|---|---|
| 2nd Floor, 45 Gee Street | c/o Martin P Hill Consulting | 4737/23 Ansari Road |
| London | 122 W 27th St | Daryaganj |
| EC1V 3RS | New York, NY 10001 | New Delhi 110002 |
| United Kingdom | USA | India |

© Charles Arthur 2018

The right of Charles Arthur to be identified as the author of this work has been asserted by him in accordance with the Copyright, Designs and Patents Act 1988.

ISBN     978 0 7494 8200 8
E-ISBN   978 0 7494 8199 5

**British Library Cataloguing-in-Publication Data**

A CIP record for this book is available from the British Library.

**Library of Congress Control Number**

2018013624

Typeset by Integra Software Services, Pondicherry
Print production managed by Jellyfish
Printed and bound in Great Britain by CPI Group (UK) Ltd, Croydon CR0 4YY

# CONTENTS

# Acknowledgements

Once again, credit must go to my publishers Kogan Page. Just as with my previous book *Digital Wars*, they contacted me out of the blue with an idea that I couldn't get out of my head: what about a book about big, important hacks? What could they tell us about hacking and business, and about hackers themselves?

Thanks to Géraldine Collard, who persisted, and Rebecca Bush, who edited, and Anna Moss, who pitched the original idea.

A countback shows me that I've been writing about hackers for about 30 years, and though the stories and methods change a little over the years, their aims (and errors) don't. Thanks to all those who have spoken to me down the years, such as 'Coldfire' in 1995, right up to the folks of LulzSec in 2011 and later, and their would-be successors. It's always fun.

Thanks to Brian Krebs, Graham Cluley, Mikko Hypponen, Troy Hunt, Matt Greene, Matt Tait and other commentators who have advised and provided input and observations, both for this book and over the years. Thanks also to the many people who I can't name who described their experiences at different organizations which were the targets of hacks.

A gigantic thank you to the queen of serendipity Aleks Krotoski, who set me off along a whole line of research and contacts after she called me about a quite different topic.

This book was largely written to the accompaniment of Steely Dan's back catalogue – thanks for everything, Walter Becker; keep going, Donald Fagen – and also Dutch Uncles and Joni Mitchell.

My biggest thanks of course to Jojo and to the children, who tolerated me turning on two-factor authentication for their email and other accounts. I think that's what's called love.

# Introduction: 01
# The cyber wars

Being hacked is embarrassing. To discover that your email or social media account or website has been taken over by someone and used for their own purposes, without your knowledge and certainly without your permission, prompts reactions of horror, outrage, frustration and anger. Your illusion of control was conferred only by knowing a username and password, which have now passed to someone else. It's a challenge to your view of the world. Not only were you not as safe as you thought, but now your privacy has been invaded, and who knows how long it will take to recover that? For the average person and business, being hacked is a shocking, unexpected incursion. It attacks what we think valuable. Yet for hackers, what they do is akin to a game, played with varying levels of professionalism and determination. The very best do it for their country, like athletes competing at the Olympics.

Yet although you value them highly, your individual credentials have almost zero value to criminals and hackers. For example, in March 2017, a hacker using the handle 'SunTzu583' was offering the usernames and passwords for 500,000 Gmail accounts on a dark website for just 0.02198 bitcoins – which at the time translated to $28.24. In effect, every $1 bought 16,667 user ID/password pairs; every cent bought 166 of them. If yours was among them, it was worth about 0.006 of a cent. The only thing cheaper is one of the transistors in a computer's CPU (where the same amount of money buys billions of them).[1]

Barely a week now passes without news of some big hack or other briefly making headline news about millions of credentials being leaked or stolen. It feels like we're awash in hacking.

The original meaning of 'hacker' was 'someone who makes furniture with an axe'. We hack away with a knife at something stubborn – plastic, glue, wood – and try to get it to conform to the shape we desire. To hack is to force, to compel, to oblige a communion, an accommodation between square peg and round hole.[2]

Computer hacking as we know it today is much the same. Though the phrase 'hackers broke in to a computer system' is frequently used, it's not really accurate. Computers do exactly what they are told to do, and they do only what they are programmed to do. When a hacker gets access to a system without the owners' permission, it happens because he (and it is usually a he) has found a way to tell the computer to do something that it is perfectly capable of doing; it's just the owners didn't expect anyone to tell it to do that in that way. 'How is that possible?' is a common exclamation among those discovering an intrusion. But computers don't know about possibility, just as they don't know about intent. All they do is respond.

In its earliest uses among computer programmers, in the 1960s, 'hacking' had much the same meaning as the original word: a 'hack' was a piece of code or a method of getting something done which, while not elegant, did actually work. That meaning is still in use – 'hack days' have become popular methods to try to find quick solutions for puzzling problems in businesses or non-governmental organizations.

There were malicious actors too. Those who broke in to systems were known as 'crackers', and The Jargon File, created in 1975 to offer a glossary of useful words for those trying to understand computer hackers, tried to corral those with bad intent into that definition. It was too late. 'Hackers' had first been used in 1963 to describe people who had messed up the MIT phone system (though the preference might have been to call them 'phreakers' – phone hackers). By 1976 'hacker' had entered the media lexicon to describe someone who broke into computer systems. The journalist Steven Levy tried to turn the tide in 1984 with his book *Hackers*, about 'heroes of the computer revolution' who did good things, but it only made the word better known. Meanwhile, news organizations adopted the unfamiliar word eagerly as stories began to appear about this new world as computers began invading offices, and soon homes.[3]

Despite that, it's easy to think that 'bots', 'malware', 'ransom-ware' and hacker groups only began to be a problem in the past few years, and that the hassle they cause is difficult to stop only because it is all so recent. But that isn't true at all. As is clear, hacking – as in breaking into systems – is many decades old. But more importantly, many of the apparently novel attacks described in this book were outlined in academic research as much as 20 years before, or stem from errors in coding that date back decades. Hacking isn't new, and neither are the techniques being used to carry it out.

For example, the idea of a computer 'virus' – code which could persuade the machine that it ran on to make more copies of that code, so it replicated as a virus does in a cell – was first proposed by John von Neumann, seen by many as the father of the modern computer, in a scientific paper in 1949. But that was theory; find-ing a computer with enough spare power to do so was a different matter. When the PC came along, it created the opportunity to test the idea to its limits. The first self-replicating 'virus' code in 1982, called 'Elk Cloner', targeted the Apple II computer, infect-ing it via the floppy disk that was then needed to load programs. In 1983 a graduate student at the University of California, Fred Cohen, demonstrated the same idea and infected a Unix mainframe computer within five minutes. In 1986 his PhD thesis offered a formal proof of the concept. The same year saw the first PC viruses which couldn't simply be wiped by restarting the machine because they edited parts of the 'Master Boot Record' (read at start-up to instigate essential system programs). In 1988 the first internet 'worm' appeared, and spread from machine to machine by copying itself until it crashed due to an error in its code after infecting about 3 per cent of all connected machines.[4, 5, 6]

The arrival of the PC in businesses and then homes in the 1990s helped create fresh new targets for malicious exploitation. The explosion of the internet also created new ways to reach those targets. Just as building the first ships led to the first shipwreck, so the spread of computing created the opportunity for hackers of every level to discover what they could do.

While the threat of 'hackers' has been around for decades, and the method and avenue of attack have shifted over the years, our understanding of them mostly hasn't, and nor has the average person's understanding of computers – where one of the biggest misconceptions is that eventually, someday, we will have completely secure devices.

The reality is that you can't guarantee that any software which does anything useful can ever be rendered totally secure. Any computing system, whether PC, phone, or dumb device, comprises layers of programs, from the chip's inbuilt methods of addition and subtraction (known as the 'microarchitecture'), to the 'firmware' which coordinates and runs all the pieces of hardware, to the operating system (OS) which sits above the firmware and provides a software layer for interaction, to the applications that run on the OS. Any of those can contain bugs; Intel famously had a bug in the microarchitecture of the first Pentium microprocessor in 1994 which returned wrong answers for certain floating-point calculations. But while the FDIV bug, as it was known, was essentially harmless unless you were building spacecraft whose path would rely on those specific calculations' results, the next bug to be discovered in the Pentium microarchitecture – called F00F – could make the processor halt, regardless of the operating system being used. For a while, it posed a risk to the entire infrastructure of the web, since someone malicious who could get a program to run on a vulnerable machine would be able to turn it off. There wouldn't be any harm done to the data, and nothing would be released; but it would force a restart, which on important servers could be a problem.[7, 8]

F00F turned out to be a risk, but not a calamity. Such dangers lurk everywhere, in every system, like rocks making up the contours of the seabed, and occasionally rising to shipwreck. Hackers are the explorers who find them in the systems that have become crucial in our lives.

Like any dedicated explorers, hackers also know the lore of their craft; they know the history of the great exploits, the people (or at least the pseudonyms) of those who did them, the effects they had, the companies or organizations laid low or embarrassed by their handiwork. 'Right back to the Morris worm in 1988,' one said to me when I interviewed him for this book – correctly citing both the year and name and effects of one of the most famous accidental hacks ever. 'Oh,' he continued, hearing that the TJX hack would be covered, 'that's Albert Gonzalez – he really screwed up, he was doing that stuff while he was meant to be working for the Feds.'

Hackers often talk about the thrill of what they do, of getting carried away with breaking into places where they're not strictly allowed; some go on to discover the very different thrill of acquiring money they haven't strictly (or even approximately) earned. What they tend not to talk about is the paranoia that soon becomes a constant companion; they find themselves worrying about whether, though it's more usually when, their past will catch up with them. Successful hackers have to have started somewhere, and these days nobody can avoid leaving footprints online. Hackers nowadays realize that everything you do can, and perhaps will, be held against you. It didn't matter that in May 2017 the British malware researcher Marcus Hutchins had stopped the Wannacry ransomware from destroying PCs around the world by registering the apparently nonsense web domain name which disabled it; three months later he was arrested by the FBI after he had been to a security conference in the US, and charged with 'creating, developing and selling' malware called Kronos, which stole bank details. (Hutchins pleaded not guilty.) The case seemed to be built on some Internet Relay Chat (IRC) logs showing Hutchins discussing code, and the use in Kronos of some code which he had previously made public. It seems far from the chain of evidence needed for a conviction. Even so, the court appearance was calculated to frighten any would-be hackers: the eminently non-violent Hutchins appeared in a yellow jumpsuit, shackled hand and foot. Governments want us to think that they take hackers and what they do very seriously indeed.

Yet businesses struggle with the responsibility that hacking puts on them. Companies badger us to hand over personal data – names, addresses, phone numbers, transaction details, payment card details – but are prone to overlooking the fact that the internet exposes them to every single person in the world who might have an interest in getting access to that data. Many companies believe the now-ageing aphorism that 'data is the new oil', a potential source of riches. But just as burning oil contributed to global warming, collecting data without care isn't good for business; data isn't just oil, 'it is also the new asbestos,' said Christopher Graham, the UK's Information Commissioner, responsible for policing the data security of organizations in Britain. 'It is a risk, potentially toxic, to the company.'[9]

This book will look at how businesses and individuals have been caught out by the rise of hacking, and the inventiveness and determination that hackers bring to their targets. It ranges across the spectrum: from break-ins which lifted money from ordinary people's credit cards, to silent access to individual political operatives' email accounts, to the subversion of devices which aren't directly controlled by any person, to vicious destruction with political ends that were never publicly acknowledged.

Just as the targets and effects vary broadly, so does the intent of the hackers. It is a spectrum of desire. Those at the lowest level (who are usually the youngest) find pleasure simply in breaking into systems, and seeing what is there. This quickly becomes competitive, and so the next stage is to wage keyboard wars with peers where nothing is at stake except pride. Yet the methods can be brutal in hacking terms, deploying hugely powerful systems to achieve nothing more than what is in effect a playground fight carried out with key strokes. Such tussles can escalate into 'botnets' of thousands of PCs and internet-connected devices being used just to make a point, such as knocking a service offline. But once someone can do that, the temptation to use those skills to go further – to make money – becomes enormous.

Crossing over to hacking for financial gain is a Rubicon. E-commerce relies on credit cards, which have poor security: a 16-digit number, a date and a name often suffice to let you order goods or services. For example, there is a huge trade in Amazon vouchers bought by stolen credit cards, and then sold at a markdown, thus turning a stolen credit card's details into an almost untraceable stream of cash.

The scams become more and more complex, always with the aim for the criminal of leaving the minimum possible audit trail back to them. That's why hackers' early experiences of breaking into systems and later battling rivals are a crucial testing ground. Criminals who can't cover their tracks don't stay criminals for long.

The biggest boost to the illegal business element of hacking has been the rise of bitcoin, which allows the almost anonymous transfer of funds over the internet without requiring either side to know or trust the other. Each bitcoin (or subdivision of one) is in effect a token confirming the answer to a difficult cryptographic calculation. It's purely digital, and can be sent to an internet address, and then laundered into real money. Bitcoin is heaven for hackers seeking to extort without being traced.

But there's another group of hackers who aren't necessarily interested in financial gain. Nation-state hackers – who operate with the backing of their country's government, often well-resourced – have been the stuff of rumour for years. Only in recent years have their activities become more visible. When Google's operations in China were hacked in 2010, the company's chiefs angrily denounced the government there, claiming it had been behind the attack – a conclusion driven by the email accounts that had been targeted, which belonged to political opponents of the administration. (Google withdrew from China as a result.) When Iran's nuclear arms programme stuttered, it turned out that a joint US–Israeli team had built a computer virus, Stuxnet, which infected the computers controlling its uranium separation centrifuges and made them self-destruct.[10]

The idea that hacking could be used by governments for political ends has come into sharper focus. As will become obvious, publicly breaking into the computers of enemy countries to create havoc has become a new weapon of nations.

It's not a cold war. But it's not a hot war either. These are the cyber wars, being fought by individuals, groups and countries against individuals, businesses and other governments – with us somewhere in the middle.

# References

**1** Ashford, W (2017) More than a million Gmail and Yahoo account credentials on sale, *Computer Weekly*, 6 (3). Available from: www.computerweekly.com/news/450414335/More-than-a-million-Gmail-and-Yahoo-account-credentials-on-sale [last accessed 11 December 2017]

**2** 'The Jargon File (version 4.4.7)' (2003) 29 December. Available from: www.catb.org/jargon/html/H/hacker.html

**3** Levy, S (2010) *Hackers: Heroes of the computer revolution: 25th anniversary edition*, O'Reilly Media, Sebastopol

**4** Skrenta, R, Elk Cloner (circa 1982) Available from: www.skrenta.com/cloner

**5** Cohen, F (1986) *Computer Viruses*, a dissertation presented to the Faculty of the Graduate School University of Southern California. Available from: http://all.net/books/Dissertation.pdf [last accessed 11 December 2017]

**6** Spafford, E (1988) *The Internet Worm Program: an analysis*, Purdue University, 8 December. Available from: http://spaf.cerias.purdue.edu/tech-reps/823.pdf

**7** Koncaliev, D (1998) *Bugs in the Intel microprocessors*, Earlham University research. Available from: www.cs.earlham.edu/~dusko/cs63/fdiv.html

**8** Collins, RR (1997) *The Intel Pentium F00F Bug: description and workarounds*, December. Available from: www.rcollins.org/Errata/Dec97/F00FBug.html

**9** Graham, C (2016) Oral evidence: cyber security: protection of personal data online, Culture, Media and Sport Committee, 27 January. Available from: http://data.parliament.uk/writtenevidence/committeeevidence.svc/evidencedocument/culture-media-and-sport-committee/cyber-security-protection-of-personal-data-online/oral/28091.html

**10** Broad, W, Markoff, J and Sanger, DE (2011) Israeli test on worm called crucial in Iran nuclear delay, *New York Times*, 15 January. Available from: www.nytimes.com/2011/01/16/world/middleeast/16stuxnet.html

# Lights out                    02

## Sony Pictures

*Governments love cyberattacks because they're effective,*
*affordable and deniable. A great combination. 'Deniability'*
*is the most important property.*
MIKKO HYPPONEN, chief research officer, F-Secure

24 November 2014 was the Monday before Thanksgiving, one of
the busiest days in the American calendar as everyone tries to get
a week's worth of work done in three days ahead of the nation's
biggest family holiday, which would effectively start on Wednesday
evening. For 6,500 staff at Sony Pictures Entertainment, though, the
short work week was about to get even shorter.

At about 8.15 am, the screens on every working PC went black.
Then they lit up with a red script on a black background – an image file
saying 'Hacked by #GOP' (which turned out to stand for 'Guardians
Of Peace' rather than the Republican Party) – which continued:

> Warning:
> We've already warned you, and this is just a beginning.
> We continue [*sic*] till our request be met.
> We've obtained all your internal data including your secrets and top
> secrets.
> If you don't obey us, we'll release data shown below to the world.
> Determine what you will do till [*sic*] November the 24th, 11:00PM
> (GMT).

The next line said: 'Data Link' followed by links to files on five
different sites, two of them being Sony and Sony Pictures sites,
another in Russia, but all with the same filename – SPEData.zip.

SPE stood for Sony Pictures Entertainment. The copies were identical: three files – a 638Mb text file called LIST1 and a 398Mb text file called LIST2 – which together contained about 37 million different file names – and a 'readme' file with a list of 10 email addresses at disposable domains, urging anyone who wanted access to the data in any of those files to get in touch.

While people looked at the screens, the computers were wiping every single file they held, and then the 'boot' sector that let them start up.

The first the outside world knew of the attacks was via Twitter. The attacker, or attackers, had also taken control of a number of accounts used for promoting Sony films, and on each posted the same message: 'You, the criminals including Michael Lynton' – SPE's chief executive – 'will surely go to hell. Nobody can help you.' An image showed Lynton's head in a dark blue and green nightmarish landscape that looked like something from a cheap game.

The combination of the unsophisticated images and poor English seemed to imply amateurish Anonymous-style hackers, doing it perhaps for a laugh or because of some odd grudge against Lynton. It wasn't the first time SPE had been attacked by hackers, though previously the target had been its gamer network, rather than its internal corporate one. Corporate Twitter accounts getting hacked was nothing new, so that didn't indicate quite how badly amiss things were inside the company.

Lynton, who had arrived as usual not long after 6.00 am, already had some clue of the extent; he had been called by the chief financial officer, David Hendler, and told that there was a hack in progress and that the systems might all have to be shut down to protect their data.[1]

SPE employees from the time say that on arriving at the gates of the 44-acre lot there were no obvious signs of disruption; the security guards only ever looked for an entry badge, rather than requiring a swipe-in. (Turnstiles requiring a swipe were eventually installed, but not until some time after the hack.) Most buildings didn't require swiping in, apart from some areas with sensitive information. 'You could just get up to the chief executive or the head of TV without having to badge into the building,' one recalled to me. (As with all those I contacted who were there, this person preferred to remain anonymous in talking about the experience.)

But once inside, it became clear how awry things were. As each of the 3,500-odd staff arrived they were told, as another explained to me, 'No opening of laptops. No access to anything. I began to walk around and see the – I can't call it mayhem, because it wasn't like that, but we were talking in the hallways, and saying "What do we do?"... You had access to nothing – no calendars, no archives, no online folders, no emails, no email addresses, nothing. You had access to nothing for a very long time.' Staff were told not to connect to the company corporate network, nor to check email, not to turn on their computers, and turn off Wi-Fi on their smartphones. The system running Sony Pictures Entertainment's worldwide network had died. More than 3,000 PCs and 800 servers had been wiped. Backups had been wiped. In Japan, London, New York and the Culver City site in Los Angeles, Sony had an unprecedented problem.

Though it was obvious there had been a hack, Sony's IT department downplayed the seriousness. Sony told staff that it was 'working on an IT issue'. When Amy Pascal, the SPE co-chairman, arrived on the lot that morning she was told that it would be a 'one-day problem'. When the screen message's 11.00 pm GMT deadline – 3.00 pm in Los Angeles – came and went, the notion that it had all been a one-off was strengthened.

But the impact on the company, its staff and its finances would be far-reaching. And Sony would unwittingly become a pawn in a new alignment of the geopolitical balance.

## You've got mail

The story of the hack and Sony's paralysis spread quickly on the first day: some of Sony's own staff posted pictures of their hacked PC screens on social media. Though the pictures were quickly removed, nothing ever vanishes from the internet, and screenshots – with the fateful links to the sites – began to circulate virally. Aware of the depth of the problem, employees were reluctant to talk publicly.

(Many still are; apart from one, all those I spoke to declined to be quoted by name.) Sony's management was struggling to do the simplest tasks. That left the news agenda open to the hackers – except nobody had ever heard of them and had no idea what they wanted until they began emailing journalists on a number of different technology sites, offering leaked data.

The day after the hack, the *Verge*, a technology news site, said that in an email the hackers had told its reporters that 'We Want equality. Sony doesn't. It's an upward battle.' (The choice of words sounds like someone translating towards English; the normal phrase would be 'uphill battle'.) 'Sony doesn't lock their doors, physically, so we worked with other staff with similar interests to get in. Im [*sic*] sorry I can't say more, safety for our team is important.'[2]

Russell Brandom, the *Verge* journalist who sent the enquiry to seven of the email addresses contained in the 'readme' file linked from the hacked PCs' screen, quickly realized that the accounts were open to anyone; you didn't even need a password to access them. That meant anyone could have read the documents and written or read the emails. But the phrase that 'we worked with other staff with similar interests to get in' raised early suspicions the hack was an inside job, or the hackers at least had an accomplice. On Tuesday, the company put out a brief official statement confirming the problem: 'Sony Pictures Entertainment experienced a system disruption, which we are working diligently to resolve.' Sony's executives meanwhile set up a telephone tree, used Gmail accounts, broke out notepads, and called in the cybersecurity company Fireeye – and the FBI.

Even so, as they headed off on Wednesday for the long Thanksgiving weekend, most staff expected everything would be fixed quickly. (The IT department didn't hurry to correct them.) 'It wasn't until Monday or Tuesday of the following week when we realized the extent of it,' one employee later told *Fortune*. 'That's when we got word that it might take weeks to get things back up.'[3]

But as Lynton later recalled, he had realized this by the second day: 'It took me 24 or 36 hours to fully understand this was not something we were going to be able to recover from in the next week or two.' One SPE employee told *Slate* that the initial experience was 'like getting hacked in the early 90s ... The message [on the screens] looked like something out of *Hackers*, the movie. Like, "You've been hacked, bitch!" It was a throwback. Almost cute.' But the staff were discovering how far they had come since the 1990s. Rather than credit cards or tokens, the cafeteria could now only take cash. Voicemail, which relied on the internet-based phone system, didn't work. The phone system still did, but only if you knew the correct extension to dial; the electronic phone directory had been zapped. There was no repository of contracts or film stock. People took to actually talking to each other in corridors.[4, 5]

Then the hackers began doing what hackers usually do – leaking content.

Even if the graphics around the screen that was displayed to would-be users looked amateurish, the method that had been used to penetrate and spread through the network was not. US-CERT, the US's Computer Emergency Readiness Team which evaluates online threats and tries to coordinate responses, later determined that the malware was new, and multi-functional. First it tried to get access to the target computers using the Windows SMB protocol (for providing shared access across a network to printers, ports and particularly files). For this key first step, it simply used a brute-force method, trying huge numbers of username/password combinations until it finally was given access to the network. Then the malware installed itself and deployed its other elements: what CERT called a 'listening implant, backdoor, proxy tool, hard drive destruction tool, and destructive target cleaning tool'. In other words: surveillance, copying and destruction.[6]

The destructive elements were odd inclusions for any sort of malware. In general, hackers don't try to destroy content. They want to capture it, copy it, and (threaten to) spread it. Alternatively, with ransomware they lock it in so you have to pay to get it back.

But the wiped boot sectors and the breadth of spread meant Sony's IT group struggled to get its systems back to work. At the time of the attack there were only 11 people on the cybersecurity team. And the old network was now, in effect, a crime scene, so bringing it back up might wipe important clues about what had happened. Meanwhile there were hundreds of people and contractors who had to be paid. Without the computers normally used by staff to process those payments and receipts, the business could grind to a halt. Accountants always say that the two most dangerous times for any company in financial trouble are Friday afternoon and the last working day of the month, when payrolls come due and huge amounts of cash are needed: if you fall short, the company is at serious risk of going under.

Over the Thanksgiving weekend, the IT team deployed a new email server with duplicate email accounts for the staff. Old BlackBerry smartphones were recovered from storage and pressed into service. But there was still the problem of the enterprise systems which had been wiped. Paper cheque cutters were deployed to help make the payments – but what were people owed? There was no way to access anything that happened before the attack. It was unlike anything the staff had ever experienced. In fact it was unlike anything that most people ever experience.

'My friends were saying things like "Oh God, I heard Sony got hacked," and I told them: you don't understand from the inside what it looks like,' one former employee told me.

> Imagine waking up tomorrow morning, going to your computer and seeing a black screen and knowing that you can no longer get access to what meetings you have that day or coming up, what contacts you have, anything you've done in terms of PowerPoint presentations, contracts you've written, research you've done, anything on a file in a share drive that you thought was safe – even if it was saved in an archive, you no longer have access to it. How would you feel?
>
> Of course you'd go to your backups … except these no longer existed. Any course of action you'd take, now multiply that by two, three, four months… Then what do you do?

People I spoke to praised the chief information officer for motivating people by setting up regular briefings which explained what was and wasn't known, and what could and couldn't be done. Making payroll was critical (remarkably, Sony Pictures didn't miss a single payroll payment); making outside payments was critical; but other business processes faced triage. The sustained effect both of the lack of systems and the pressure to work around them was exhausting.

'This was like a home invasion where after taking the family jewels the hackers set the house ablaze,' observed Tom Kellermann, chief cybersecurity officer at the cybersecurity company Trend Micro.[7]

Because its online backups had been wiped, Sony had to resort to offline backups, usually stored on tape. While more robust, it's much slower to transfer and restore data. And there was also concern that any malware planted by the hackers might have been stored with the backup; simply restoring it might allow them straight back in. Even by the end of December, Fireeye wasn't completely certain that the wiped PCs and network were really clean.

## Inside out

The links that had been in the original image file, being public sites, attracted immediate attention. Reddit, the discussion board which draws millions of readers, fell upon the content of the files (quickly downloaded), and began to tease out the contents. Even the names of the files, without the contents (which would follow in the days to come) were revealing: passwords, salaries, and more.

Most hacks include the stealthy removal of megabytes, often gigabytes, of data. This hack was special: the hackers had taken terabytes – thousands of gigabytes – of data.

On the Wednesday, four links were sent to film filesharing sites. They linked to three as-yet unreleased films – *Fury* (a World War Two film starring Brad Pitt), *Annie* and *Mr Turner* – and the March 2015 film *To Write Love on Her Arms*. They had come from inside Sony; they were the digital files that would be used to create DVDs to send to voters in the Oscars to watch. Most embarrassing was that Sony's own servers had silently been used to 'seed' the films for filesharing.

The choice of films seemed to suggest opportunism rather than planning. While *Fury* would be popular with typical filesharers – young males – the same couldn't be said of the others. Someone who had been searching through Sony's systems trying to find the most potentially popular unreleased films might not bother with anything but *Fury*. (A week after the hack, *Fury* had been downloaded 1.2 million times, while *Annie* had 0.2 million; the others had fewer than 0.2 million in total.)

On 1 December, the Monday after the attack, FBI agents were noticeable on the Sony Pictures lot in Hollywood, interrogating the systems, and holding meetings in which staff were lectured on data security (best practice for passwords, and how to recognize suspicious emails – both of which looked like classic cases of shutting the stable door long after the horse had bolted). 'The FBI will continue to identify, pursue and defeat individuals and groups who pose a threat in cyberspace,' the Bureau said in a statement.[8]

That didn't slow the hackers down. On the same day they released a huge spreadsheet with salaries and home addresses of 6,000 SPE staff, including 17 executives whose annual pay was over $1 million. The careful timing of the leaks, and their detail, pointed to someone, or some group, with a marked dislike of Sony.

The next day, more corporate documents came out – these ones with the personal information about SPE employees, including salaries, names, birthdates and Social Security numbers. The files were posted on Pastebin (a text-pasting site popular with hackers for providing proof of break-ins). Links to them were sent to multiple journalists, who found themselves competing to slog through huge volumes of information for anything incriminating – but not about the hackers; instead, they began examining what had been going on inside Sony, revealing race and gender pay gaps, sexism and executives' dislike of various actors, films and politicians. The hackers didn't have to do the hard work of digging up the dirt. The media did it for them – a pattern that is repeated again and again in hacking incidents.

'The [news] blogs were the ones giving us all the information,' one employee told *Fortune*. 'We got more information from blogs and websites than we did from Michael [Lynton] and Amy [Pascal, SPE's co-chair].'[3]

Sony instituted multiple measures to deal with the human impact, introducing identity theft protection, the FBI lectures, a hotline for staff worried by the data release, counselling, and an insistence at a town hall meeting from Lynton that though 'there is no playbook for us to turn to', 'this won't take us down' – though he wouldn't answer questions.[1]

Externally, there was plenty of criticism for Sony, based on the discoveries inside the leaked files. The login credentials for thousands of computers, social media accounts and web services such as Facebook, YouTube and Twitter were stored in a series of Word documents, Excel spreadsheets, text files and PDFs. The files had convenient names such as 'password list.xls' or 'YouTube login passwords.xslx'. In some cases, password-protected documents included the password in the document name. And the passwords were stored in plain text.

## The hidden fortress

The question was still: how had the hackers done it? As organizations get larger, they generally become easier to hack into. That's a consequence of the spread of systems, and the increasing difficulty of securing the 'attack surface' – the number of devices, operating systems and versions, and programs and apps which are used on a network. One flaw might let an attacker into the network; another might let them gain access to administrative rights on a machine that is otherwise inaccessible from outside; that then lets them make a change internally which provides access to all areas. Hacking is almost always a multi-step process. But the first step is to get in.

Sony Pictures, and Sony in general, was not the computing fortress it might have seemed. The company had become notorious over the years for its struggles with its own corporate structure, where successive chief executives had tried to break down the way that the separate divisions often worked as competing silos and sometimes hobbled rival divisions' ideas if they might hurt their own financial performance.

Sony's Playstation Network (PSN), separate from the Pictures group, had famously been hacked in April 2011, when 77 million accounts were accessed, possibly including their credit card details. In June 2011 the amateur hacking group LulzSec used a simple SQL injection attack on a database to access Sony Pictures' systems, and leaked thousands of personal details – but those were of people who had entered contests with the company, not its employees. 'From a single injection [attack], we accessed EVERYTHING,' wrote the group. 'Why do you put such faith in a company that allows itself to become open to these simple attacks?' And LulzSec got nowhere near as deep into the system as whoever had hacked it now.[9, 10]

When Kazuo Hirai took over at Sony in June 2013, promoted from Sony Computer Entertainment, he inherited a company still infused with a Japanese culture – hierarchical and averse to firing people – which struggled to cope with the modern internet culture that the company was both trying to exploit and, in its computing systems, defend itself against.

Sony had been badly embarrassed by the PSN and LulzSec hacks, and had beefed up its security, moving its cybersecurity monitoring to an in-house team in late 2013. There were 42 firewalls, and a 24-hour online security centre in Washington, DC – though in the shift to the in-house team, the monitoring of one firewall and 148 other bits of kit was lost.

'Security incidents impacting these [overlooked] network or infrastructure devices may not be detected or resolved,' an audit report in 2014 (released with the emails) noted. By 2014, the cyber-security team comprised: three information security analysts, three managers, three directors, one executive director and one senior vice-president, as documents leaked from the hack showed.[11]

Rodolfo Rosini was at Storybrucks, a gaming development company, when he began working with Sony Online, a subsidiary of Sony Pictures. He had 10 years' experience with online security, but now was working on a machine learning and artificial intelligence system which was being integrated into Sony's systems for game playing. As 2014 began:

> we had access to all the [computing] assets and everything; though
> we were an external company, we had computers provided by [Sony]
> connected to the network, we had sony.com email accounts, all that.
> Essentially, the same access as someone on the inside. So I basically had
> the privilege of seeing how information security was handled internally.

Rosini was appalled by what he found. But Rosini felt that little had changed at the company, which in the US came under the umbrella of Sony Pictures Entertainment. '99 per cent of exploits come via PDFs, Flash and Java,' he told me. 'They weren't even updating machines centrally. It was being done at the workstation. And you could run all this stuff [your own programs] locally.' Without central updating, there would be no way to know whether all of your machines were protected from any piece of malware. Allowing programs to run which people might not need or which had security flows increased the 'attack surface'.

He told me that he had tried to feed this information upwards, but been ignored. 'Nobody in this company had ever been fired, ever… there was a lot of incompetent behaviour which was not punished, and people who really couldn't do the job were not pushed out.'

As an example of how easy he found it to route around the security, he installed Dropbox – a file storage program which synchronizes local files on a PC with off-premise cloud storage – on a PC. 'There was a block on the firewall, and I had to bypass it. And I did that in, like, 30 seconds.'

Then in February 2014 he discovered that the entire network map had been published on Pastebin.

Rosini was horrified, and tried to raise his concerns with the IT group:

> I informed the IT manager [of Sony Online] and said, 'Look, someone has accessed your internal network. There is something inside your network that is phoning home and that is mapping your network to the outside world, which means that the network could be compromised.'
>
> And then it turned out IT couldn't really look at Pastebin, because it was blocked for them.

Soon after he received an email from a senior member of the team: 'He basically told me to shut the fuck up. Said in very clear terms that I didn't know what I was talking about. That I had no idea about the back end and the security that they had. That I had no clue.'

Stung, Rosini checked for himself. 'I could download executables' – programs which can then run on a PC – 'I could execute code, I could access all these files and folders, everything.' The key point being that any malware or hacker able to get the same user privilege as him could do the same.

Rosini was still there in November 2014 when the hack occurred. None of the documents he could normally access were in the stash of stolen data. 'They hadn't gone into the subsidiaries.'

Rosini wasn't the only one frustrated by Sony's security. Another former employee called it a 'complete joke', speaking to *Splinter* a week after the hack, saying that reports of security violations had been repeatedly ignored. They cited a case where an online contest had collected personally identifying information, but failed to encrypt it; another where a file server had been hacked because one of the European employees had gone to a cybercafe and logged into the server – and then forgotten to log out, so the person who next sat down there had full access.[12]

Late in 2013 an outside contractor found suspicious traffic on Sony's network; an investigation discovered that gigabytes of data were regularly being encrypted and then copied externally – 'exfiltrated'. The source of the hack never seemed to be identified. The timing, though, is notable because by that time the filming of one particular film – *The Interview* – had been completed.[13]

Sony Pictures was also aware that it was hacked in February 2014. Its head of legal compliance Courtney Schaberg had emailed three colleagues on 12 February, saying that 'regarding the possible hack of an SPE server, at this point it looks like credentials for two external corporate user accounts (rather than admin accounts) for an SPE system may have been obtained by an unauthorized party, who then may have uploaded malware.' Two days later, Schaberg was playing down what had happened: personal data about 759 people 'associated with theaters in Brazil' had been exfiltrated but since there was no legal requirement to notify anyone in Brazil, it wouldn't say anything.[14, 15]

But what might have raised concerns was that the data had been taken from SpiritWORLD, 'a central system for distributing media across the world for Sony Pictures' (according to the company's description).[16]

A hack followed by the upload of malware is exactly how any large-scale exfiltration will be accomplished; rather than repeatedly breaking into the system, hackers find it much simpler and safer just to leave a piece of software running on servers, stealthily gathering data. And this wasn't any old piece of malware. On 10 December, just over two weeks after the hack, the assistant director of the FBI's cyber division told a Senate committee that it would have penetrated 90 per cent of defences.[17]

Instead, the FBI and Fireeye team on the spot concluded that the hackers had stolen the login details of a systems administrator with top-level access to the systems. This was why some whispered about an 'insider' attack. But it was a classic, external hack.

How did they get those details? One suggestion came from Stuart McClure of Cylance. He analysed the emails, and found a number of phishing emails targeting high-level executives which pretended to be from Apple, demanding that users verify their Apple IDs – but Apple doesn't send out such emails. McClure emphasizes that it's speculation. But it might have been a way in.

The November 2014 leaks revealed a deep structural failure at Sony. Plaintext passwords in files called 'Passwords' were the keys to the kingdom; no wonder the hackers had been able to range so widely. Firewalls hadn't helped. Providing easy access to all the passwords certainly hadn't helped. The hackers had achieved god-like status on the network, and soon it was clear that denying Sony's staff access to their network and data was only part of the attack's intent. Another was to embarrass Sony and to lay every-thing bare, to publicize all of the company's most precious secrets: more than 100 terabytes of data, including four not-yet-released films, 30,000 financial documents and internal reports, that master password set, and 170,000 emails – many of the latter containing painfully personal judgements by top executives about actors, other executives, and the quality or otherwise of Sony's own films.

The leaks kept coming – eight tranches in all, containing 38 million files. Emails arrived at specific websites: *Buzzfeed*, the *Daily Beast*, *Gawker*, *Mashable*, *Recode*, the *Verge*, and more, pointing them to the filesharing sites where they would find each successive leak. Sony hired lawyers to send letters to news organizations demanding they destroy the 'Stolen Information' and telling them Sony 'will have no choice but to hold you responsible for any damage or loss arising from such use or dissemination by you'. It didn't stop the stories. American news organizations in particular could largely ignore the threat, because the First Amendment offers broad protections to the press; and it would be almost impossible for Sony to prove that any particular organization's publication of data led to damage or loss.[18]

The revelations in the emails, and the eagerness with which they were written up by news organizations, had a particularly corrosive effect on morale inside the company in the weeks after the hack. 'Some of the emails that came out made you want to crawl under the table,' one former employee told me. And though the internal network was still dead, smartphones worked: 'I remember being in an office with a couple of people and we just kept Googling people's names to see what would come up.' Just as the first reaction to discovering Google Street View is to look at where you live, everyone inside SPE was doing searches against their own names: had they written something that was about to make them notorious? Or, perhaps worse, had someone written something about them? 'You want to work with someone you're inspired by, that you trust, that you're motivated by, that has credibility and treats others with respect, and some of the things that were coming out were horrible,' one person who was there told me. Part of the attraction was the implicit trust that people wrongly put in the security of email – a medium which is not encrypted by default, and where security usually consists of an easily guessed username and a password whose strength is often dubious, especially where people are able to create their own.

'Rule No.1 when I entered the business world was: if you're not comfortable with what you write in an email being on the front page of a newspaper, do not put it on an email,' one of those who went through it told me. Clearly, Sony's executives didn't follow that dictum.

It's a natural outcome of the way that work has evolved: people do 'work' in all sorts of places, fitting in responses to email in the interstices of their lives and travel. Because a smartphone or PC is secure, the natural thinking is that every part of the chain of communication is. It would have been far better for Sony's bosses if they had communicated using a messaging app such as WhatsApp or Signal, which can't be hacked in the same way. For Pascal and Lynton, who often seemed to write their emails on the move – hers are brief, snatched, often with misspellings or oversights ('I'm took tired lets talk I. Am' for 'I'm too tired, let's talk in a.m.'), with 'Sent from my Sony Xperia Z2' appearing again and again – a secure messaging app would have been both an acknowledgement of their mobility and the confidentiality of their discussions.[19]

In fact Sony's lawyers had previously discussed whether they were storing too much email. Leah Weil, SPE's general counsel, had noted earlier in 2014 that while some might need to be retained, 'many can be deleted and I am informed by our IT colleagues that our current use of the email system for virtually everything is not the best way to do this'.[20]

Pascal suffered the most from the email leaks, being revealed making racist jokes about what films Barack Obama might like. In a written apology, she said the emails were 'insensitive and inappropriate but are not an accurate reflection of who I am'. She also apologized in front of a town hall meeting of staff: 'I'm so terribly sorry. All I can really do now is apologize and ask for your forgiveness,' she said. Lynton told people not to read the emails because of their potentially divisive effect internally and externally.[21, 1]

People read them anyway.

'About a month after the hack I definitely went through thinking "Oh my God, this is going to shut this entire business down, this is doomsday, Sony [Pictures] will not survive this,"' a former staffer recalled to me. 'Who would sign a deal with Sony now? From a trust point of view, I certainly wouldn't have.'

Staff, meanwhile, used their smartphones to look for any morsel of information about who was behind the hack. If 'Guardians of Peace' (a fairly standard, if unambitious, name for a group of amateur hackers) wanted money, wouldn't they have issued a blackmail demand? Wouldn't they have sought to deal with the Sony Pictures management, threatening to release emails and other content and demanding a price to be paid in bitcoin which, suitably anonymized and redirected, could have enriched them? Why wipe machines and reduce the company to working on paper and pencil? You'd have to have a gigantic animus against the organization to do that; it wouldn't be a business transaction at all, but one motivated by hate, and the company management would be wary that anyone who would wipe their machines and then ransom the stolen contents would be likely to double-cross them on any deal. The psychology made no sense if the aim was to make money from Sony Pictures.

One theory quickly took hold and was hard to shake: that, as the GOP message to journalists had implied on the second day, the hack was an inside job by someone who was about to be or had recently been fired. 'Everyone was kind of eyeing IT, wondering if one of them had a hand in it,' one staffer told *Slate*.[9]

Whenever a hacking attack occurs, there is a small number of options to explain it. Those behind the hack could be outside or inside the organization; and the motive could be to cause trouble, or to make money, or – much more rarely – to carry out state-sponsored espionage or damage. Each part of this six-way matrix (amateur, mercenary, state; internal or external) also has its own inherent list of motives. By looking at what has been done and how, one can generally figure out the intent, and what sort of actor one is dealing with.

Thus an attack which steals data and threatens to release it unless some sort of ransom is paid – usually, nowadays, in a cryptocurrency – is commercially aligned. One which simply spreads data around or wipes computers is amateurish, perhaps 'hacktivism'. One which silently siphons data and seeks to remain unnoticed is probably commercial or state-sponsored espionage.

This wasn't quite any of those. But Sony and Fireeye soon thought they knew. On 28 November, just four days after the attack, Arik Hesseldahl at the *Recode* tech news website reported that 'Sony and outside security consultants are actively exploring the theory that the hack may have been carried out by third parties operating out of China on North Korea's behalf.' But it was only one of the possible reasons: 'The sources stress that a link to North Korea hasn't been confirmed, but has not been ruled out, either.'[22]

By 3 December, Reuters reported that a 'person familiar with the company investigation' said that the investigators had linked the attack to North Korea based on 'evidence' left behind by the hackers.[23]

Fireeye was also certain that this was no common hack. 'The attack is unprecedented in nature,' Kevin Mandia, its chief operating officer, wrote to Lynton, in an email which was forwarded to staff. 'This was an unparalleled and well-planned crime, carried out by an organized group, for which neither SPE nor other companies could have been fully prepared.' By mid-December, Fireeye was almost certain that North Korea was behind it, because of the similarities in code between that and past hacks in South Korea.[24]

The FBI used its confidential malware warning network to issue a 'flash warning' to cybersecurity officers about the malware it had identified. Though it didn't say it had been found at Sony, the timing and the malware's description as 'destructive' and 'written in Korean' made it obvious. The computers would sleep for two hours, and then shut down, reboot and begin wiping all their files.

Predictably, North Korea denied any involvement. 'Linking the Sony hacking to the DPRK [Democratic People's Republic of Korea] is another fabrication targeting the country,' a North Korean diplomat told *US Voice of America* on 4 December. 'My country publicly declared that it would follow international norms banning hacking and piracy.' But it also called the hack 'a righteous deed'.[25]

On 8 December the 'Guardians of Peace' sent a new email, which went to all SPE's staff: 'Stop immediately showing the movie of terrorism which can break the regional peace and cause the War!' it said.[26]

The focus turned at once towards a film called *The Interview*, due to be released worldwide on 25 December. It was a Seth Rogen schoolboy farce, in which the comparatively new leader of North Korea was lampooned and insulted, and then shown being blown up in cartoonish, grisly detail.

# North by north where?

The idea that North Korea, or hackers loyal to it, might be behind the attack was not at first an idea that many people outside the online security business – nor, particularly, inside it – took seriously. The 'Hermit Kingdom' was the punchline of jokes: for years it had been seen as so backward due to its stringent dictator-communism that the idea it might even have computers seemed bizarre. Certainly, it had a missile programme, and yearned for a nuclear weapon; but that too was portrayed as a quixotic mission by a country which lacked expertise and resources, and was only kept going by funding from China. North Korea was recognized as cruel to its people and to visitors considered to be spying; but beyond its borders, the Western narrative early in the 21st century was that it was all bombast, no bombs.

That began to change in 2011, as the 'Dear Leader' Kim Jong-il, then 70, faded from public view. In January 2009 he had anointed one of his sons, Kim Jong-un, as his successor, and barely been seen since.

On 4 March 2011, there was a DDOS – distributed denial of service, from computers all over the world – attack on South Korea, targeting government websites and the network operated by US forces stationed in the country. Notably, it was set to run for a limited period and then completely wipe the 'bots' – malware-infected computers used to carry out the attack. 'Highly destructive code like this was common with early malware [but] has long since given way to bots that allow for long-term command and control,' commented the security company McAfee in an analysis of the so-called 'Ten Days of Rain'. The logical conclusion was that this wasn't a commercial hacker, because they like to retain infected computers for future use. Another odd point which McAfee noted: the attack came exactly 20 months after a DDOS attack on 4 July 2009, using 150,000 hijacked PCs in South Korea which had in turn attacked about 50 targets in the US and South Korea. Of those targets, 14 were common from 2009 and 2011. 'We believe that there is strong, although circumstantial, evidence to conclude that both attacks had originated from the same adversary,' McAfee's researchers noted.[27]

The timeline of those attacks makes sense if you assume that Kim Jong-un, then barely 30, was getting a team of North Korean state hackers to flex their muscles and put the country on a new footing in the growing international stage of cybersecurity and threats. In 2010 the Stuxnet virus, developed by the US and Israel to target Iran's computer-controlled nuclear centrifuges, had come to international media notice. It wouldn't have escaped North Korea's leadership that its rogue nuclear programme would be an obvious target for a similar cyberattack; developing the capability to fend off and even launch cyberattacks of its own made perfect sense.

# Gross less

Seth Rogen shot to fame with his role as a stoner slacker in the 2007 film *Knocked Up*, and subsequently scored well with goof-ball comedies aimed at young men. He, screenwriter Dan Sterling and Evan Goldberg had been developing *The Interview* since about 2010, starting with the basic idea of a TV chat show host who scores a big interview with a reclusive dictator who is secretly a fan of the show; the host is then recruited by the CIA to kill them. When Kim Jong-un, then 27, took over from Kim Jong-il they figured that the younger leader made the concept attractively plausible. The visit to North Korea by US basketball star Dennis Rodman in February 2013 – Kim Jong-un is believed to be a basketball fan – made the idea even more plausible. In the screenplay, the chat show host and his sidekick discover that people close to Kim hate him and want to kill him, humiliatingly and publicly; after much cartoonish action, they succeed and the DPRK is liberated.

It was standard escapist fare, placed firmly in the teenage boy gross-out genre. When the DPRK's third underground nuclear test in February 2013 put Kim Jong-un in the headlines, the studio saw an opportunity to capitalize on a famous face. The film was greenlit in March 2013 with a $45 million budget.[28]

On 11 June 2014, the day the film's trailer first aired, Rogen tweeted a picture of the film's poster, which had the tagline 'From the western capitalist pigs who brought you *Neighbors* and *This*

*Is The End'*. The North Korean government in Pyongyang wrote angrily to the Secretary-General of the United Nations (of which it has been a member since 1991) calling the film 'undisguised sponsoring of terrorism, as well as an act of war'. A North Korean official added: 'The enemies have gone beyond the tolerance limit in their despicable moves to dare hurt the dignity of the supreme leadership,' which sounded like a line from the film. The complaint went largely unregarded; if anything, it looked like good publicity. North Korea didn't like the film! Haha! Promoters were told to emphasize the idea to audiences that Kim was 'a recluse who can be charming at times as opposed to a person who is simply a dangerous dictator' and to emphasize 'the dictator's bizarre behaviour – he's a young, inexperienced guy with self-esteem and "daddy" issues'.[29, 30, 31]

What they hadn't realized was how different the new leader was from his father. Notably, he was more vicious, quickly moving aside family members and others who might be a threat to his increasingly totalitarian rule. Now a Japanese-owned corporation was making a film poking fun at him; even worse, suggesting his death. 'The equivalent of blasphemous,' says Paul Fischer, a filmmaker who has studied the regime. (Kim Jong-il was fascinated by films.) Would any loyal North Korean allow such blasphemy if they could stop it?

One former employee told me that the idea that North Korea might have been behind the attack, and because of *The Interview*, 'really came out of nowhere', adding that 'I had heard that there were concerns about making the movie … [but] I think it was just that they were afraid that it would cause bad relations with them. I know people had stated concerns over what it would look like to the North Korean government.'

In fact, the film's potential political impact had long been a concern at senior levels. In January 2014 when release dates for *The Interview* were being planned, an early note of caution came from Steven O'Dell, head of international releases: 'I think we NEED to be crazy in this business … but I think a S. Korea release is a bit too crazy … our guys took a real look at it but I think they are just a little too close to the DMZ' [demilitarized zone, which acts as a buffer between the two halves of the country, which are officially still at war]. After viewing an early cut, South Korea's distributors didn't want it: 'there would be a big potential to produce [a] political issue about North Korea'.[32]

Even if some employees – and Rogen – weren't aware of the ramifications of metaphorically tweaking North Korea's nose, those in Sony's headquarters in Japan certainly were. There's a century-long history of military, civilian and diplomatic tensions dating back to Japan's occupation of the country from 1910 to 1945. Japan has long been uneasy about the DPRK's military posture, because it has no formal army and is in missile range of the country.

To Rogen and Franco, looking for some gross-out fun, and seeking to make a point about human rights (and also some money), it might not have looked like an insult for a big Japanese corporation to fund and promote a film suggesting the killing of North Korea's leader. But as the film critic Ann Hornaday noted in the *Washington Post* after the hack, 'All films are political.' Particularly those about politics.[33]

After the trailer's release, Sony had hired Bruce Bennett, a defence analyst at Rand, to review the film and decide what its effect on North Korea might be. (He already thought a real-life assassination could trigger the collapse of the North Korean government.) After North Korea's angry reaction to the trailer, Bennett told Lynton he had spoken to the US's special envoy to the country, which had decided that the threat was 'typical North Korean bullying, likely without follow-up, but you never know with North Korea'. He left a decision in Sony's hands.[34]

Understandably, the equivocation made Lynton wary. On 9 July he emailed Pascal suggesting edits to the scene of Kim's death. 'What we really want is no melting face and actually not seeing him die. A look of horror as the fire approaches is probably what we need.'

Lynton wasn't the only one trying to dial back the gore. During summer 2014 Kazuo Hirai, the chief executive for the entire conglomerate, took the highly unusual step of sending a number of requests for changes to Pascal, who in turn passed them on to Rogen. The latter two tussled back and forth over email for weeks. (Rogen frequently answered Pascal's emails late, because he had switched to Gmail from Yahoo in the summer, but the autocomplete function on Sony executives' phones and PCs kept filling in his old address.) Rogen was frustrated by the pressure from Sony, feeling it was both censorship and appeasement. Making such changes would mean 'it's a compromised product', he told Pascal. But she persisted, and in the end Rogen relented, emailing a promise that 'We will play with the colour of the head chunks to try to make them less gross.'[35, 36]

Yet if North Korea was behind the attack, what did it want? Surely not to pirate copies of a Brad Pitt film. The answer came on 16 December, when the 'Guardians of Peace' dumped 12,466 emails from Michael Lynton's account, covering a six-year period up to November 21 – the Friday before the hack – and then threatened that 'We will clearly show [the remainder of the Christmas gift] to you at the very time and places "The Interview" be shown, including the premiere, how bitter fate those who seek fun in terror should be doomed to.'

It continued that:

> Soon all the world will see what an awful movie Sony Pictures
> Entertainment has made. The world will be full of fear. Remember
> the 11th of September 2001 [the date of the terror attacks on the
> World Trade Center and The Pentagon, usually known as 9/11]. We
> recommend you to keep yourself distant from the places at that time.
> (If your house is nearby, you'd better leave.)[37]

Immediately, the four largest cinema chains in the US announced they wouldn't show the film. Hours later, Sony cancelled its distribution; there was no point sending films to cinemas that weren't going to screen it.

The threat of terrorism on US soil changed the outlook for the spies watching the to-and-fro of the hacking world. The intelligence agencies of the largest countries, and particularly the members of the 'Five Eyes' intelligence sharing group (the US, Canada, UK, New Zealand, and Australia) are frequently aware of who is doing what in the hacking world. It is, after all, their job. That doesn't mean, though, that they will intervene to prevent a hack, nor publicize who was behind it; sometimes it's sufficient to watch who does what, and gather clues in order to pinpoint or forestall the source of future attacks. Intervening can be impossible, and publicizing the source of a hack unambiguously will generally mean revealing a lot more about the capability of their own surveillance techniques than they would like.

The next day, 17 December, a story in the *New York Times* with the roundabout headline 'US Said to Find North Korea Ordered Cyberattack on Sony' quoted 'senior administration officials' who were pointing to North Korea as the source of the hack. Barack Obama's White House was considering what response to make, the story explained, outlining the possible approaches being considered.[38]

Barely three weeks had passed since the hack. Short of delivering a letter, leaking a story to the *New York Times* was the clearest method for the US government to tell North Korea, which monitors US media output closely, that it knew what was going on. One part of the *New York Times* story suggested that the NSA had put 'implants' in the country's computer networks that 'like a radar system, would monitor the development of malware transmitted from the country'.

Mikko Hypponen, chief research officer at Finnish company F-Secure, told me later that 'the reaction from the whole industry, including myself, was really a sense of disbelief when US intelligence [said] they believed this is North Korea almost immediately after the breach'. He pointed to the attack's 'unusual' aggression – 'not just did they delete a lot of data, they leaked employee emails, they leaked employee health records, leaked unreleased movies. And almost immediately, US intelligence says it's the North Koreans because of *the goddamn movie*.' He emphasizes the last three words, his eyes wide behind his round glasses.

'I was dumbfounded,' Hyponnen said:

> How on earth could they know? How could they be so certain that they could make a statement like that, because we all know that one of the main properties of cyberattacks is deniability. Governments love cyberattacks because they're … [he held up three fingers and folded each down in turn] … effective, affordable and deniable. A great combination. 'Deniability' is the most important property.[39]

The point about deniability is one that runs through the diagnosis of all hacking attacks. To the untutored eye, a hacking attack seems simple enough to follow. Computer servers keep logs of what devices they have connected to, and when. (Even your own PC will have a long, endlessly lengthening list of such communications.) Surely all you have to do is look at the logs to find out which machines connected, and when, to find out the culprit?

However, there are two complications. First, if a hacker can break into one machine – the final target – then logically they could do the same to another machine first, and use that for the attack. Worse, if the machine that they have subverted connects via the Tor network, which anonymizes the location of the connecting server, then there is effectively no way of knowing which machine on earth made the first connection.

The second complication is that some hacks bypass the attacked computer's logging systems; in that case, it won't be clear when or where the attack happened. (Often, hackers who get access like this will also wipe the logs to cover their tracks.) Computer forensics on hacking attacks thus has to rely on very different techniques.

Sony cleaned itself up, and got systems back online. But the question of whether it had really been North Korea which carried out the attack still lingered for some people. Within the cybersecurity space, though, the doubts began to vanish.

By the middle of 2017, people had found the fingerprints of the 'Lazarus Group' in multiple attacks. Besides the Sony Pictures hack – now called the 'Sony Wiper' hack – there was a hack in February 2016 of the international SWIFT banking system targeting the Bangladesh central bank (it aimed to steal a billion dollars; it failed after a few million), and in early summer 2017 the 'Wannacry' ransomware which hit millions of systems.

Looking back over past attacks revealed similar fingerprints in the code going back to 2009, before Kim Jong-un took over. However, said Kaspersky, which carried out the analysis, 'their activity spikes starting in 2011', when the number of malware samples leaps from eight in 2010 to 105.[40]

Some of the fingerprints were simple to spot: misspelling 'Mozilla' (the browser) as 'Mozillar'; the reuse of self-deleting scripts; reuse of shared passwords; and a list of virtual machines, commonly used by antivirus researchers, that the malware would watch for and refuse to run in.

This template made it clear that the same group had been behind a March 2013 attack which wiped tens of thousands of PCs at three South Korean broadcasters and two banks. Then, screens on affected computers showed skulls and a message from the 'WhoisTeam', with a message saying it was the beginning of 'our movement'. McAfee also spotted the same group's fingerprints in an analysis of the attack, which it dubbed 'Dark Seoul', and said that 'one of the primary goals of this group was a covert military spying operation that attempted to target military forces in South Korea'. McAfee felt there were two groups at work, based on differences between the content of the malware; but both had the same aims, and suspicious overlaps in timing, method and – wrapping it up – code. Moreover, the element targeting the military, which had been running since 2009, was only aimed at South Korea. And there is only one nation directly concerned with stunting the military power of South Korea. An HP Security Research briefing published in July 2014 – after the trailer, but before the hack – pointed out that in November 2013, Kim Jong-un had referred to cyberwarfare capability as a 'magic weapon' along with nuclear weapons and missiles as part of a plan to ramp up attacks on South Korea.[41, 42, 43]

Within the security world, the linking of those hacks changed minds dramatically. 'This is one of the few cases I know of where there actually is a smoking gun and you actually know for a fact who's doing something,' Hyponnen told me. 'However, it also changed the narrative.' It wasn't just that his thinking had to incorporate the idea that North Korea had the capability to carry out cyberattacks on companies in the US; it was also that the NSA was capable of seeing it happen.

But he is satisfied about the source of the attack. 'Whether it's coming from the government, or some loosely linked group – that's much harder to tell. Inside North Korea, yes.' And once you accept that Sony Pictures was a North Korean hack, then other dominos fall, he explained: 'We have fairly strong links between Sony Pictures and Swift [the banking hack], proving that Swift is fairly likely to be North Korea as well, and if we believe that, then it's fairly likely that Wannacry [the ransomware attack of May 2017] is North Korea as well.' He continued:

Now, every link is a little bit weaker, and these become hard-to-believe cases. Is it really possible that a government is distributing ransomware Trojans to try to steal money? Are we really supposed to believe that? However, that's what it looks like. It's unbelievable, but that's what it looks like. And we have to remember that North Korea is not a normal country. I mean, their governmental money printing presses have been printing fake money for a decade.

Pardon? 'Do a search on "superdollars". North Korea has been printing fake $100 bills for over a decade.' (This is true: the 'super-dollars' got the name because their quality is higher than the original. The purpose is generally to fund overseas operations; debasing the currency would be impossible. Iran has also been accused of doing the same in the past.)

'If a government is so fucked up and is ready to do stuff like that,' says Hyponnen, 'maybe then we can believe that they would be ready to do stuff like Wannacry. With the Swift attack, they tried stealing almost a billion dollars.' That's substantial compared with the country's GDP – estimated at $28 billion in 2016 – and especially its government budget. More importantly, because North Korea runs both a spending and trade deficit but has no access to international debt markets, it needs every possible source of foreign currency. If that includes hacking interbank transfer systems, issuing fake currency or creating a ransomware worm, it all helps. 'It's thinking out of the box,' says Hyponnen. 'How do we fix our budget deficit? Well, I have an idea…'

It's a surprising chain of logic; but, in the words of Sherlock Holmes, once you've removed every other explanation, what remains – however improbable – must be the answer. The Sony Pictures attack doesn't fit into the matrix of budget resolution; but it does fit into the reaction of a proud leader and his concerned subordinates who do not want him to be made a figure of fun on the world stage. In that sense, the Thanksgiving attack is explicable.

Did Sony's executives overlook the threat from North Korea? Building a 'threat model' about the country's new, aggressive leader would have required state-level knowledge about the capabilities of the country's hackers and the changing focus of its leader. After all, there hadn't been a whisper from North Korea in 2013 when the film *Olympus Has Fallen* posited a brutal North Korean terrorist group taking the US president hostage, requiring a *Die Hard*-style rescue by Gerard Butler as a secret service agent. But in retrospect, one can see that dictators and their followers don't mind being portrayed as ruthless. What they can't bear is being portrayed as nincompoops.

## Counting the cost

In the immediate wake of the hack, big numbers were thrown around to estimate its cost. Macquarie Research, a financial research company, estimated that the theft of the five films that were pirated and the losses on the combined film and promotional budgets for *The Interview* would total about $95 million. In mid-December, Jim Lewis, senior fellow at the Center for Strategic and International Studies, suggested that Sony's eventual costs would be $100 million, but that it would take six months to become clear.[44]

On 4 February 2015, Sony published its quarterly results for the quarter including the hack. Its assessment of the cost was nowhere near the numbers Macquarie or Lewis had suggested. Sony put the figure at $15 million for the quarter during which it occurred, and another $20 million for the remainder of the financial year. 'The figure primarily covers costs such as those associated with restoring our financial and IT systems,' said a spokesman for Sony in Tokyo. It suggested the overall effect on the Sony group's results 'will not be material'. The film group was expected to actually increase its operating profits year-on-year by 5 per cent to $460 million, though the disruption had meant it wasn't able to pull together its formal results to the end of December 2014 by that time. In March 2015 it did: revenues and profits at the Pictures division were down, but the impact of the hack amounted to less than 10 per cent of profits.[45, 46]

A few months later, the fiscal full-year results (to the end of March 2015) showed that the problems at the Pictures division – total assigned cost 4.9 billion yen, or about US$41 million – were minimal compared with the costs of withdrawing from the PC business after years of losses, and Sony's struggles in the smartphone business. Those lost US$529 million and $370 million respectively, as well as a $1.5 billion writedown in the value of the mobile phone division. In fact, the film division had done okay: revenues for the year were up 6 per cent, and operating profit up 13 per cent. If the hackers had really wanted to wipe the company out, they had failed.[47]

Those at the top were affected. In February 2015 Amy Pascal stepped down as co-chair of the studio, trailing a jetstream of embarrassing emails whose release detailed just too much of her company's thinking about its male and female stars. She was also left standing when the music stopped: she had approved the making of the film that had so infuriated the North Korean leader. But it wasn't all bad. SPE had a four-year agreement to finance her new production venture with the studio, for which it would retain distribution rights.

Meanwhile, the personal data, including Social Security numbers (essential for identity theft in the US) of about 47,000 staff had been distributed around the net. In September 2015, Sony settled a group of lawsuits brought by employees with a $15 million payment. The total cost had been around $56 million – plus the unquantifiable losses of not showing *The Interview* in more cinemas. It still went to DVD. Some were floated into North Korea on balloons in a publicity stunt.[48]

For Sony Pictures employees, though, the effects were long term. Staff who had been issued with security monitoring for their bank accounts fretted that they might be hacked. 'Do I have to worry about someone getting a random medical procedure with my benefits?' one asked rhetorically in *Fortune*. 'I'm never going to access any of my financial accounts on my work computer ever again.' In future, they told the magazine, they'd use their smartphone or home computer for anything personal: 'It's not worth the risk … you always have to look over your shoulder. This is forever.'

The challenge of having had to work under such conditions had a polarizing effect on staff at all levels, who discovered whether they really were positive, flexible and creative – or not. One told me that the experience was, for some, an ultimate test. The human resources department brought in therapists and counsellors. One ex-employee recalled: 'it taught us that we need to have a little bit of compassion because almost no one was without their little freak-out moments. Something we learned was just to give people the permission to be able to do that.' Typically those moments would be triggered by trying to cope with personal and work challenges, and leave people overwhelmed. 'We learned that okay, that's going to happen, and it kind of happened to everyone on their own time,' they recalled.

Yet perversely, those I spoke to seemed to have been uplifted by the experience. 'I think it was a really good thing to get through as a company, and I learned so much from it,' another told me. 'The company learned from it as well – a lot of valuable lessons that made them better.'

Lynton himself said that the most important lesson he learned was that what mattered was making decisions, not dithering: 'You can't be caught in the headlights doing nothing,' he told the *Wall Street Journal*.[4]

It also reminded people that films aren't just light on a wall, suggested Hornaday in the *Washington Post*, finding a silver lining of sorts: 'As depressing as *The Interview* spectacle has been as political theater, at least it has reinvested otherwise trivial, disposable cultural products with the meaning they've had all along.'[33]

Did the Sony hack achieve North Korea's aims? If one assumes those were simply to stop the widespread release of the film, then yes. But it also tipped off the rest of the world to the country's growing expertise in hacking. However, for a country and a dictator seeking above all to be taken seriously, demonstrating one's power in that way might not after all be the worst outcome.

# References

**1**   Cieply, M and Barnes, B (2014) Sony cyberattack, first a nuisance, swiftly grew into a firestorm, *New York Times*, 30 December. Available from: www.nytimes.com/2014/12/31/business/media/sony-attack-first-a-nuisance-swiftly-grew-into-a-firestorm-.html?_r=0

2   Kastrenakes, J and Brandom, R (2014) Sony Pictures hackers say they want 'equality', worked with staff to break in, TheVerge.com, 25 November. Available from: www.theverge.com/2014/11/25/7281097/sony-pictures-hackers-say-they-want-equality-worked-with-staff-to-break-in

3   Marikar, S (2014) I work at Sony Pictures. This is what it was like after we got hacked, fortune.com, 20 December. Available from: http://fortune.com/2014/12/20/sony-pictures-entertainment-essay/

4   Fritz, B, Yadron, D and Schwartzel, E (2014) Behind the scenes at Sony as hacking crisis unfolded, *Wall Street Journal*, 30 December. Available from: www.wsj.com/articles/behind-the-scenes-at-sony-as-hacking-crisis-unfolded-1419985719

5   Hess, A (2015) Inside the Sony hack, *slate.com*, 22 November. Available from: www.slate.com/articles/technology/users/2015/11/sony_employees_on_the_hack_one_year_later.html

6   Alert (TA14-353A) *Targeted Destructive Malware*, US Computer Emergency Readiness Team, 19 December 2014. Available from: www.us-cert.gov/ncas/alerts/TA14-353A

7   Barnes, B and Perlroth, N (2014) Sony films are pirated, and hackers leak studio salaries, *New York Times*, 2 December. Available from: www.nytimes.com/2014/12/03/business/media/sony-is-again-target-of-hackers.html

8   Bond, P (2014) Sony hack: FBI confirms investigation, *Hollywood Reporter*, 1 December. Available from: www.hollywoodreporter.com/news/sony-hack-fbi-confirms-investigation-753067

9   Finkle, J and Baker, L (2011) Hackers attack another Sony network, post data, 3 June. Available from: http://uk.reuters.com/article/uk-sony/hackers-attack-another-sony-network-post-data-idUKTRE75178X20110603

10  Williams, M (2011) PlayStation network hack will cost Sony $170m, *Computerworld*, 23 May. Available from: www.computerworld.com/article/2508315/computer-hardware/playstation-network-hack-will-cost-sony--170m.html

11  Chmielewski, D and Hesseldahl, A (2014) Sony Pictures knew of gapsin computer network before hack attack, *Recode*, 12 December. Available from: www.recode.net/2014/12/12/11633774/sony-pictures-knew-of-gaps-in-computer-network-before-hack-attack

**12** Hill, K (2014) Sony Pictures hack was a long time coming, say former employees, *Splinter News*, 4 December. Available from: https://splinternews.com/sony-pictures-hack-was-a-long-time-coming-say-former-e-1793844351

**13** Robertson, J and Riley, M (2014) Sony said to learn last year about large network-security breach, *Bloomberg News*, 16 December. Available from: www.bloomberg.com/news/articles/2014-12-16/sony-said-to-learn-last-year-about-large-network-security-breach

**14** Wikileaks Sony emails, *Wikileaks*, 12 February 2014. Available from: https://wikileaks.org/sony/emails/emailid/106672

**15** Wikileaks Sony emails, *Wikileaks*, 14 February 2014. Available from: https://wikileaks.org/sony/emails/emailid/113480

**16** Biddle, S (2014) Sony was hacked in February and chose to stay silent, *Gawker*, 11 December. Available from: http://gawker.com/sony-was-hacked-in-february-and-chose-to-stay-silent-1670025366

**17** *Cybersecurity: Enhancing coordination to protect the financial sector*, US Senate Committee on Banking, Housing & Urban Affairs, hearing on 10 December 2014. Available from: www.banking.senate.gov/public/index.cfm/hearings?ID=1632C6B0-843F-4B9B-9DF2-0A5322324070

**18** Fleming, Jr, M (2014) Read David Boies' legal letter on Sony hack attack coverage, *deadline.com*, 15 December. Available from: http://deadline.com/2014/12/sony-pictures-letter-david-boies-deadline-1201326203/

**19** Wikileaks Sony emails, *Wikileaks*, 23 July 2014. Available from: https://wikileaks.org/sony/emails/emailid/55690

**20** Feinberg, A (2014) Sony Pictures top lawyer's emails exposed in latest leak, *Gizmodo*, 10 December. Available from: https://gizmodo.com/sony-pictures-top-lawyer-s-emails-exposed-in-latest-lea-1669594084

**21** Fleming, Jr, M (2014) Amy Pascal formally apologizes for racially insensitive e-mail, *deadline.com*, 11 December. Available from: http://deadline.com/2014/12/amy-pascal-formally-apologizes-for-racially-insensitive-e-mail-1201320544/

**22** Hesseldahl, A (2014) Sony Pictures investigates North Korea link in hack attack, *Recode*, 28 November. Available from: www.recode.net/2014/11/28/11633356/sony-pictures-investigates-north-korea-link-in-hack-attack

**23** Finkle, J (2014) Sony investigators find links to North Korea, *Yahoo Finance*, 3 December. Available from: https://finance.yahoo.com/news/sony-name-n-korea-source-behind-cyber-attack-184619626-finance.html

**24** Richwine, L and Finkle, J (2014) Sony investigator says cyber attack 'unparalleled' crime, *Reuters*, 7 December. Available from: www.reuters.com/article/us-sony-cybersecurity-probe/sony-investigator-says-cyber-attack-unparalleled-crime-idUSKBN0JL00720141207

**25** Sungwon, B (2014) Exclusive: North Korea denies involvement in cyber-attack on Sony Pictures, *Voice of America*, 4 December. Available from: www.voanews.com/a/exclusive-north-korea-denies-involvement-in-cyber-attack-sony-pictures/2545372.html

**26** Pagliery, J (2014) Message to Sony: don't show 'movie of terrorism', *CNN*, 8 December. Available from: http://money.cnn.com/2014/12/08/technology/security/sony-hackers/index.html

**27** Ten Days of Rain: Expert analysis of distributed denial-of-service attacks targeting South Korea, McAfee Security, 28 June 2011. Available from: https://securingtomorrow.mcafee.com/wp-content/uploads/2011/07/McAfee-Labs-10-Days-of-Rain-July-2011.pdf

**28** Siegel, T (2013) Seth Rogen to direct, star in 'The Interview' for Columbia Pictures (exclusive), *Hollywood Reporter*, 21 March. Available from: www.hollywoodreporter.com/news/seth-rogen-direct-star-interview-430224

**29** Rogen, S (2014) Here's the poster for my next movie #TheInterview, *twitter.com*, 11 June. Available from: https://twitter.com/Sethrogen/status/476859502059601922

**30** Mullen, J (2014) North Korea: James Franco, Seth Rogen movie is 'undisguised terrorism', *CNN*, 25 June. Available from: http://edition.cnn.com/2014/06/25/world/asia/north-korea-the-interview-reaction/index.html

**31** Biddle, S (2014) Leaked emails: Sony execs scared of 'desperately unfunny' Interview, *Gawker*, 15 December. Available from: http://defamer.gawker.com/leaked-emails-the-interview-sucked-for-sony-even-befor-1671234001

**32** Wikileaks Sony emails, *Wikileaks*, 10 June 2014. Available from: https://wikileaks.org/sony/emails/emailid/200677

**33** Hornaday, A (2014) Sony, 'The Interview' and the unspoken truth: All movies are political, *Washington Post*, 18 December. Available from: www.washingtonpost.com/lifestyle/style/sony-the-interview-and-the-unspoken-truth-that-all-movies-are-political/2014/12/18/406f84c6-86ca-11e4-b9b7-b8632ae73d25_story.html

**34** Boot, W (2014) Exclusive: Sony emails say State Department blessed Kim Jong-un assassination in 'The Interview', *Daily Beast*, 17 December. Available from: www.thedailybeast.com/exclusive-sony-emails-say-state-department-blessed-kim-jong-un-assassination-in-the-interview

**35** Shorrock, T (2017) How Sony, Obama, Seth Rogen and the CIA secretly planned to force regime change in North Korea, *AlterNet*, 5 September. Available from: www.alternet.org/grayzone-project/how-sony-obama-seth-rogen-and-cia-secretly-planned-force-regime-change-north-korea

**36** Wikileaks Sony emails, *Wikileaks*, 25 September 2014. Available from: https://wikileaks.org/sony/emails/emailid/22450

**37** Lang, B (2014) Sony hackers threaten 9/11 attack on movie theaters that screen 'The Interview', *Variety*, 16 December. Available from: http://variety.com/2014/film/news/sony-hackers-threaten-911-attack-on-movie-theaters-that-screen-the-interview-1201380712/

**38** Sanger, DE and Perlroth, N (2014) U.S. said to find North Korea ordered cyberattack on Sony, *New York Times*, 17 December. Available from: www.nytimes.com/2014/12/18/world/asia/us-links-north-korea-to-sony-hacking.html?_r=0

**39** Personal communication

**40** Guerrero-Saade, JA, Raiu, C and GReAT (2016) Operation Blockbuster revealed: a glimpse at the spider web of the Lazarus Group APT campaigns, *Kaspersky Securelist*, 24 February. Available from: https://securelist.com/operation-blockbuster-revealed/73914/

**41** McAfee Labs (2013) Dissecting Operation Troy: Cyberespionage in South Korea, *McAfee.com*, 8 July. Available from: https://securingtomorrow.mcafee.com/mcafee-labs/dissecting-operation-troy-cyberespionage-in-south-korea/

**42** HP Security Briefing, episode 16 – Profiling an enigma: North Korea's cyber threat, *Micro Focus*, 27 August 2014. Available from: https://community.saas.hpe.com/t5/Security-Research/HP-Security-Briefing-episode-16-Profiling-an-enigma-North-Korea/ba-p/268893

**43** N. Korea boosting cyber warfare capabilities, *chosun.com*, 5 November 2013. Available from: http://english.chosun.com/site/data/html_dir/2013/11/05/2013110501790.html

**44** Araquel, E (2014) Sony hacker attack will cost company tens of millions of dollars, *Associated Press and Bloomberg*, 18 December. Available from: www.thestar.com/business/2014/12/18/sony_hacker_attack_will_cost_company_tens_of_millions_of_dollars.html

**45** Hornyak, T (2015) Hack to cost Sony $35 million in IT repairs, *NetworkWorld*, 4 February. Available from: www.networkworld.com/article/2879814/data-center/sony-hack-cost-15-million-but-earnings-unaffected.html

**46** Consolidated financial results forecast for the third quarter ended December 31, 2014, *Sony*, 4 February 2015. Available from: www.sony.net/SonyInfo/IR/library/fr/150204_sony.pdf

**47** Consolidated financial results for the fiscal year ended March 31, 2015, *Sony*, 30 April 2015. Available from: https://www.sony.net/SonyInfo/IR/library/fr/14q4_sony.pdf

**48** Patten, D (2015) Sony hacking class action lawsuit reaches settlement, *Deadline*, 2 September. Available from: http://deadline.com/2015/09/sony-hacking-lawsuit-settlement-employees-identity-theft-1201513280/

## **LESSONS** FROM THE SONY PICTURES HACK

- Hackers acting for nation states read the news just like everyone else – and they're particularly focused on what they perceive as threats to, or opportunities for, their ambitions.

- If you think you might be a target for nation-state hackers, you need to contact your own government. There is a continual mutual surveillance of other countries' activities online.

- Then again, don't expect governments to step in to prevent a hack, because that's extraordinarily difficult to do. Instead, they may give guidance on where the threat lies. But security is still your responsibility.

- Prepare and rehearse for the possibility that one day your entire company's on-site computing infrastructure might be wiped out. It might not be hackers; it might be a fire or other disaster.

- Prepare and rehearse for the possibility that your offsite backup servers will be wiped out, possibly at the same time.

- In such an event, realize that the organization's staff and their motivation will determine whether or not recovery is ultimately successful. Organizations do survive catastrophes, but it depends on how determined the people who work for them are to bring it through.

- Don't put things in email that you wouldn't be happy to see reprinted on the front page of the newspaper, and on a million news websites. Email isn't a secure medium, and a throwaway remark from a year ago could come back to haunt you in times to come. Use a different method instead: face-to-face, or on the phone, or a secure messaging app, on a phone with sufficient security.

- Listen to warnings which filter up from lower in the organization. Expertise in hacking and security is widespread nowadays.

- Don't hold passwords in single files which are convenient to access by multiple people. They'll be one of the first things hackers will look for.

# Anonymous attacks

# 03

## HBGary

*Nobody would think to do this.*

UNIDENTIFIED MICROSOFT PROGRAMMER, on being shown the SQL injection hacking technique in 1995

It was Sunday evening, 6 February 2011: the night of the 45th Super Bowl, the most-viewed event in the US TV calendar, with the Pittsburgh Steelers playing for the title against the Green Bay Packers. But Aaron Barr wasn't watching it, not even for the adverts. Instead, he was trying to connect to the email server for his work at HBGary Federal, a cybersecurity company which focused on contracts with the US government.

Barr was revising a big presentation that he was going to give at a conference in the coming week; as he had explained in an exclusive interview published online in the *Financial Times* on Saturday, he would present research about the security risks to organizations posed by social media and their associated networks. He'd explain how someone's separate postings on Twitter, Facebook and LinkedIn could yield enough clues, once tied together, to identify someone who wanted to remain anonymous. He had told the *FT* he had penetrated the identities of the members of a US military group and of staff at a nuclear plant in the US so thoroughly that he could have sent them emails with links to malware – 'phishing' emails – that, once clicked, would install sypware on the recipients' PCs.[1]

He had also, he said, used the same technique to identify key members of Anonymous, the amateur hacking collective which had become famous for breaking into various sites, spreading videos, and in December 2010 even knocking PayPal and Visa offline. The latter had been in retaliation for those organizations withdrawing the ability to make donations to Wikileaks; they, in turn, had been pressured into the withdrawal by the US government, angered by Wikileaks' publication in November of thousands of leaked US diplomatic cables. (PayPal later said that the Anonymous attacks cost it £3.5 million in lost business and mitigation spending.)

However, that evening Barr couldn't connect to the HBGary Federal server. That was a problem. It was also peculiar.[2]

In 2003, cybersecurity was already a booming business. As broadband got faster and companies tooled up with more computing power, the potential for security lapses and loopholes to leave companies open to fraud and theft was becoming more and more obvious. Stories were beginning to emerge of companies losing serious amounts of money to hackers. So Greg Hoglund, already a noted security researcher who had contributed under his own name to *Phrack* magazine in 1999 on installing a rootkit that could silently watch activity in Windows NT, and made a number of conference presentations on technical hacking methods at the official BlackHat conference, set up a cybersecurity company, which he called HBGary.[3]

As its business grew, though, Hoglund increasingly found that he was chasing lucrative US government contracts which could bring him into conflict with his existing clients; and the government also demanded very high security clearances. The business opportunity was there, but the company structure wasn't right.

So in December 2009 he set up an offshoot, HBGary Federal, specifically to chase work offering cybersecurity – both defensive and offensive – to US government agencies. The company was set up with $250,000 of capital – $35,000 from the newly hired chief executive, Aaron Barr; another $35,000 from Ted Vera, who was chief operating officer; $87,500 from Penny Leavy-Hoglund, Hoglund's wife; and $62,500 from HBGary itself. Two other smaller shareholders put in another $30,000.[4]

Barr had spent 12 years in the US Navy as a cryptologist, programmer and systems analyst, and then worked at Northrop Grummans, a big defence contractor, latterly as chief engineer of its cybersecurity efforts. He could see the opportunity: he wanted to be part of a start-up culture, rather than a big defence contractor, and get the chance to develop software in that field. With two decades of experience in computing, he knew about hacker culture, but only at the state level; Anonymous was a comparatively new phenomenon, and barely studied. Anyway, it wasn't really relevant to a federal cybersecurity company's focus; that was about stopping the bad guys – a classification that didn't yet include Anonymous – from doing bad things to you.

But though things had looked promising, by January 2011 the outlook was mixed. HBGary Federal was competing in a crowded market. Contracts were hard to come by, and the business had missed internal projections for revenues; informal talks had begun with two potential buyers. What it needed was a big business win: that would either prove its long-term potential, or make it a juicier acquisition.

HBGary Federal was deeply entwined with multiple government projects, in partnership with a number of secretive companies. Its key partnerships, it explained in a PowerPoint presentation, were Palantir Technologies (which provided 'big data' analysis to both government and private clients), Fidelis Cybersecurity, and EndGame, another cybersecurity company based in Arlington, Virginia (where the biggest employer is the US Pentagon).

Barr, meanwhile, had become interested in Anonymous – the amorphous hacking collective which had begun on the messaging board 4chan, and gradually moved onto a network of IRC (Internet Relay Chat) servers where they would try to set the world to rights.

Casting around for topics for a presentation at BSides, an information security conference aimed at 'grassroots' users, Barr decided that the risks of social media would make a good topic.

In internal emails to Leavy-Hoglund and copied to Hoglund and Vera, he said that he intended to illustrate how it posed a risk to people who wanted to stay unknown: if you used it, you could be identified. 'Social media represents our next great vulnerability,' wrote Barr. 'When considering my research topic for the BSides security conference, I wanted to demonstrate why social media poses great risk to organizations.' He would focus on three organizations: a 'critical infrastructure facility', a military facility and the Anonymous Group.[5]

Barr told the executives in the email group that he knew that by choosing Anonymous he was picking a controversial subject, but had used 'proprietary' analytic tools and a 'social media analysis methodology' to tie their online IRC nicknames to their real names. Of the 30-odd he said 'managed' the Anonymous group, he reckoned he could identify 'over 80 per cent', and had in effect unmasked many more ordinary members but hadn't bothered to research them further.

His intent, he emphasized in the email, wasn't 'malice of intent or aggression, it was research to illustrate social media is a significant problem that should worry everyone', he continued. He didn't intend to release names; he just wanted to make the point that if he could deduce the identities of people who wanted to remain unknown, what did that mean for people in important industries who might be targeted by more nefarious criminals? 'I hope that the Anonymous group will understand my intentions and decide not to make this personal.'[6]

Hope, as they say, springs eternal.

# Don't bug the hive

Anonymous had attracted widespread attention through a couple of notable actions: first in 2008 by spreading a video which the Church of Scientology had had removed from YouTube, and then by supporting the June 2009 Iranian election protests through a website set up to try to help protesters in the country.

But defining who 'controlled' what the group did was difficult. Anyone could join an Anonymous chatroom, and choose whether just to observe events or join in. Among those who did were skilled amateur hackers with wide ranges of expertise. There were, however, plenty of others with little or no actual hacking knowledge or experience, but a long list of suggestions about targets and methods. The signal-to-noise ratio in any Anonymous chatroom was thus minimal. The talented hackers tended to find each other and shift their focus to private chatrooms on IRC – an old and simple but widely used bare-bones chatroom system – where they could discuss tactics and strategy with little disturbance.

Anonymous was something of a hive mind, in both senses. First, its approach to external events emerged organically from its internal discussions. Second, if the swarm was annoyed, it could get extremely aggressive towards its targets. And if enough hackers tried to sting you, bad things would happen.

Joseph Menn had joined the *Financial Times*, one of the world's most prominent business newspapers, in March 2009, covering the technology beat, with a focus on security and privacy; he already had years of experience at the *Los Angeles Times* and *Bloomberg News* writing business and technology news. He was increasingly interested by the emerging hacker culture, and the commercial hackers who were making millions exploiting flaws in PCs and websites.

One day an email arrived from HBGary's press officer: would he like to talk to Aaron Barr, who was going to give a talk at BSides on how he had tracked down the real names of key members of Anonymous?

'I agreed to interview Barr because I thought the premise was interesting, because it was offered as an exclusive [in] advance [of the talk], and because Anonymous and the authorities' attempts to stop it was one of the biggest stories going around at the time,' Menn explains. It wasn't the sort of in-depth investigation he usually did, but:

> probably the deciding factor was that I knew Greg Hoglund, the founder of HBGary. Gary was deeply technical, and extremely smart, and well respected by long-time top security people. I guessed that if he was a partner with Barr, then Barr was probably decent at his craft.[7]

From pitch to conversation to write-up was less than 24 hours, Menn recalls; a quite typical turnaround time for a story with an interesting news element but minimal investigative content. 'He seemed to have reasonable answers. I thought it was worth a modest story about what he said he could do, and my editor agreed … a routine story.'

The 'routine story' appeared on Saturday, 5 February, in the paper and online. 'An international investigation into cyberactivists who attacked businesses hostile to Wikileaks is likely to yield arrests of senior members of the group,' the story began. It quoted Barr saying that he had figured out the hierarchy and location of senior members of the group, and that they were in the UK, US, Germany, Netherlands, Italy and Australia; though only about 30 of 'a few hundred' members were steadily active, led by a core of 10 who 'are the most senior'. He said he had penetrated the group as part of a project to demonstrate to other organizations the security risks of social media and networking.

But to Anonymous, the story looked anything but routine. There had already been arrests of some alleged members in the UK over the PayPal and Visa attacks (which would later lead to court cases). The suggestion that Barr had penetrated Anonymous and identified its members – 'doxxed' them – was dramatic; and the story pointed out that he would be presenting his research later that month. For any group worried about getting infiltrated, Barr's claims were a cattle prod. The IRC chatrooms hummed.

For himself, Barr wasn't trying to identify Anonymous members to help the US or UK governments; he was doing it because he thought it was possible, and to show that people in business and government should know it was risky to have too public a profile. Despite the entreaties of the social networking companies, which encouraged people to share everything – life details, photographs, thoughts, experiences – Barr's reasoning was that you couldn't be sure who you were sharing that information with, and how they might use it; to illustrate the points, he created a number of fake Facebook profiles to observe and interact with people. He just needed to finish his presentation.

The server wasn't responding, though, and Barr felt vaguely uneasy. But at first his only concern was that the system wasn't behaving. 'Then I started getting messages from people on IRC as well as on Twitter.'

Twitter was the big clue. His account had been hacked, and the hackers were announcing themselves through it. A couple of phone calls later it became clear that it wasn't just his account. Someone had broken into the HBGary Federal company systems and was apparently rifling through everything on its servers: emails and presentations and more.

The question of who was behind the hack was quickly answered. It was Anonymous. But how had they got into the servers and records of a cybersecurity company?

To understand that, we need to rewind, to 1995.

# 95 ways to read your database

Andrew Plato's job at Microsoft was not the most exciting. On the plus side, it was the mid-1990s, and Microsoft's Seattle campus was one of the most exciting places in the world to be: it wrote the software which powered almost all the PCs being sold, and Windows 95, its new consumer operating system, had had people literally queuing around blocks at midnight waiting to buy it and install it on their machines at the first opportunity. An operating system. A few years before, nobody would have known what an operating system was.

Plato, then aged 26, was a 'technical writer', but that didn't mean he wrote software. Instead, he was documenting what the software did and how it worked, so that people coming cold to the product could understand how to use it. 'I did documentation in support of product development,' he recalls. 'Like, operators' manuals and user manuals for developers and for database administrators. One of the things I did quite a bit of is data dictionaries – we would document the structure of a database.'[8]

Despite the success of Windows 95, Microsoft had been 'blindsided' (as Plato puts it) by the rise of the internet, and was hurrying to integrate its products with the new, democratized network. One of those products was SQL Server, Microsoft's system for relational databases. SQL stands for Structured Query Language, and is usually pronounced 'sequel'. SQL is a language for interrogating and updating databases; while outwardly simple, its commands can be chained together to create remarkably precise queries of complex sets of interlinked databases.

Plato's job was not complex. It was a drudge. He had to write 'SQL queries' – commands that the system could interpret as queries or commands for the database – and test them for the expected response. 'It was a bit of a slog,' he says. 'I was always trying to find something to make the job go a little faster. Sometimes I was validating hundreds, if not thousands, of tables in a database.'

To save time, he stored some of the queries on Notepad, the simple Windows text editor, and then copied that and pasted it into the program that connected to the SQL Server database. Doing that was tedious.

Except one day in late September 1995 he made a mistake: he pasted the query into a webpage, on Microsoft's new MSN Plaza site in a space for user input. 'I was on a screen where you enter information about yourself, a screen where you set up your account.' Not realizing his error, he hit enter. The query intended to check the inner workings of the database was passed to programs (called interpreters) linked to the live database where millions of MSN users had already registered.

'These interpreters – they saw a SQL query, and when they see a SQL query, they just execute it. So they did, and returned it to me. This screen, it just returned all the data from that field in the database.'

In one sense, that was exactly what he had been expecting. But he shouldn't have been able to do it from a webpage accessible to the world. Plato had hacked the database. More precisely, he'd carried out 'SQL injection' – discovering a weakness in the protection around the database by entering a SQL command into a web browser.

Plato didn't realize this at first:

I'm like, 'Oh wow, that's cool, I didn't know it would do that.' And for me, it was making the job easier – rather than having to copy and paste stuff out of a command line window, which was always a pain because you couldn't drag and drop [the text], I could do it in the browser where I could copy and paste much easier.

But after a day or so, a thought occurred to him. 'If I can do it on this site,' he thought, 'why couldn't I do this elsewhere? If I can just submit a SQL query to a website and it just executes it, then I could see *anything* inside the database.'

Over the weekend, he tried his technique on a number of websites, including Oracle, IBM and HP:

> I hacked probably about 20 or 30 websites, and got data out of them.
> I could get user accounts, I could get all sorts of stuff. I just had to
> figure out the database structure, which typically wasn't very difficult,
> because you could submit a query that actually gives you the database
> structure.

Then he came back to the MSN Plaza site. 'I knew there was a place in the table where they stored all the credit card numbers.' He entered a carefully tailored SQL query on the site: 'And I just had this big long huge list, I mean, thousands of credit cards displayed in the browser window.'

A world of possibilities – most of them bad – opened up before him like a door yawning open above a canyon. The obvious thought arose: 'I could take these credit cards and go buy things with them.' But also, he says, 'it occurred to me that this isn't good, because if I can do this, anybody can do this, and so I should probably show this to somebody.'

He took his discovery to his superior, who suggested he should explain it to the Microsoft developers – the people building the tools and the site. One developer said he should bring it to the 'Tuesday Standup Meeting', where the developers would gather to discuss progress and problems. The next available one was 10 October.

The Tuesday Standup Meeting was where the developers would plan what areas were more and less important, and what subjects were stumbling blocks and which were promising. Microsoft developers were, at the time, the crème de la crème, picked from thousands of applicants, and riding high. The growing dominance of Windows meant there was also a tendency towards arrogance. Microsoft was sweeping all before it in computing, and they wrote the code that powered the machines, so their confidence was high. 'They were the gods, they got to do whatever they wanted, especially the higher-end developers, or in any sort of group where there was a lot of money pouring in,' says Plato. 'And at that time, there was a lot of money and research coming in.'

He was nervous, but also excited:

I was beside myself. I'm, like, 'Wow, they're going to see this, they're going to be impressed by me, I get to show off my coding skills.' I'm imagining I'm going to get promoted, I'm going to be hanging out with Bill [Gates, the chief executive and then one of the most powerful men in the technology business]. All these things are going through my head.

Tuesday morning arrived, and Plato turned up nervously at the meeting. One of the managers called him forward: 'Hey, Andrew, why don't you come up and show us this bug you've got.' That didn't concern Plato; the Tuesday meeting would often talk about bugs in the site and how they'd fix them.

'I go up there, get on the site, type a very basic SQL query, select "all" from users – some basic table – put some basic table command into a form field, hit "enter" and like clockwork, it brings up all the data, shows it all,' Plato recalls. He explained how he had originally been doing that query into the database, but had now used the site to do the same. He'd been able to query the database directly through the site. If he could, anyone could.

He waited for realization to dawn, for the gods of the programming world to see that there was a gaping hole in the security of their systems which could be exploited by anyone who knew a few SQL commands.

The silence stretched a little, and then someone spoke up. 'I don't get it, what do you mean?'

'You can query the back-end database directly through the web browser,' Plato replied. 'I could do this at home.'

'So?'

Unsure whether to be rattled, exasperated or astonished, Plato upped the ante. 'I did this and queried all the credit card databases right in the browser. This is a pretty serious' – he hesitated to call it a vulnerability; it felt like more than a bug – 'this is pretty serious. *Anyone* could do this.'

Even more than 20 years later, his heightened emotion at the time means Plato recalls the detail of the moment. The silence stretched once more:

At that moment there's this one developer – I recall he had a big shaggy beard and I kind of looked up to him. I mean, the guy never showered, he was always in sweatpants, but he was an uber-developer. I recall his office at Microsoft was full of pop cans, stacked like twelve high. I mean the guy was basically a bum, but he was super-smart.

The super-smart never-showered developer fixed his gaze on Plato:

I remember him sitting back and saying, 'This is a waste of time. This is nothing.' The minute he did that, everybody else joined in, because everyone looked up to him, so the minute he put me down, it became time to put me down.

I distinctly remember him saying, 'Nobody would think to do this.' And another guy said, 'Aren't you a tech writer? Go back to writing docs, this is a waste of time.' And that was it. I felt like I'd done something wrong, I felt like an idiot.

He still recalls the feeling of humiliation.

Plato wasn't wrong, though. He had uncovered a serious vulnerability which could affect any database-driven system that was exposed to the internet, where there would be lots of people who might think to try a SQL query on a form field. Even so, history did manage to spite him once more a few years later. He was working at a network company when he noticed the security consultant Rob Graham talking about a 'new' hacking technique: 'You take SQL commands and you can put them through a browser.' Plato thought: 'Browser SQL? That sounds really familiar.'

The technique had been written up in *Phrack*, an online 'magazine' by and for hackers, by someone under the handle 'rain.forest. puppy' who had stumbled on the same method. Plato read it. 'It was essentially what I had done four years prior. I thought, "Well, there you go – now it has a name, and now it's been acknowledged in the world." And I also thought: "I really was onto something."'

So why didn't he document what he'd found? 'It's easy in hindsight to say so, but where the hell was I going to publish it? What was I going to do with that information? I didn't know.'

Thus most records suggest that a hacker with the handle rain. forest.puppy – real name Jeff Forristal, who now runs a security company – discovered SQL injection. But really it was Andrew Plato.

# Enter the bad guys

'The bad guys are going to get in. Accept it,' warned a slide from an HBGary presentation to IDC early in 2011. What the presentation showed, unintentionally, was that 'security' was treated as being synonymous with 'viruses'. 'Detect bad guys using a smallish genome of behaviours – and this means zeroday [*sic*] and APT – no signatures required … inoculate to protect against known malware.' It added that 'Security is an intelligence problem.'[9]

'Zeroday' is more usually called 'zero day', and describes an attack which hasn't been identified by anyone publicly before, and so catches the target unawares. An APT is an 'advanced persistent threat' – software that has been incorporated into the target's systems and sends out data or opens back doors. And the idea of inoculation is a clear indicator that the key threats HBGary was considering were little pieces of code in, say, phishing emails. It promised 'continuous protection' through its 'digital DNA' – a phrase that the presentation slide insisted was trademarked, though the team was distressed to discover soon afterwards that the Pentagon was using the same phrase.

What the presentation didn't consider was bad guys who got in without using malware, or indeed anything that would be distinguishable from the behaviour of fully authorized users.

The member of Anonymous who broke into Barr's system was happy to talk to me about how it came about; less so to be named, or quoted. As they recount it, someone posted a link to the *Financial Times* article – or more probably the text of it, acquired somehow despite the paywall. The effect was electric, because HBGary was known to be affiliated with other, professional, hacking teams. Barr's claims seemed bold, and nobody was keen to trust his assurance that he wouldn't go to the police. They wanted to see what he had.

The lead hacker then spent the rest of the night working through all the public information about HBGary and HBGary Federal. Then he began going to work on the HBGary Federal site itself, since that was where Barr ostensibly had the research.

The first discovery: HBGary Federal was running a custom CMS – content management system, used to put content online within a templated webpage. The second discovery: an SQL injection exploit.

How long did it take to find the SQL injection flaw? About 15 minutes, I was told.

The vulnerability was that the CMS contained 26 pages of content. If you asked it to retrieve page 27, the error message it threw back was enough for a smart hacker to figure out how to get the database to yield up its information, by putting SQL queries into the URL of the browser.

With that, the hacker was able to access the database of usernames and passwords of those allowed to post to the site – the HBGary Federal staff. The passwords were encrypted, but comparatively weakly, using the MD5 system. MD5 is a 'hashing' system: it performs a mathematical operation on the input, represented as binary bits, and outputs a single 'digest' 128 bits long. Two inputs differing by just a single bit produce results that look completely different, so there's no obvious way to reverse-engineer an MD5 hash; in theory, it would be the mathematical equivalent of unscrambling an egg. When someone logs in and gives their password, that is hashed using MD5, and the stored hash and the new one are compared. If they match, the input password was correct.

But the scrambledness depends on the cook. People tend to choose passwords they can remember, rather than which are unusual. Knowing this, hackers and security experts have investigated many methods of working backwards from a hash to the original password. The simplest is to apply MD5 to a giant dictionary of common words and passwords. Then compare what you have with those results.

The Anonymous hacker, having acquired the hashed password database, headed over to Hashkiller, a site which offers precisely those reverse lookups, and presently claims to have more than a trillion cracked hashes.

Two of the passwords, belonging to Barr and Vera, turned out to have used eight-character passwords, with six lower-case letters and two numbers. That offered only a 36-character dataset to attack; including upper-case letters would make it 62 characters, and adding ASCII punctuation would take it up to 95. Password cracking difficulty increases geometrically with length and character set; Barr and Vera had supplied low-hanging fruit.

Seconds after putting the hashes into Hashkiller, three of the passwords had been broken. In time, it was able to work through 90 per cent of the hashed passwords, but all he needed – and, at that time, wanted – was Barr's password. This turned out to be 'kibafo33'.

As passwords go, it's not a strong one: one password tester gives it a 32 per cent score (no upper case, no symbols, too short), another reckons that it would take only one minute to crack using modern techniques.[10, 11]

Barr had also made a key mistake. He'd reused his password elsewhere. His email, Twitter and LinkedIn accounts all used the same one. Vera's supplied a login to a company support server. However, that only gave access to an 'ordinary' account, without administrator permissions (which allows far more extensive control over the whole system and access to the files used by any user).

The server had not, however, been patched against a security vulnerability which let an ordinary user elevate themselves to administrator level – a so-called 'privilege escalation'. (The flaw had been publicized in October, and the software patch to close it had been released in November, three months earlier.) Meanwhile, Barr's email was the next target.

The hacker logged into Barr's Gmail account, and because the company was using Google Apps [an application suite including email, shared documents and spreadsheets], that gave him administrative control of the whole HBGary Federal domain.

Barr didn't have two-factor authentication turned on; that might have saved him, as Google's security system would have demanded the hacker supply both the password and a one-time code generated by an app. Instead the hacker now had control of the email system inside both HBGary Federal and HBGary, the senior company. He set about copying all the emails and associated files – many gigabytes of them – to his own systems, and searching them for interesting words, phrases and documents.

The hacker began keyword searching – 'Anonymous', 'FBI', 'password', 'SSH', 'FTP'. Those led to correspondence between Barr and the FBI, and between Barr and his colleagues about Anonymous. The hacker was astonished at Barr's confidence in his 'opsec' – operational security – which by then had been completely compromised. While the hacker monitored it, Barr sent an email to a friend, including a screenshot from IRC boasting that Anonymous had no idea he was watching them. (Barr was in a different, public channel, not the private one where the attack was being discussed.) That gave the hacker Barr's IRC handle. (Google doesn't alert users of concurrent logins to email, because so many people access it from multiple devices – a phone, tablet, home PC, and perhaps a work computer too. Even two-factor authentication offers only minimal protection against multiple concurrent logins, once they are authorized.)

In computing security terms, Barr was now standing in the street naked.

Finally, the hacker sought to get access to the server running rootkit.com, the site set up by Hoglund, who was known as an expert on the topic (of programs which run hidden on PCs). This had better security. The administrator had to be inside the HBGary firewall; even though he had found Hoglund's password, it wouldn't work from outside HBGary's systems.

To beat this, he had to turn to human interaction – and using Hoglund's email, contacted the support service for HBGary, pretending to be Hoglund. Such 'social engineering' attacks usually rely on the hacker giving the impression of being an executive in a rush to get somewhere, who has lost their device or forgotten their password. The hacker pretended to be Hoglund, saying he was in Europe (where it was late in the evening) and asking for a tunnel to be opened in the firewall so he could 'reset' the password.

Sometimes, humans are the most easily hacked part of a system because people on helpdesks like to help. The support service didn't have any reason to doubt the source of Hoglund's email – though a more cautious person would have wondered why he was asking first for external access, and then needed a new password, and had forgotten his username. Because the hacker had had access to Hoglund's emails, he could see what past conversations looked like, and produce a passable simulacrum of their conversational style.

There wasn't a routine in place for checking such details with a phone call or other system. So the support desk opened up the machine and reset the password.

# The calamity of access

Given access, the hacker logged into the site, and found more data and more MD5-protected passwords. Anonymous stripmined the site – emails, documents, presentations were all copied and then made available through filesharing torrents. (Wikileaks eventually made its own copy.)

On many commercial sites, such a cascade of bad security would be bad enough. For a company ostensibly in the cybersecurity business, though, it was calamitous.

And yet the mistakes that led to the downfall – an SQLi vulnerability, reused passwords, a three-month-unpatched vulnerability – are far from uncommon. SQLi is the second most common method of intrusion. Industry estimates suggest that about 30 per cent of users reuse passwords somewhere. And social engineering is probably the oldest form of 'hacking' – usually known as a con trick.

On Sunday night, at about 10.00 pm US Eastern time, Anonymous gathered in an Internet Relay Chat (IRC) chatroom named '#ophbgary' – Operation HB Gary – to discuss the spoils and celebrate. The first stories had begun appearing on news sites as they spread the word to interested journalists, and in one case by Barrett Brown, a journalist and activist who was interested in the development and sale of surveillance technologies by American companies to foreign countries and governments. Brown's story on the hack appeared at Daily Kos at 8.29 pm EST with the headline 'Anon pwns HBGary Federal UPDATED w/PRESS RELEASE'. ('Pwns' is the hacker lingo for 'takes over', usually pronounced as 'own').[12]

Anonymous had indeed done precisely that, said Brown: 'An hour ago, Anon seized control of the internet security firm's website, defaced its pages, acquired 60,000 company emails, deleted backup files, seized Barr's Twitter account, and took down the founder's website rootkit.com.' It had also acquired a document apparently written by Barr containing his notes attempting to both name and locate a number of the key Anonymous members.

Hackers worry about 'doxxing' – documents and details which tie their online identity to their physical identity and location – for obvious reasons: the police can track you down. But on reading the presentation Barr had been working on, it seemed there was little for the hackers to worry about. The names the Anonymous members had used were in some cases obviously made up (such as someone allegedly in Germany calling themselves 'Rerhuf Arthur' – the first name backwards suggests a weak joke), and generally incomplete. A couple of the names, it turned out, were correct, in one case because the hacker had used his real name to register a web domain that he later referred to online.

The HBGary Federal main page, meanwhile, had been replaced by a screenshot mostly full of text, which said in part, 'You've tried to bite at the Anonymous hand, and now the Anonymous hand is bitch-slapping you in the face. You expected a counter-attack in the form of a verbal braul [sic] (as you so eloquently put it in one of your private emails), but now you've received the full fury of Anonymous.'[13]

They also used Barr's password, duplicated on his iCloud account, to remotely wipe his iPad.

The hack threw Barr, Vera, Hoglund and Leavy-Hoglund into crisis mode, said Barr:

> We had talked internally about what was the worst that was going to possibly happen from my activities at the talk, and because of previous activities by Anonymous, we thought they might DDOS [distributed denial of service, effectively taking offline] our site for a while. We had customers that were using both of the sites, so we thought that might cause some problems, and we did stuff to try to mitigate that. But we did not expect – nor was there really a lot of historical precedent – that they were going to do what they did.

The underestimation resembles that of the disdainful programmer at Microsoft. He couldn't see that exposing an insecure web interface to the internet meant that you were opening it up to the entire bell curve of expertise and malice – including the most skilled and greedy – because he had grown up in a world where access to computers was limited. For HBGary's principals, who thought they were familiar with the internet and its threats emanating from commercially oriented or state-backed hackers, the idea of crowdsourced attacks by amateurs who would post and expose everything about a company online simply hadn't existed 10 years earlier. It didn't really exist in their threat models; Wikileaks and the Anonymous crew had seen the possibilities of the new computing landscape, and they were using them.

# Handling the crisis

The problem was that HBGary Federal didn't have an emergency response plan. 'We were a start-up, we'd been in business less than a year, and we only had five employees. As is typical of most start-ups, you don't really build those things inside the first year. That all comes later,' Barr said.

But now his Twitter account had been taken over, and was being used to tweet abuse and emails, and his LinkedIn account had been hacked, as had Vera's:

> I remember feeling a sense of dread that Sunday, once we realized that all of our emails had been stolen and they had control of them and were threatening to release them publicly … it's like having your house broken into, right? You feel very violated. You feel very exposed.

But the difference from a burglary is that the content hadn't just been taken; it was going to be shown off, piece by piece, to the world; death by a thousand cuts.

Penny Leavy-Hoglund, Hoglund's wife, was invited by Barrett Brown to come into an Anonymous chatroom where the hack and discoveries were being chewed over. She logged on at 11.00 pm EST, apologizing for being unfamiliar with the IRC system: 'First time using this so forgive me if I'm slow,' she wrote. 'Not the sophisticated computer user like you guys and girls.'[14]

She was asked if she knew that Barr had been collecting data about Anonymous, and collecting a list of names. 'He was never planning on giving to the gov't,' she wrote. But, she added, 'we have not seen the list and we are kind of pissed at him right now.' The *FT* article, she said, 'was to get more people to the event'.

Her purpose in being there, she said, was to get the HBGary emails removed from the downloads. That wasn't possible; the emails were inextricably bundled into the torrents that were being downloaded on multiple machines.

The conversation looped around ineffectually. Anonymous members were certain that Barr had a meeting planned with the FBI for the Monday, and inferred that he was going to sell his findings about them to it. Leavy-Hoglund was overwhelmed by the volume of text; there was just one of her, and more than a hundred of them throwing in accusations, questions, insults and general chatter. Though she stayed there for just over 90 minutes, she didn't persuade anyone, nor get the HBGary emails withdrawn from public torrents. They didn't persuade her to fire Barr – 'I can't fire someone that owns a portion of the company,' she protested. 'What you did was illegal and it will hurt you guys as well,' she argued. (She also noted that the HBGary Federal site, with its SQLi vulnerability, had been written by an outside company: 'We fired them.')

After 90 minutes, Hoglund himself took over her handle. 'You Realize that releasing my email spool will cause millions in damages to HBGary?' he asked.

'Sabu', the most forthright of the Anonymous team, replied, 'Relax, we aren't releasing your spool. Depending on what YOU and YOUR WIFE do.'

To which Hoglund replied, 'Do you realize that attacking a US company and stealing private data is something you have never done before?'

That was, indeed, the Rubicon that Anonymous had crossed. The hacker's reaction moved from curiosity, and self-preservation – worrying about what Barr might have found out – to the thrill familiar to hackers of taking over a company's entire system within an hour.

Within Anonymous there was a recognition that the HBGary hack changed the landscape of amateur hacking, and the position of Anonymous. They had attacked a US federal contractor, and done it with a mixture of techniques, such as social engineering along with SQLi and password cracking, that could look like a Chinese or Russian nation-state attacker.

Menn, who now works at Reuters, covering the same field, looks back on the events of that weekend as significant in a way nobody could have guessed. What he thought was a routine story 'destroyed Barr, and created [the hacking crew] LulzSec, which went off on the most spectacular hacking spree – a politicized Bonnie and Clyde performance artwork like the world had never seen'.

Indeed, LulzSec – composed of a number of the participants from that chatroom, particularly 'Sabu', 'topiary' and 'tflow' – arguably found their feet in the havoc wreaked in those 48 hours, and would go on to hack into multiple government sites. All but one would also be caught and sentenced.

But at the time, Barr, Vera, Hoglund and Leavy-Hoglund were trying to work out what to do. Anonymous was releasing everything, including the internal documents from HBGary Federal, and then from HBGary. That created a cycle in which they could either explain the context behind a document, or ignore it. But if they ignored it, wouldn't that give free rein to those who were misinterpreting it? Barr struggled with that:

> When private or direct communications get released to the public, there's always some level of misinterpretation. Then you have to try to deal with that, which means you're always starting inside a hole, trying to work your work out. Every single story, trying to have to explain or not explain, and then trying to develop a strategy as to what do you do? Do you just keep your mouth shut, because you have to consider – especially when you're dealing with customers or partners – what type of legal liability do you have? It was very, very challenging.

He found the experience frustrating: the gigantic flood of attention, and the number of articles written, would have been challenging for someone with long-term media experience. Barr was a relative newcomer, and this was a new chapter in hacking by Anonymous. Looking back on it, he says there was enough information for journalists to work with: 'We had something like 66,000 emails in the public domain. If you're going to do a story on it, do your research and get it right. I don't expect you to paint a picture that's exactly the way I want it to be pictured, but I at least expect you to get the facts right.' (He praises the work of the *Wall Street Journal* and *Ars Technica*.)

In retrospect, he also thinks that he should have stayed silent, and declined interviews in the aftermath. That was difficult, as more of the emails were published on Project PM, Barrett Brown's personal project to monitor the 'intelligence contracting industry, the PR industry's interface with totalitarian regimes, the mushrooming infosec/"cybersecurity" industry, and other issues constituting threats to human rights, civic transparency, individual privacy, and the health of democratic institutions'. The discovery that a law firm retained by Bank of America had contacted HBGary Federal, seeking ways to discredit Wikileaks through a propaganda campaign aimed at American journalists, meant that the trouble would not quickly abate.[15, 16]

Barr says that he gave interviews to try to give his position, 'but when you have that much of a wave of contrary opinion, there's only so much you could fight it. I think eventually you just need to let it wash over you and then let it pass.'

# Aftermath of a hack

There was a lot to wash over, though. The hack, and the associated questions as the emails leaked out about the work HBGary was doing, forced the company to cancel speeches and withdraw its stand from the prestigious RSA security show in late February. 'In addition to the data theft, HBGary individuals have received numerous threats of violence including threats at our tradeshow booth,' a notice posted there said. A few days later, the comedian Stephen Colbert tore into HBGary Federal, and Barr, in a segment on his evening show.[17, 18]

On 1 March 2011, three weeks after the attack, Barr stepped down from his post as CEO of HBGary Federal. 'I've been the focus of much of the bad press,' he told *Threatpost*. 'I hope that, by [my] leaving, HBGary and HBGary Federal can get away from some of that.'[19]

On 29 February 2012, HBGary – which had seen an unexpected growth in business in the year after the hack – announced that it had been acquired by ManTech International, an IT services company with a number of government customers, for an undisclosed sum. 'This is great news. We have a billion-dollar company backing us,' said Hoglund. HBGary Federal wasn't part of the deal. It had closed.

(ManTech's Cyber Solutions division, including HBGary, was subsequently acquired in 2015 by another company, CounterTack.)[20, 21]

The hacker who broke into HBGary Federal was caught for other crimes, and sentenced to jail time. He now works for a penetration testing company – essentially, discovering how easy it is to break into companies' systems and move through them. The difference is that he now gets paid for doing what he used to do for free.

Plato too now runs a security company, and sees SQLi attacks happen regularly:

> We have to remember how a lot of software is built. It's built to get it to market fast so that you can get funding, you can get customers, you can get clicks, and please your investors, and become a real company. And when you're racing to make something work, it's really easy to push aside anybody who says 'whoa, whoa, whoa, that's dangerous – you sure you know what you're doing here? You're exposing yourself to problems.' It's really easy to take a lot of shortcuts, borrow people's code from places you shouldn't, hack together solutions that are flimsy. We see this all the time in organizations when they get frustrated and they need to just get something to work, and they're under pressure to perform. And rather than try to really solve the problem, they eventually just sort of go nuclear on the option, and open everything up. Then once they get it working, well, they never go back and close all those doors, because then they're onto the next problem.
>
> So this is a problem that affects any IT and software development. Which is this – the firefighting mode of development or systems management. You're constantly always onto the next problem, being driven on. And the number of problems you have is unlimited. You can almost never get a hold of them.

# References

**1**   Menn, J (2011) Cyberactivists warned of arrest, *Financial Times*, 5 February. Available from: www.ft.com/content/87dc140e-3099-11e0-9de3-00144feabdc0

2   Laville, S (2012) Anonymous cyber-attacks cost PayPal £3.5m, court told, *Guardian*, 22 November. Available from: www.theguardian.com/technology/2012/nov/22/anonymous-cyber-attacks-paypal-court

3   Hoglund, G (1999) A *REAL* NT Rootkit, patching the NT Kernel, *Phrack*, 9 September. Available from: http://phrack.org/issues/55/5.html

4   Burke, K (2009) HBGary launches HBGary Federal, *Forensic Focus*, 9 December. Available from: www.forensicfocus.com/index.php?name=News&file=article&sid=1314

5   'Re: Better?', HBGary emails, *Wikileaks*, 6 February 2011. Available from: https://wikileaks.org/hbgary-emails/emailid/5874

6   'Better', HBGary emails, *Wikileaks*, 5 February 2011. Available from: https://wikileaks.org/hbgary-emails/emailid/6505

7   Personal communication

8   Personal communication

9   'HBGary IDC Presentation 122310' via Wikileaks. Available from: https://wikileaks.org/hbgary-emails/fileid/47245/13888

10  How secure is my password?, *Dashlane*. Available from: https://howsecureismypassword.net

11  Password strength tester, *PasswordPal*. Available from: www.Passwordpal.net/strength-tester.php

12  Brown, B (2011) Anon pwns HBGary Federal UPDATED w/PRESS RELEASE, *Daily Kos*, 7 February. Available from: www.dailykos.com/story/2011/2/6/20216/40699

13  HBGary: security firm investigating 'Anonymous' hacked and exposed, *Security Generation*, 10 February 2011. Available from: www.securitygeneration.com/security/hbgary-security-firm-investigating-anonymous-hacked-and-exposed/

14  'Chatlog Mon Feb 07 03:17:59 2011 Session Ident: #ophbgary', 7 February 2011. Available from: https://pastebin.com/x69Akp5L

15  'Project PM', Free Barrett Brown, undated. Available from: https://freebarrettbrown.org/project-pm/

16  Masnick, M (2011) Leaked HBGary documents show plan to spread Wikileaks propaganda for BofA … and 'attack' Glenn Greenwald, *Techdirt*, 10 February. Available from: www.techdirt.com/articles/20110209/22340513034/leaked-hbgary-documents-show-plan-to-spread-wikileaks-propaganda-bofa-attack-glenn-greenwald.shtml

**17**  Roberts, P (2011) RSA 2011: winning the war but losing our soul, *Threatpost*, 22 February. Available from: https://threatpost.com/rsa-2011-winning-war-losing-our-soul-022211/74958/

**18**  Stephen Colbert: Wikileaks and Anonymous, *YouTube*, 25 February 2011. Available from: www.youtube.com/watch?v=kaoGZJCaZXM

**19**  Roberts, P (2011) HBGary Federal CEO Aaron Barr steps down, *Threatpost*, 28 February. Available from: https://threatpost.com/hbgary-federal-ceo-aaron-barr-steps-down-022811/74971/

**20**  Anderson, M (2012) Cyber security firm HBGary bought by ManTech International, *Sacramento Business Journal*, 28 February. Available from: www.bizjournals.com/sacramento/news/2012/02/28/hb-gary-sacramento-man-tech-cyber-securi.html

**21**  Creighton, N (2015) Cybersecurity firm CounterTack makes first acquisition, *Boston Business Journal*, 15 July. Available from: www.bizjournals.com/boston/blog/techflash/2015/07/cybersecurity-firm-countertack-makes-first.html

## LESSONS FROM THE HBGARY HACK

⬧ Hackers tend to be at least a bit paranoid, and sometimes very paranoid. If you're going to claim you have details about their identities, be very sure it's correct; if you're going to do so publicly, check your defences.

⬧ Don't reuse passwords. It's unnecessary – password managers are plentiful – and can lead to the compromise of all your accounts.

⬧ Use two-factor authentication on email and other systems. Ideally, don't use SMS-based authentication, because it can be bypassed or hijacked; use an app or key system.

⬧ Investigate how easy it is to 'social-engineer' your systems. If someone rings up your support centre and pretends to be you, saying you've lost your password, how easy – or difficult – is it for them to get access to your account?

⬧ If someone emails your support centre ('From:' emails are easy to spoof), how easy is it for them to get access to your account?

⬧ Assume – as always – that your emails could be hacked and spread far and wide.

⬧ Hackers aren't always malicious, but they can be vengeful.

# John Podesta's inbox    04
## The Democratic presidential campaign

*The takeaway is this: your personal email is the portal to*
*everything you do online. If it is compromised, \*all\* of*
*your other accounts fall.*
MATT TAIT, ex-GCHQ information security specialist[1]

It's quite rare that a hack changes the course of history. But that
may have been the case with John Podesta's email.

Email has been the lifeblood of communication on the internet
ever since people realized they needed a way to get in touch across
time zones, and set up ways to send information asynchronously
over the network. Many people over the age of 30 couldn't compre-
hend trying to organize any tasks electronically without the use of
email. Its drawbacks – lack of encryption, the difficulty of verifying senders' identities, potential for being tapped at some point
on the way, and the problem of knowing whether a recipient has
received it or read it – have all been solved by other systems, which
offer encryption, verification and delivery/read receipts. Yet email
survives, the veritable cockroach of the internet.

But if you were running a US presidential campaign, you'd need
email – wouldn't you? A campaign is a tremendously complicated
undertaking. There are teams throughout the US at the local level,
and the need to both tailor messages to individual states and neigh-
bourhoods, allied to the need to have a national message for TV
and newspapers. And in the early stages, the fight is not against

the other party; it is against a rival from the same party, so that messages and speeches have to be subtly tweaked to appeal to the existing voters, not the swing voters in the broader nation. Coordinating what will be said, and when, is crucial. Secrecy, too, matters: letting the other side know what you're planning would let them prepare their response, or simply beat you to the punch in announcing initiatives. Hundreds of millions of dollars are spent chasing the most powerful job in the world. It's not a business for amateurs.

In January 2015, Hillary Clinton hired John Podesta, who had just turned 66, as her campaign manager, and then as her chief of staff for the campaign once she formally announced she was running. They knew each other well: Podesta had been President Bill Clinton's chief of staff from October 1998 to January 2001, managing a period of crises which included impeachment proceedings against the president. Those began in December 1998 and marked a tumultuous time in American politics, full of division and rancour. Later, Podesta had also worked for President Obama, and was a visiting professor of law at Georgetown University. In short, he had been through it all before.

In April 2015 Hillary Clinton announced (via YouTube) her second attempt to become the Democratic candidate for president. After a bruising winter campaign, the outcome of the first Democratic primary in Iowa on 1 February 2016 left her unexpectedly in a two-horse race against 74-year-old Bernie Sanders, six years her senior yet touting a left-wing agenda that resonated with much younger voters.

Six weeks later, on 15 March, Clinton won the Democratic primaries in Missouri, Ohio, North Carolina, Florida and Illinois – but by narrow margins, notably just 0.2 per cent of votes in Missouri.

On Tuesday 22 March there would be primaries in Arizona, Idaho and Utah which would favour Sanders, even though Clinton had in theory got enough candidates to wrap up the nomination. The pressure was enormous. Clinton was in the lead on delegates – but the campaign was unsettled by Sanders' determination, and the level of support he was drawing. The Republican Party's problems with the insurgent candidacy of Donald Trump seemed far away, though members of Clinton's team kept an eye on it.

In a campaign team comprising hundreds of people, like a medium-sized business, Clinton was akin to the chief executive, and Podesta effectively the chief operations officer, responsible for making everything run smoothly. From the core group, the organization fanned out into state-based and topic-based groups, a complex web of interlocking tasks, with one single aim: getting Hillary Clinton elected president in November. Podesta was at the centre, directing operations which included deciding which states to visit, what policies to promote and which to downplay, and gathering 'opposition research' about likely opponents, both in the primary stage and the head-to-head race for the tape.

There was also to some extent a generational divide within the campaign. Those at the top had grown up and seen the internet grow from an academic oddity to this year's wonder and then into a more and more important part both of campaigning and organizing. Those at the bottom were part of a smartphone generation to which the internet was a background hum. They were used to apps such as Facebook and Snapchat; email wasn't their thing. But the campaign's thinking and organization flowed from the top, and from the people brought in to help organize it.

What everyone knew was that security mattered. In an age of Anonymous and of Wikileaks – which had published thousands of leaked US government emails (or 'cables') in 2010 – you needed to guard your electronic data as carefully as possible.

Thus the email that popped up in Podesta's inbox on Saturday, 19 March 2016 was concerning. The 'From:' address was 'no-reply@accounts.googlemail.com', a legitimate sender email for Google. The subject line said: '*Someone has your password*'.

The content itself was just as worrying. 'Someone has your password' it said in white text, in a box with an alarming red background.

'Hi John,' the message continued below, in plain text. 'Someone just used your password to try to sign into your Google Account john.podesta@gmail.com.' It then detailed an apparent attempt from the Ukraine to access the account: the IP address matched that of a Ukrainian mobile phone operator. 'Google stopped this sign-in attempt. You should change your password immediately.' It then offered a link to do so.

Right from the start, one of the biggest problems for Clinton's campaign team had been the persistence of media coverage about 'her emails'. During her 2008 presidential campaign bid, a private email server had been installed at the family home in New York. In 2009 she was made secretary of state, yet kept using the server for accessing emails, including some State Department ones. In 2013 the server was moved to a data centre in New Jersey. In August 2015 when it became clear that Clinton had been using the machine for a mixture of official and non-official business, the FBI began an investigation. That was still rumbling on in the spring of 2016 as the primary campaign continued, with former security chiefs suggesting that the server almost surely had been hacked to spill secrets. They didn't have any *proof*, but it just seemed obvious. Clinton scoffed at the idea, suggesting that there was nothing sensitive stored on it, and no evidence of a breach. But the problem for the campaign was the words 'Clinton' and 'emails' in a newspaper headline would suck attention away from anything else until the FBI investigation was resolved.

Mindful of the forthcoming general election, which looked increasingly certain to be against Donald Trump as the Republican candidate, the campaign team was on edge over anything linking the words 'email' and security. Trump had referred to it. Sanders had referred to it. When it came to security, what you didn't want was someone compromising it by rifling through your emails. And the Clinton campaign *really* didn't want any publicity about emails and hacking.

Podesta was asleep when the email arrived. It was 2.34 am in San Francisco, where he was staying with a friend, prior to flying back to Washington, DC's Reagan Airport in the afternoon.

However, on the east coast, people were already up and at the Clinton headquarters in Brooklyn; presidential campaigns don't take days off. As is common for high-level members of a campaign, at least three people had access to Podesta's personal inbox, including his chief of staff, Sara Latham. Concerned, she forwarded the email to the campaign's operations helpdesk for advice. Was it something that Podesta needed to be worried about? If his email had indeed been compromised, there was no knowing where the contents might end up. Or was it a phishing email – something just trying to get his login details by fooling him with an authentic-looking email?

Phishing has a long, inglorious history. In September 1995, America Online was the US's biggest internet service provider: Steve Case, its chief executive, proudly announced that there were now a remarkable 3.5 million members. But Case also had some concerning news: users would be asked to change their passwords regularly, because hackers were trying – and succeeding – in stealing people's login details. 'There have been some cases where certain individuals are passing themselves off as employees or representatives of America Online and then asking members at random for their passwords.' This was not AOL policy, he explained: 'under no circumstances will anyone from AOL ever ask you for your password.'[2]

The hackers, meanwhile, had almost industrialized the process of capturing those details from unsuspecting users who were new to the internet and unschooled in the pitfalls of online communication. The hackers would send messages to novice users via AOL Instant Messenger or email, posing as AOL staff and requiring people to confirm their details – usually their username and password, and for good measure name, address, credit card number, bank name and expiration date – for vague, computer-y reasons ('We have detected hackers using your account… We have lost your account information… We did not receive your billing information…'). While many of those receiving the messages would ignore them, enough would bite and hand over the goods that it was worthwhile for the scammers.[3]

The practice was called 'phishing' – fishing with a phone twist, since everyone used dialup connections on their phone lines – and the first recorded use of the word online seems to have been in February 1996.[4]

Phishing wasn't, and isn't, hacking in the strict sense; there's no subversion of a computer to do something that it's not expected to do. Instead the subversion is of the user's expectation of what the computer will show them. Subconsciously, we expect that because the computer is trustworthy, it won't allow false messaging to appear; that in the same way it rejects a malformed email or web address, it will spot a faked email or website. But computers only do what they are told, and if they're told to display a message intended to deceive the reader, they dutifully will.

AOL struggled to clamp down on phishing. The problem was always how to educate users in what was real and what was fake, and how to guarantee that people wouldn't fall for the latter. It's trivially easy for any competent web developer to copy the HTML for almost any login page, but with the entry fields linked to their own collection points. It looks real, but isn't. The growth in the use of SSL, which certifies the security of a connection to a site, and of browsers which could use the SSL certificate to identify whether a site was masquerading, helped; but people didn't always know what signs to watch for.

Phishing didn't go away. By 2015, Canada's government estimated there were 156 million phishing emails being sent every day, of which 16 million would reach people's inboxes and 8 million would be opened. Of those, one in ten, or 800,000, would click the links in them, and one in ten of those would enter their details in the phishing site. That's only a 0.05 per cent success rate; but it's still 80,000 per day. In 2017, Google published a study of the 'dark web' where credentials are sold which found more than 4,000 'phishing kits' – prefabricated sites which look like Gmail, Yahoo or Hotmail logins – and that the most popular was used by 2,599 different hackers to steal a total of 1.4 million login credentials of username/ password pairs in the course of a year. In all, they saw 12.4 million credentials phished.[5]

Even so, that paled in comparison with the number of credentials exposed by data breaches, which amounted to 1.9 *billion*. The problem that poses for account security is that usernames can be guessed, or are often public. (Often they're just an email address.) Passwords can only be drawn from a limited number of characters, and humans tend to want to choose something that they can remember easily. This makes even encrypted passwords vulnerable to a 'dictionary attack' in which a computer slogs through possible combinations of existing words and characters, running them through the same algorithm that encrypted the original password, to try to find a match. The advent of high-performance graphics processing units (GPUs) has been a boon for password cracking because they can execute simple programs at extraordinary speeds. With those billions of username/password credentials drifting around on the web, and given people's tendency to reuse passwords, there's often a good chance someone has reused the password for their email at, say, LinkedIn, Adobe or Uber – all of which have suffered gigantic data breaches. A successful phishing attack on any single service that someone uses may yield access to many of their others too.

Phishing has been classified into a number of forms, including 'whaling' (aimed at the very biggest, often richest, targets), and 'spearphishing', targeting specific people in an organization because of their position. Emails which pretend to be from someone inside the organization and have links to malicious sites, or 'invoices' sent to accounts departments whose attachments are actually malware, are a common form of attack.

When someone else gets phished, the tendency is to think they're fools; but when you get phished, it's because you were caught off guard, or it's the service provider's fault for not having better protections against fake logins. In reality, it's always about misplaced trust. Sometimes, successful phishing is just about hitting the correct psychological buttons. In 2013, just after the Snowden leaks, Robert Johnston, then working for the Marine Corps (and who would later head Crowdstrike's inspection of the hacking of the Democratic National Congress), investigated how many military personnel would be susceptible. His team sent out a phishing email with the subject line 'SEAL team six conducts an operation that kills Edward Snowden'. It worked scarily well: 'The click rate was through the roof,' he told Buzzfeed.[6]

So now the problem for the Clinton campaign team members, as they considered the email with its worrying message, was: is this phishing? Or did someone actually have access to Podesta's personal emails?

At 9.29 am on the east coast, Latham sent the email on to Charles Delavan, the IT helpdesk manager who was second-in-command of the four-strong IT team. Within half an hour he responded: 'This is a legitimate email. John needs to change his password immediately, and ensure that two-factor authentication is turned on on his account.'[7]

Two-factor authentication (2FA) is an added layer of security for any sort of account normally protected only by a username and password. When you try to log on from a new device, it demands a code which is sent separately to, or generated on, an already trusted device. The ring of trusted devices or apps is then widened either by generating one-off passwords to be used on specific devices, or entering the original password followed by an 'authorization code' generated by an app or sent from the server to a phone, and which is typically valid for about 30 seconds.

Once set up, 2FA tends to stay out of the way; it doesn't interfere with getting or sending email, or signing into a social media or other account, as long as you're doing that on a device already given your imprimatur. Only when you're trying to log into a new or different device does it turn into a roadblock. (To guard against the possibility that you've lost your phone and don't have access to any other trusted device, Google and others let you generate 'anytime codes' to print out and keep.)

But the roadblock for you becomes an almost impenetrable wall for a would-be hacker. If they need a one-time code which will be sent to a device (itself typically secured by another, different code, or biometrics), hacking into the account becomes a far different challenge. The only way around it then is either to steal the device, or somehow get hold of a code that will allow them into the account.

Getting the code isn't easy. The 30-second code system, known as 'Timed One-Time Passcodes', or T-OTP, is increasingly popular for 2FA systems. The code can either be generated by the login server and sent via SMS to the owner's phone, or generated by an app on the phone. (SMS is viewed as less secure, because phone numbers can be stolen without stealing the device itself; the codes can then be intercepted.)

The code is generated from a 'seed' number provided by the login server, which is usually read into the app by scanning a QR code or typing in a sequence of characters. The seed number is also stored on the login server. When the user tries to log in, the app and the server both apply a predetermined algorithm using the seed and the time, to the nearest 30 seconds, to generate a 40-character code which is then boiled down to a six-digit number. Enter that number and you're in. Every 30 seconds, there will be a different number;

without knowing the seed, you can't predict what the next number will be. In theory, as long as the seed is secure on the server and inside the app, you have authenticated the user.

Well, almost. The problem is that the server allows for the device's clock to drift slightly, and calculates not only the current code, but also the code for the previous 30-second segment, and for the following one. That creates a 90-second window for hacking. It's comparatively easy to build a webpage which looks like Gmail's login, and asks for a code – and passes those elements on to the real Gmail page. Such a 'man in the middle' attack lets the hacker validate their own system against Gmail's challenge; now they're logged in, and have captured the user's password (which has just been typed in) so they can access the email settings to grab a set of anytime codes. (A quick web search turns up readymade exploit kits to phish 2FA-protected credentials.)

But hacking a 2FA-protected account is not trivial, and if the phishing isn't done well it will trigger suspicion both at the email provider and with the user who is being phished. In general, 2FA reduces the chance of being hacked by 90 per cent or more, and if you try to phish someone without realizing they have 2FA turned on, the credentials you get are essentially useless.

Even so, roughly 70 per cent of email users don't use 2FA, according to a survey of 2,000 adults in May 2016. (The countries covered were the US, UK, France, Germany, Australia and New Zealand.) Just over half weren't sure how it worked; 41 per cent had no idea what it was.[8]

That means scammers can rely on seven in ten recipients of their phishing emails having no protection as long as they click through to the fake page and enter their login details.

Podesta's personal Gmail account was one of the 70 per cent: it didn't have 2FA enabled.

Delavan later said that he had mistyped in his reply to Latham: he'd meant to say that it was an illegitimate email, not a legitimate one. In his reply to Latham, he included the correct link to reset Podesta's password and turn on 2FA. But that wasn't the link that was clicked; instead, it was the convincing-looking link in the original 'Someone has your password' email.

The link led to a page which appeared to be a standard Google sign-in page. But it wasn't. It had been created with the bit.ly link shortening service, which can take a gigantically long URL and generate a shorter version beginning with bit.ly; a 255-character URL can be boiled down to just 13 characters. When you click on the bit.ly URL, the browser requests it from the service, which checks the database entry for that string of characters, and redirects the browser to the original URL. (Twitter uses the same method for every URL posted on its service; that lets it remove spam and malicious links immediately, by stopping the lookup or addition of identified malicious URLs to the database.)

The original URL stored at bit.ly led to 'myaccount.google. com-securitysettingpage.tk'. At first glance, legitimate – except the '.tk' at the end is suspect; it's for the island of Tokelau in the Pacific. The URL was also carefully encoded so that the page, mimicking a Google sign-in, would be pre-populated with Podesta's email address and Google profile photo. To the unwary, it would look just as it should, and they would go ahead and enter a password.

By 10.10 am, 2FA had been turned on for the account. But it was too late. His entire email archive, going back to 2009 – helpfully saved online by Google – had been made accessible to a team of Russian hackers known to those tracking them as 'Fancy Bear', or APT28. They downloaded the lot.

And yet there were subtle hints that the email to Podesta was not legitimate. One was in the subject line itself. '*Someone has your password*' it seemed to read. But what looks like the English letter 'o' in the words 'someone' and 'password' is actually a completely different character: a Unicode character which looks like an English 'o' to a human reader in most computer fonts – such as that used on an iPhone – but, to the computer itself, isn't the same at all. (Ironically, the difference is most apparent when viewing the email on the Wikileaks site, which uses the Courier font and makes the fake 'o' look more like a zero.)

Why use that different character? The best explanation is to evade Google's spam and phishing detection systems, where the phrase 'someone has your password' coming from a non-Google address would be blocked. The Fancy Bear team had probably already experimented with this; and if one unusual character had failed, there would be a multiplicity of others to swap in for a fresh attempt at getting past the filters and hooking a victim.

But even as the hackers were targeting the DNC and the campaign team, they too were being observed. SecureWorks, a cybersecurity company, had been following the hackers' work as they moved around the net. Bit.ly lets users set up accounts so that they can monitor clickthroughs on their links. But it also lets anyone else track how many have clicked it, and what the original URL was, and what other URLs that account has created shortened links for.

SecureWorks was able to pick out roughly 9,000 more links created by the same team. Between October 2015 and May 2016 those were sent to around 3,900 people in the US military, government, and suppliers, as well as journalists, members of the US Democratic National Committee, which organized the caucuses and would coordinate with the winner of the race for delegates, and other members of Clinton's campaign team. All had been the target of similar 'spearphishing' emails. Viewed in a browser, the 'Someone has your password' element was in white text on an urgently red background; the 'CHANGE PASSWORD' link in white text inside a web-link-blue box. Though the URL changed, the layout was consistent.

According to an analysis of SecureWorks' research by the Associated Press of 19,000-odd malicious links created by Fancy Bear between October 2015 and May 2016, the first set was sent on 10 March targeting dozens of people apparently because they had worked on the 2008 Clinton campaign. Most of those failed; though some of the links were clicked, that doesn't indicate whether credentials were entered. In each case, just as with the phishing message sent to Podesta, the original URL was pre-encoded with the email address of the person being targeted so that those details would be filled in on the fake login page.[9]

Another round followed the next day, targeting the Clinton inner circle. But emails in the hillaryclinton.com domain used Google's email systems, and already had 2FA turned on, so staff knew that a warning about someone having their password could be ignored. Some of the phishing attempts faked coming from other members of staff, to try to get them to send information or passwords. The staff were aware of the ongoing attempts, and that they were also targeting the DNC.

The phishing attempts continued through March and into May, when scores more were aimed at the Clinton campaign and the DNC, even though the latter was already hacked; analysts reckon there were two groups at work, with the same aims but separate operations. SecureWorks saw them spread their net wider, aiming at Democrats well beyond the Brooklyn headquarters; in an analysis published in June 2016, it said there were 213 links created between March and May targeting 108 different hillaryclinton.com email addresses. The targets for the spearphishing campaign ranged from junior personnel in charge of travel to the finance director. But the campaign's security was effective. Only 20 of the links had been clicked; and that doesn't of itself indicate that they entered their credentials. A few of the links were clicked more than once – which could indicate suspicion more than gullibility. Those I talked to from the campaign team subsequently were adamant: they were aware of phishing attempts, and they wouldn't fall for it.[10]

Fancy Bear didn't restrict its phishing to the central team, though. Its broad range of phishing emails caught some in regional groups, such as one working in Chicago whose emails were hacked in late March. The DNC's director of voter protection, Pratt Wiley, was targeted 15 times between October 2015 and March 2016. The phishing also targeted people at companies working with the campaign, such as 270 Strategies, a campaign-building organization allied to Clinton, and the Clinton Foundation, a charitable organization set up by Bill Clinton in 1997. One of the people I spoke to who worked closely with the campaign thought Podesta's account might have been compromised before the March emails; there's no way of knowing whether earlier phishing emails weren't simply removed from the subsequent data dump.

That the Clinton campaign would be targeted wasn't surprising. The question was, by who? There was an undercurrent of unease among some in the campaign. Although there were hundreds of staff, there was nobody dedicated to the job of cybersecurity – an omission that younger members of the team felt unhappy about. There were only four people in the full-time IT side of the team, none specifically charged with the cybersecurity role.

By April 2016, some in the DNC realized that it had been hacked, possibly for some time; the FBI had been warning it for six months that there were hacking attempts under way against its servers.

In mid-May, the Clinton campaign team took a key step by telling the staff to use Signal, an end-to-end encrypted app which offers text, voice and video calling to authenticated phone numbers. It's almost immune to spoofing, and doesn't store anything on servers. Staff were told not to discuss anything sensitive via email; instead anything contentious, especially about Donald Trump, had to go via Signal.[11]

On Friday 10 June the DNC leadership told its 100-odd staff to hand in their laptops. Though they didn't say why at the time, a breach of the DNC's servers had been confirmed by Crowdstrike, which had been retained by the organization once its suspicions about hacking were too big to ignore. Crowdstrike was confident that the hacking had been done by Fancy Bear, aka APT28, a Russian state-linked group that it had been watching, and for even longer by another group which they called Cozy Bear.

On Sunday, 12 June, Julian Assange, the founder of Wikileaks, told the *Peston on Sunday* TV news programme in the UK that 'we have upcoming leaks in relation to Hillary Clinton, which are great. Wikileaks has a very good year ahead of it… we have emails relating to Hillary Clinton which are pending publication'. In retrospect, was he talking about the DNC emails, or the Podesta ones?[12]

Assange harboured a longstanding resentment of Clinton because of the threats made against him by the US State Department when she was in charge after his publication in 2010 of the US diplomatic cables. As the 2016 campaign crescendoed, Assange was in his fourth year of self-imposed austerity inside the Ecuadorian embassy in London, where he had sought and been given political asylum in June 2012 while facing rape charges in Sweden. He feared being extradited from Sweden to the US to face trial for espionage.

Unable to leave the embassy grounds – which consisted of a ground floor flat, where his single room (one of the embassy's six) was described as 'threadbare' – Assange's resentment had distilled and crystallized. Whatever hurt Hillary or limited her horizons was fine by him. And Wikileaks had hardly been worried about publishing personal emails before.

On Tuesday 14 June, the DNC announced that its computers had been hacked by Russian sources. Crowdstrike said that two different Russian groups had broken in.[13]

Within 24 hours, an online character called 'Guccifer 2.0' sent a number of news websites a small dump of documents and emails, and claimed 'this is me who hacked Democratic National Committee'. (The choice of name was an interesting reference: the first Guccifer was an unemployed Romanian taxi driver who hacked and dumped the contents of a number of US and Romanian politicians' emails in 2013 and 2014. He was extradited to the US and indicted there in May 2016. He claimed he had previously hacked Hillary Clinton's email server, but offered no proof. In September that year he was jailed for just over four years.)[14]

Guccifer 2.0 set up a Wordpress blog and proclaimed that despite Crowdstrike's report of 'sophisticated hacker groups' breaking into the DNC, it wasn't really that hard: 'Guccifer may have been the first one who penetrated Hillary Clinton's and other Democrats' mail servers. But he certainly wasn't the last. No wonder any other hacker could easily get access to the DNC's servers.' He strenuously denied being anything to do with Fancy Bear or Cozy Bear; he was Romanian and worked alone, he insisted.

He claimed to have been inside the DNC's systems for more than a year, and displayed documents, including an opposition analysis of Donald Trump's likely strengths and weaknesses. 'The main part of the papers, thousands of files and mails, I gave to Wikileaks. They will publish them soon.'[15]

The documents weren't all authentic, though; some had been tampered with. And some of the details about the hacker raised suspicions. He didn't understand Romanian when it was put to him. Some of his email metadata showed it had come via a VPN service popular in Russia. He used brackets rather than colons in smiley emoticons, more typical when using the Cyrillic keyboard than the Romanian layout. The documents had been opened on multiple machines, and the metadata showed Russian names and Cyrillic settings. There was even the use of a pirated version of Office 2007 – popular in Russia – to process the documents. It all pointed strongly to Russian state-backed hackers as the source. Because why would amateur or commercial Russian hackers want to break into the DNC's servers? There was no money there. The details of what was happening were political arcana.

Thomas Rid, a cybersecurity expert who was then at the Department of War Studies at King's College London, thought that the timing was 'too smooth for one hacker', noting how Guccifer 2.0's publication of the DNC's emails distracted from the organization's announcement of a hack. He agreed with Crowdstrike: Guccifer 2.0 was closely linked, if not part of, Cozy Bear and Fancy Bear.[16]

In late June Guccifer 2.0 provided the website The Smoking Gun with a big file containing the emails of one of the DNC's Chicago regional staff members from a period up to 22 March (when she was hacked). This made the idea that he was separate from Fancy Bear even less tenable. But it also showed how strangely some campaign staff were using email. The Smoking Gun reprinted a series of emails sent as staff prepared to corral reporters at a rally in Las Vegas attended by Clinton. The back-and-forth of one-line emails sent over the course of 10 minutes looked bizarre in the modern smartphone world: the conversation would make more sense as a texting, WhatsApp or Signal exchange, and would have been faster, unhackable and left fewer traces. The *Washington Post* wrote up the leak and commented that it would 'reinforce the fact that Clinton prefers to campaign in a bubble. She rarely takes questions from the travelling press corps.'[17, 18]

The same was true of Trump. But there weren't leaked emails about Trump's campaign.

On Friday, 22 July, just as the Democrats were gathering for their convention to confirm Clinton as their candidate, Wikileaks published a dump of 22,000 DNC emails, including some where Bernie Sanders was disparaged by party members. The Democratic hierarchy and Sanders supporters were quickly at each other's throats again, and the DNC chair was forced to resign.

The campaign had moved into a new phase: information war. For Clinton, the hack meant yet another excuse, or reason, why the words 'Clinton', 'hacking' and 'emails' might be in headlines again. But there was also something strange about the documents in the dump: some of them looked as though they didn't come only from the DNC.

Writing in August 2016, when he first revealed the Clinton campaign's use of Signal, Nick Bilton of *Vanity Fair* observed that the risk of email hacking left people with two options: 'either delete everything (and hope it's also deleted from the server) or leave it all, cross your fingers, and hope for the best.'[11]

His article was titled 'How the Clinton campaign is foiling the Kremlin'.

## October surprise, surprise, surprise

American presidential election campaigns have developed the idea of the 'October surprise', a revelation about one of the candidates which is unveiled with just a month to go to polling day. It turned out that 2016 wouldn't offer the vanilla version.

Friday 7 October, just four weeks before voting, turned out to be a busy news day. At about 2.00 pm, the US Department of Homeland Security and the Office of the Director of National Intelligence (DNI) released a joint statement. It read:

> The US Intelligence Community is confident that the Russian Government directed the recent compromises of emails from US persons and institutions, including from US political organizations. The recent disclosures of alleged hacked emails on sites like DCLeaks.com and Wikileaks and by the Guccifer 2.0 online persona are consistent with the methods and motivations of Russian-directed efforts... We believe, based on the scope and sensitivity of these efforts, that only Russia's senior-most officials could have authorized these activities.[19]

On most days, such an unambiguous report about the target of Russian hacking made by the US intelligence community – which takes in the FBI, CIA and NSA – would have held headlines for the rest of the day.

But at 4.00 pm, the *Washington Post* broke a far more dramatic story: an audio tape of Donald Trump talking about how he would sexually assault women and use the power of his position to over-whelm them. The story exploded like a bomb across news sites and TV networks.

Less than an hour later, Wikileaks released a dump of 2,060 of Podesta's emails and 170 documents. It claimed the first tranche showed Clinton had appeased Russian interests in 2015 by approv-ing the sale to a Russian business of a Canadian uranium mining company called Uranium One, which had mines in the US.[20]

Though the Trump tape was blitzing the airwaves, hundreds of user accounts on Twitter suddenly picked up the topic of the Podesta emails – even though the details of who had said what to whom over a uranium deal were complex, to put it mildly.

Twitter later suspended almost all of those accounts: it had determined they were linked to Russian interests, and particularly a disinformation group called the Internet Research Agency (IRA), based in St Petersburg, which is reckoned to have more than a thou-sand staff blogging and tweeting in the guise of other countries' nationals.[21]

For staff on the campaign, the day was a rollercoaster; one described it to me as the craziest day they had ever experienced. On getting the news of the email dump – which some, from Clinton on down, had suspected might happen after the DNC hack and then the regional staff phishing had hinted at broader compromises – Podesta and his communications staff sat down for a conference. They realized it would mean that 'Clinton' and 'emails' would keep appearing in the headlines. But there was nothing they could do.

The media narrative took on a life of its own, fuelled by access to Podesta's emails. 'Most of John's emails were … boring,' Clinton commented in her post-election book, *What Happened*. 'They revealed the nuts and bolts of a campaign at work.' None of it was about *her* personal email. But the shorthand of news writing meant it looked that way. And, Clinton observed, 'Anything said behind closed doors is automatically considered more interesting, important and honest than things said in public.' Her evident anger at the distortion of the content, and the outright lies in some of the repetition, comes through.[22]

That didn't stop the drip-drip-drip. On 12 October at 8.46 am EST, Trump himself tweeted 'Very little pick-up by the dishonest media of incredible information provided by Wikileaks'. What makes this notable is that just 15 minutes earlier Wikileaks had sent a private direct message to Trump's son, Donald Jr: 'There's many great stories the press are missing and we're sure some of your follows [sic] will find it,' the Wikileaks message read. 'Btw we just released Podesta Emails Part 4.'[23, 24]

Assange released selections of emails every day up to the election, carefully picked to cast Podesta and especially Clinton in the worst possible light. There was no way to know how complete the release was.

Podesta's emails did include some catches for Clinton's critics. There was the content of a paid speech she had given to Goldman Sachs. 'Forget the FBI cache; the Podesta emails show how America is run,' said the headline on an article in the *Guardian* by Thomas Frank at the end of October. He was outraged by what he felt the emails revealed: 'it is when you search "vineyard" on the Wikileaks dump that you realize these people truly inhabit a different world from the rest of us'. (He was outraged by references to Martha's Vineyard, 'the ritzy vacation resort island off the coast of Massachusetts'.)[25]

The question of what might have been found by trawling through the emails of Donald Trump Jr, or his sister Ivanka Trump, or her husband Jared Kushner – none of them strangers to money, having been born into millionairedom – didn't arise, of course, because their emails hadn't been published. (That was to change, partially, as an FBI investigation into collusion with Russia got under way in 2017.)

The bigger problem for the campaign, whose cybersecurity had become completely solid since shifting to Signal, was that the constant release tied together 'Clinton' and 'email' and now 'hacked'. Because those three words would appear together, the average person wouldn't distinguish between using a private server for emails (of which Clinton had been exonerated in July, and of which there was no direct evidence of hacking), and a commercial email service where one user had been hacked.

'What Leaked Emails Reveal About Hillary Clinton's Campaign,' read the headline at *Time*. At the *Washington Post*, it was 'Hacked emails appear to reveal excerpts of speech transcripts Clinton refused to release.'[26, 27]

The campaign was stymied, and tried to avoid the topic by releasing what seemed a self-contradicting statement: 'We are not going to confirm the authenticity of stolen documents released by Julian Assange, who has made no secret of his desire to damage Hillary Clinton,' said Glen Caplin, for Clinton. By calling them stolen, he seemed to be verifying their authenticity.[28]

Caplin was also given the unenviable task – described as 'the most spirit-crushing job in modern political history' in the book *Shattered*, about the unsuccessful campaign – of trying to sift through all of Podesta's emails to find the ones that would be used against Clinton, her staff and the wider aims of the Democratic Party. His team worked on a mobile whiteboard, on which each of the mounting list of 'scandals' emerging from the email dump was recorded, and tried to figure out what their rebuttal was, while others worked through the email corpus looking for old comments, observations or discussions which might rise zombie-style to infect the news cycle anew.[29]

The problem was that there were a lot of zombies. Podesta and the rest of the team had, as is common in many workplaces, treated email as a completely secure space in which to vent their opinions. Those were now being aired in the most public places at the most embarrassing time possible. Attempts to deny the veracity of the emails – suggesting that they might have been faked – fell flat because Google had itself effectively verified many of them through one of its anti-spam systems called DKIM, for 'DomainKeys Identified Mail'.

A DKIM signature consists of a cryptographic hash (a one-way calculation) of parts of the email, creating a unique string which is then included in the email's header. The parts of the email used to calculate the hash depend on the particular implementation of DKIM; it can be all of the body and the header (excluding the DKIM hash itself), or just a few parts of the header. Google's system, used on Gmail and by the hillaryclinton.com server, does it for the body.

So why didn't Google's DKIM system spot that the original phishing email sent to Podesta, claiming to be from a specific Google address, was fake? Why wasn't that rejected at the server, or dumped into a spam folder where it might never have been seen? The problem is that DKIM is limited. If there isn't a DKIM system built into the *sending* server, there's no simple way to generate the hash.

And just when it seemed it couldn't get worse, it did. One of the email dumps included an email with Podesta's iCloud password. On the discussion site Reddit, activity on the /pol group (or 'subreddit'), ostensibly dedicated to the discussion of politics, exploded as one of its users logged in and was able to locate and wipe Podesta's iPhone. They also hacked his Twitter account and posted a pro-Trump message. 'This is the exact moment in history where they will pinpoint the fall of hilary's [*sic*] campaign,' wrote one anonymous 8chan user.[30]

# The final countdown

When the votes were counted, three states – Michigan, Pennsylvania and Wisconsin – turned out to be the hinges on which the door of history turned. They controlled 16, 10 and 20 Electoral College votes; a candidate needs 270 to win. Trump won Michigan by 10,704 votes, or 0.25 per cent of the votes cast, over Clinton. In Pennsylvania, he won by 44,292 votes, a 0.75 per cent margin. In Wisconsin, he won by 22,748 votes, a 0.81 per cent difference. In each of the three states a third candidate, Gary Johnson, received more votes than the winning margin – though of course it's impossible to know how those votes might have been distributed if he had not run.

The total difference in those three states was just 77,000 votes out of 13.2 million for the two main candidates, or 0.6 per cent – six people in a thousand. Barack Obama won all three states in 2012, by margins of between 5 and 10 per cent. But in 2016 Clinton received 600,000 fewer votes there than Obama did, while Trump saw a surge of 400,000 compared with the losing Republican candidate Mitt Romney in 2012. Had Trump only garnered as many votes as Romney, Clinton would have won Michigan and Pennsylvania, but not Wisconsin. That would have left her on 268 Electoral College votes – and Trump on 270, still the victor.

Did Podesta being hacked make that difference by keeping 'email', 'hacked' and 'Clinton' in the headlines? Was it FBI Director James Comey's reopening of the Clinton investigation just over a week before the election, propelling the email story back into the headlines? Was it something in Trump's vague and hyperbolic promises to voters? Did Clinton's lack of a powerful message to compare with Obama's 2008 cry of 'Yes we can' handicap her? Was it the Russian propaganda coursing like an infection through the bloodstream of social media?

It's impossible to be certain. But with any complex system, each element can play a part. In a chaotic system, a tiny shift in the input can create a huge variation in the output. And the 2016 US presidential election was, without doubt, chaotic.

Nor did the election result itself stop the phishing. Less than six hours after Trump had sealed the necessary Electoral College votes to win, five waves of phishing emails were sent to US-based think-tanks and NGOs, with attachments or links claiming to contain 'shocking' analysis of the outcome. Volexity, the security company which spotted them, reckoned it was the work of Cozy Bear, based on the malware that the files would install.[31]

On 29 December, nearly two months after Donald Trump's election, the US Department of Home Security and the FBI jointly released a report on what they called 'Grizzly Steppe'. Unlike many intelligence project codenames, which mash together two quite random words such as 'Pensive Giraffe' or 'Cloudy Cobra' to create their words, the names here were carefully chosen to evoke Russia. The Joint Analysis Report – JAR – would, however, be little use to any but a security administrator.[32, 33]

One attached file points to a number of IP addresses said to have been used by the hackers (these ranged around the world, from the US to Canada to Swaziland to Luxembourg to Venezuela) along with MD5 hashes, a form of mathematical fingerprint, to identify rogue files inside an organization.

What the JAR did not provide was an audit trail: there were no times and dates, no names, no explanations for how the conclusions had been reached. This made it easy to deny, as the Russian Foreign Minister Sergey Lavrov was happy to do.[34]

Aaron Barr, who like Podesta saw his emails spread far and wide across the internet, watched what happened with enlightened interest:

> If I'd had a chance to talk to him, we would have [had] some very similar emotional experiences, where there are a set of things that happen in discussion internally that you just say to yourself. When they see the light of day, and everybody else gets to read those and interpret those, and you watch the discussion and you're thinking to yourself, 'Wait, no, but that doesn't mean that', or there's a whole other set of things and you can't … [he pauses]. There's just no way you can try to deal with that in a public venue to try to change that opinion.

What's the answer, then?

> I think not to acknowledge it, to just be silent about it, is unfortunately – I wish it was very different because I would much rather have a public discussion, especially in my emails, some of the more salacious or controversial material, I'd much rather have a public discussion and hear the anger or the disagreement and debate it. I would much rather do that than be silent. But I do think to be silent is the best approach.

Speaking in May 2017, Podesta expressed his frustration at the way that the FBI investigation overshadowed much of the campaign – and the shock of its reopening just 11 days before the election, even though that was quickly closed. 'If I had to do it over again, I wouldn't have returned the emails to the State Department,' he told *Der Spiegel*. 'I would've just released them. Perhaps we could have ended the whole thing with it.'[35]

It probably wouldn't have. But it's a nice thought. One point, though, remains true: the Clinton campaign itself wasn't hacked. The combination of 2FA and Signal kept its secrets safe. Podesta's personal email, replete with special offers from online stores, messages about his professorial work, and all the other detritus of an inbox, was hacked. A few of the people in regional areas were too. But none of the central group was. Hillary Clinton's campaign server wasn't hacked. Nor were her emails.

# References

1  Tait, M (as @PwnAllTheThings on Twitter) (2017) The takeaway is this: your personal email is the portal to everything you do online. If it is compromised *all* of your other accounts fall, *Twitter.com*, 16 August. Available from: https://twitter.com/pwnallthethings/status/897932050111406081

2  Langberg, M (1995) AOL acts to thwart hackers, *SF Mercury News*, 8 September. Available from: https://simson.net/clips/1995/95.SJMN.AOL_Hackers.html

3  Amato, J (1996) LA Times story on AOL phishers, *alt.aol-sucks newsgroup*, 13 May. Available from: https://groups.google.com/forum/m/#!search/phishing$20aohell$20alt.aol-sucks/alt.aol-sucks/dc5ll928b2U

4  barton (1996) How AOL could stop account phishing tomorrow, *alt.aol-sucks newsgroup*, 5 February. Available from: https://groups.google.com/d/topic/alt.aol-sucks/eNjlyDPjtEo/discussion

5  Thomas, K, *et al* (2017) Data breaches, phishing or malware? Understanding the risks of stolen credentials, *google.com*, 30 October. Available from: https://static.googleusercontent.com/media/research.google.com/en//pubs/archive/46437.pdf

6  Leopold, J (2017) He solved the DNC hack. Now he's telling his story for the first time, *buzzfeed.com*, 8 November. Available from: www.buzzfeed.com/jasonleopold/he-solved-the-dnc-hack-now-hes-telling-his-story-for-the

7  Lipton, E, Sanger, D and Shane, S (2016) The perfect weapon: how Russian cyberpower invaded the U.S., *New York Times*, 13 December. Available from: www.nytimes.com/2016/12/13/us/politics/russia-hack-election-dnc.html?mtrref=t.co&_r=0

**8**  Gott, A (2016) New study: the one big security trick people aren't using, *LastPass blog*, 2 August. Available from: https://blog.lastpass.com/2016/08/new-study-the-one-big-security-trick-people-arent-using.html/

**9**  Satter, R (2017) Inside story: how Russians hacked the Democrats' emails, *Associated Press*, 4 November. Available from: https://apnews.com/dea73efc01594839957c3c9a6c962b8a

**10**  Threat Group-4127 targets Hillary Clinton presidential campaign, *Secureworks Counter Threat Unit Threat Intelligence*, 16 June 2016. Available from: https://www.secureworks.com/research/threat-group-4127-targets-hillary-clinton-presidential-campaign

**11**  Bilton, N (2016) How the Clinton campaign is foiling the Kremlin, *Vanity Fair*, 26 August. Available from: www.vanityfair.com/news/2016/08/how-the-clinton-campaign-is-foiling-the-kremlin

**12**  Assange on Peston on Sunday: 'More Clinton leaks to come', *ITV News*, 12 June 2016. Available from: www.itv.com/news/update/2016-06-12/assange-on-peston-on-sunday-more-clinton-leaks-to-come

**13**  Alperovitch, D (2016) Bears in the midst: intrusion into the Democratic National Committee, *Crowdstrike blog*, 15 June. Available from: www.crowdstrike.com/blog/bears-midst-intrusion-democratic-national-committee/

**14**  (unsigned) (2016) DNC hacker releases Trump oppo report, *The Smoking Gun*, 15 June. Available from: www.thesmokinggun.com/documents/crime/dnc-hacker-leaks-trump-oppo-report-647293

**15**  Guccifer 2.0 (2016) Guccifer 2.0 DNC's servers hacked by a lone hacker, *Guccifer 2.0 blog*, 15 June. Available from: https://guccifer2.wordpress.com/2016/06/15/dnc/

**16**  Franceschi-Bicchierai, L (2016) 'Guccifer 2.0' is likely a Russian government attempt to cover up its own hack, *Motherboard*, 16 June. Available from: https://motherboard.vice.com/en_us/article/wnxgwq/guccifer-20-is-likely-a-russian-government-attempt-to-cover-up-their-own-hack

**17**  (unsigned) (2016) Hack yields Clinton campaign e-mail, records, *The Smoking Gun*, 28 June. Available from: http://thesmokinggun.com/documents/crime/hfa-gmail-attack-723571

**18**  Borchers, C (2016) Reported email hack purports to show Clinton campaign tracking snoopy reporters, *The Washington Post*, 28 June.

Available from: www.washingtonpost.com/news/the-fix/wp/2016/06/28/
reported-email-hack-purports-to-show-clinton-campaign-tracking-
snoopy-reporters/

19  DHS Press Office (2016) Joint statement from the Department of
Homeland Security and Officer of the Director of National Intelligence
on Election Security', US Department of Homeland Security,
7 October. Available from: www.dhs.gov/news/2016/10/07/joint-
statement-department-homeland-security-and-office-director-national

20  Assange, J (2016) The Podesta emails; part one, *Wikileaks*, 7 October.
Available from: https://wikileaks.org/podesta-emails/press-release

21  Nakashima, R and Ortutay, B (2017) AP exclusive: Russia Twitter
trolls deflected Trump bad news, *Associated Press*, 10 November.
Available from: https://apnews.com/fc9ab2b0bbc34f11bc
10714100318ae1

22  Clinton, H (2017) *What Happened*, Simon & Schuster, New York

23  Trump, D (2016) Very little pick-up by the dishonest media of
incredible information provided by WikiLeaks. So dishonest! Rigged
system!, *twitter.com*, 12 October. Available from: https://twitter.com/
realDonaldTrump/status/786201435486781440

24  Ioffe, J (2017) The secret correspondence between Donald Trump Jr.
and WikiLeaks, *The Atlantic*, 13 November. Available from: www.
theatlantic.com/politics/archive/2017/11/the-secret-correspondence-
between-donald-trump-jr-and-wikileaks/545738/

25  Frank, T (2016) Forget the FBI cache; the Podesta emails show how
America is run, *Guardian*, 31 October. Available from: www.
theguardian.com/commentisfree/2016/oct/31/the-podesta-emails-
show-who-runs-america-and-how-they-do-it

26  Frizell, S (2016) What leaked emails reveal about Hillary Clinton's
campaign, *Time*, 8 October. Available from: http://time.com/4523749/
hillary-clinton-wikileaks-leaked-emails-john-podesta/

27  Heiderman, RS and Hamburger, T (2016) Hacked emails appear to
reveal excerpts of speech transcripts Clinton refused to release, *The
Washington Post*, 7 October. Available from: www.washingtonpost.
com/politics/hacked-emails-appear-to-reveal-excerpts-of-speech-
transcripts-clinton-refused-to-release/2016/10/07/235c26ac-8cd4-
11e6-bf8a-3d26847eeed4_story.html

**28** Allen, C and Przybyla, HM (2016) Report: Wikileaks releases what appear to be excerpts of Clinton's paid speeches, *USA Today*, 7 October. Available from: www.usatoday.com/story/news/politics/elections/2016/10/07/clinton-paid-speech-transcripts-wikileaks/91751472/

**29** Allen, J and Parnes, A (2017) *Shattered: Inside Hillary Clinton's doomed campaign*, Crown Publishing, New York

**30** (anonymous) (2016) Internet people need hotpockets and a holocaust, *Reddit /pol/*, 12 October. Available from: https://web.archive.org/web/20161020092103/http://web.archive.org/web/20161012202517/https:/8ch.net/pol/res/7831536.html

**31** Adair, S (2016) PowerDuke: widespread post-election spear phishing campaigns targeting think tanks and NGOs, *Volexity blog*, 9 November. Available from: www.volexity.com/blog/2016/11/09/powerduke-post-election-spear-phishing-campaigns-targeting-think-tanks-and-ngos/

**32** NCCIC and FBI (2016) GRIZZLY STEPPE – Russian malicious cyber activity, *US CERT*, 29 December. Available from: www.us-cert.gov/sites/default/files/publications/JAR_16-20296A_GRIZZLY%20STEPPE-2016-1229.pdf

**33** Enhanced analysis of GRIZZLY STEPPPE activity, *US Department of Homeland Security*, 10 February 2017. Available from: www.us-cert.gov/sites/default/files/publications/AR-17-20045_Enhanced_Analysis_of_GRIZZLY_STEPPE_Activity.pdf

**34** Executive summary of Grizzly Steppe findings from Homeland Security Assistant Secretary for Public Affairs Todd Breasseale, *US Department of Homeland Security*, 30 December 2016. Available from: www.dhs.gov/news/2016/12/30/executive-summary-grizzly-steppe-findings-homeland-security-assistant-secretary

**35** Brinkbäumer, K and Sandberg, B (2017) It is soul-crushing! Clinton campaign chair John Podesta on President Trump, *Der Spiegel*, 5 May. Available from: www.spiegel.de/international/world/clinton-campaign-chair-john-podesta-on-president-trump-a-1146317.html

## LESSONS FROM THE JOHN PODESTA HACK

- Learn what phishing looks like. Always be suspicious of warning messages about hacks. Don't click links on a PC; enter URLs.

- Enable two-factor authentication on all the accounts – corporate and personal – of people who are going to be in the public eye.

- Don't rely on a text message authentication system: it can be spoofed or hijacked by someone taking over a SIM card or phone number. Use apps which generate codes, or physical devices which generate codes.

- Don't send passwords to other accounts in email, because if that gets hacked, so potentially does the other account.

- If at all possible, don't use email. Apps such as Signal offer real-time connection which works even better than email. They can also send attachments.

- Assume that at some point in the future your email is going to be hacked and spread far and wide because you've become famous (or notorious), for reasons you don't yet know. Consider whether you're happy with the content to be found there.

- Media and social media narratives around data leaks, especially of email, gain a life of their own. You won't be able to put out the fires individually. Focus on another narrative.

- With that in mind, if you face such a situation, try to work out what the worst outcomes could be by examining the contents that you think have been compromised. Build strategies for dealing with customers, suppliers and media based on what you think might happen. (See too whether executives in your company are willing to submit to this in an exercise. If not, how will they cope if it does happen?)

# Open house      05

## TJX

*They wouldn't even know we were in [the systems], if we didn't deface [them]... I'd rather have root.*
A HACKER CALLING HIMSELF 'SOUPNAZI' TALKING TO ZDNET IN 1999

It was July 2007, and Maksym Yastremskiy had enjoyed his evening at the Club First Aura nightclub in Kemer, a coastal resort in Turkey. Then, as he and a friend arrived back at his hotel, the men surrounded him, and he found himself handcuffed and bundled into a car.

The Turkish security detail who arrested the Ukrainian under an Interpol warrant couldn't get past the encryption protecting the contents of Yastremskiy's computer. So, as a US Secret Service agent later recounted it, they forcefully interrogated him until he revealed the passphrase to unlock it. There they found the sorts of incriminating details they had been expecting about his life as a credit card criminal, dealing in and creating 'clones' of millions of cards from around the world. The process is straightforward enough: given a credit card number, expiry date and user's name, you can create a fake card – magnetic stripe and all – which in the US and many other countries lets you make fraudulent transactions for hundreds of dollars.

Buying and selling such details was a thriving business, the fraudster's form of a short-lived commodity market, such as milk: stolen card numbers generally had a limited life, and overuse could bring problems for the purchaser and others up the chain. So the value was to be found in dealing in large numbers, as anonymously as possible, and ideally not using them yourself.

But as any commodity dealer will tell you, trading can be profitable. Yastremskiy, from Ukraine, was reckoned to have earned around $11 million from trading credit card data. He was in Turkey, far away from the safety of Ukraine, because he thought he'd meet someone who could deal more data. Even though Yastremskiy, who went by the online handle of 'Maksik', was reckoned by authorities to be 'the world's most prolific vendor of compromised card details', he always wanted more contacts with more stolen data.[1]

Yastremskiy's computer also contained details which linked him back to a gang of credit card data thieves. The US Secret Service had previously tempted him to meetings with other 'contacts' – in fact their agents – in Thailand, the United Arab Emirates and Turkey. They had cloned his hard drive in 2006, but had been unable to get into it. With the passphrase detail from Turkey, the US Secret Service were able to follow the details about the rest of Yastremskiy's connections.

Among the people who the hard drive provided connections to was an American called Albert Gonzalez. He, it turned out, had been instrumental in the biggest theft of credit card details that had ever been recorded. The commodity market was about to turn spectacularly sour.

# Airborne money

The US company TJX is, and was, a retailing giant. In the financial year to the end of January 2006, the TJX group of companies encompassed more than 2,300 stores in the US, Puerto Rico, Canada, Europe and Australia under the various brands of TK Maxx, TJ Maxx, Marshalls, Winners, HomeGoods, AJ Wright, HomeSense, and Bob's Stores. Revenues were over $16 billion, 80 per cent of which was from the US, but margins were thin: net profit was just $690 million, representing a 5 per cent return on sales – roughly consistent with the group's long-term figure. There was $465 million of cash in the bank, up from $307 million a year before.

TJX's business is high-turnover clothes retailing: its 2002 annual report explained that 'our mission is to deliver a rapidly changing assortment of quality, brand name merchandise at prices that are 20–60 per cent less than department and speciality store regular prices, every day'. Sales and profits had grown rapidly since 1996. At that time, its position as a low-cost retailer reliant on rapid inventory and merchandise turnover meant TJX was continually looking for cutting-edge technologies to give it an edge over other organizations. In 2000 it was an early adopter of Wi-Fi, buying into the first generation which was installed at all of its retail stores – more than 1,200 of them – replacing the older wired system. Wireless connectivity for computing was then unfamiliar to most people; in June 1999 Apple's Steve Jobs had shown off the 'iBook' laptop, with Wi-Fi capability, and released the first 'Airport' base station for connectivity; for security, it offered a system called 'WEP', for Wired Equivalent Privacy, which was the standard agreed by the world body for securing wireless networks.

In 2000, most people didn't understand or use Wi-Fi. TJX was ahead of that curve. Its new Wi-Fi-enabled point-of-sale systems, which handled millions of credit and debit card transactions, were linked by WEP-secured systems to its mainframe computers, which stored details of those transactions, in some cases going back years. TJX was, like many retailers in the early years of the century, trying to fight on the streets and online. It had opened e-commerce stores, and was desperate to capture as much data as possible about its customers, as online retailers had begun to show that they could use data about past sales to nudge customers to buy extra items (notably at Amazon, where the 'people who bought X also bought Y' system seemed especially effective).

That prompted the creation of 'data warehouses' – ever-growing repositories of information about customers, stored in databases whose contents were meant to be easily accessible by design. The US did not (and still does not) have stringent data protection laws like those which were already in force in Europe, where access to personal data had to be carefully justified. So TJX collected and stored as much as it could: driver's licence details when people returned goods without a receipt; names and addresses; card numbers; Social Security numbers; military ID numbers; details of purchases. It would keep those for years, because you never knew when you might find a use for them.

Yet its focus on technology wasn't evenly applied. By 2006 its systems' security lagged behind the industry standard, called PCI-DSS (Payment Card Industry Data Security Standard), for protecting credit card data. The PCI-DSS had been formed in 2004 by a group of credit card associations worried about the ease with which a hacked database might give up its data. An internal IT security audit at TJX the same year noted multiple security flaws, such as a lack of firewalls (to prevent movement of data between different parts of the organization, or out of the organization), failure to encrypt cardholder data, timeliness of uploads for antivirus software and the absence of regular tests of security systems.

But the biggest weak link was at TJX's perimeter, in the WEP system nominally 'securing' its Wi-Fi network over which those millions of cards' data passed. The problem was that WEP was about as secure as a combination lock with two dials.

## Dubious security

In 1997, a team of experts was working on the '802.11b' standard for an exciting new method of connecting computers wirelessly to the internet. It promised connectivity as fast as a wired cable, but without a cable's restriction on movement. Besides setting down the standards for how internet packets would pass over the wireless network, they had also realized that it would need to have some form of security; whereas a wired network naturally limited access to those who could plug into it, a wireless network was always broadcasting its contents. They settled on an encryption system which was dubbed Wired Equivalent Privacy, or WEP for short, and it was written into the 802.11 standard as the default method for encrypting wireless communications on one of those networks.

Though its name – Wired Equivalent Privacy – implied it was as secure as connecting with a physical wire, WEP was irredeemably flawed.

The first doubts about its security were raised publicly in October 2000 by Jesse Walker. At the time, he was a cryptographer at the chipmaker Intel. He told me:

> One day in 2000 Duncan Kitchin, the Vice Chair of the 802.11 working group and an Intel employee, walked into my office. We discussed the authentication protocol, which could be broken immediately from a high level description of the protocol. When he left he gave me a copy of the 802.11 standard. I studied the protocol definition in the standard and then deduced the consequences of its definition. It is as simple as that.[2]

The consequences, he deduced, were calamitous. WEP wasn't safe, because its essential design was completely flawed.

He submitted a critique titled 'Unsafe at any key size: an analysis of the WEP encapsulation' to the 802.11 committee.[3] The title harked back to Ralph Nader's 1965 book *Unsafe at Any Speed*, about the inherent flaws – and consequent lethal dangers – in the design of American-built cars. WEP, as Walker pointed out, had inherent flaws which rendered it useless for truly secure communication. The reasons were technical, but important.

WEP allowed passwords up to 63 characters long, which were then converted to a 40-bit binary string to be used for encryption. It also tried to raise the encryption challenge by adding to the 40-bit string another 24-bit string known as the 'Initialization Vector', or IV. The IV changed with every data packet sent. With 24 bits available, there would be about 16.8 million different IVs to add to the 40 bits. The packet and the 64-bit string were then run through a reversible encryption algorithm called RC4. (You needed a reversible algorithm; otherwise the receiver wouldn't ever be able to decrypt the packet, and there would be no communication.)

Crucially, the IV was also sent unencrypted along with every encrypted Wi-Fi packet, so the receiver could synchronize decryption. You couldn't decrypt a single packet just by examining the unencrypted IV; you had to have the password too, because that made up the rest of the 64 bits, and cycling through every possible 64-bit combination would require an enormous number of attempts.

On paper, this might look fine. But in practice, things were very different. A Wi-Fi access point operating at 11 megabits per second, the initial Wi-Fi 802.11b standard, would work through every possible IV within about an hour, and then have to begin reusing them. (What about choosing them randomly, rather than sequentially? As Walker pointed out, this was, counterintuitively, even worse: mathematically, the chances of an IV reuse – or 'collision' – using random choice was 99 per cent within three *seconds* of normal use.) And because these were wireless networks, the data was being blasted out in all directions like a foghorn. There was no way to stop people picking up the packets and analysing them.

To break into a typical WEP-encrypted network, all a hacker needed to do was set up a Wi-Fi antenna, run a program that collected every passing packet, watch for two packets with the same IV, run that through the reverse of the RC4 encoding, and use that to figure out the remaining 40-bit password key used to encrypt the packet. And that would be the password for the entire network.

That sounds complex. But in fact it would probably only take a few minutes for an eavesdropping hacker to crack the encryption for a wireless system that a committee had laboured over for years and made standard for millions of devices around the world.

Nor would lengthening the IV change this dynamic, explained Walker; it would only slightly increase the time needed to complete the hack. 'WEP's design attempts to adapt RC4 to an environment for which it is poorly suited, with potentially catastrophic consequences for its intended users,' he wrote.

In case that language seemed too formal, his paper also pointed out that it would be simple for a determined attacker to compromise any base station, given a little determination. 'It is simply not worth trying to provide any privacy if this is the best we can do,' he wrote.

Walker's warnings were followed in 2001 by a series of academic papers re-demonstrating WEP's flaws, with titles such as 'Your 802.11 wireless network has no clothes' and the less confrontational, but still damning, 'Weaknesses in the key scheduling algorithm of RC4'. But rather like Nader's warnings, many people had to be affected before what Walker and other experts were saying was heeded by those who would lose from it.

The hacking community could read an academic paper as well as anyone. Sometimes the hackers' job was made easier by computer science students, who would spot the papers and write programs to see whether they could implement what was described; in such cases those programs, or the clearer concepts behind them, would leak out onto the wider web, where the program or the concept would soon be repurposed and weaponized as another element in hackers' growing arsenal.

By mid-2001 there were free WEP-hacking programs for Windows and even for Apple's Mac OSX (then a tiny player in the PC market). On 20 August, *Wired* ran a news article online which began, 'Wireless networks are a little less secure today with the public release of "AirSnort", a tool that can surreptitiously grab and analyze data moving across just about every major wireless network.'[4]

'WEP... is crippled with numerous security flaws,' noted the webpage for downloading AirSnort. 'AirSnort requires approximately 5–10 million encrypted packets to be gathered. Once enough packets have been gathered, AirSnort can guess the encryption password in under a second.'[5]

How long would it take to get 5–10 million packets? Between two and four hours, since the network generated about 800 packets per second. But some cracking systems could get to work on around 85,000 packets, and expect a 95 per cent success rate. Acquiring that many packets would take less than two minutes. The disclaimers that the programs were there to 'assess Wi-Fi network security' fooled nobody. If you used them, you were either trying to break into your own system to confirm how weak it was, or into someone else's system, probably with malicious intent.

One of the authors of AirSnort, Jeremy Bruestle, told *Wired* that many of those who had contacted him about the program were systems administrators thankful for at last being able to show their management that 'WEP really is insecure' by cracking it with his tool. Trusting WEP was too easy, he suggested.[4]

The noise about WEP's flaws kept growing. In June 2003, the Institute of Electrical and Electronic Engineers recommended that WEP should be abandoned as a wireless encryption standard, and people should instead use WPA – the far stronger Wi-Fi Protected Access algorithm, which used 48-bit keys and offered 50 *trillion* combinations rather than the 16.7 million of WEP, and never included the master key in the broadcast packet. The Wi-Fi Alliance, an industry body for certification and promotion, declared in February 2004 that WEP 'should not be considered a secure mechanism to protect Wi-Fi wireless LAN traffic' and that WPA should be used 'where data security is a concern'.[6] WEP was thus retired by the official body. But it lived on.

By March 2005 it wasn't only the criminals, lay hackers and experts who knew about WEP's flaws. That month a small team of FBI agents demonstrated to a meeting of the Information Systems Security Association in Los Angeles how they could break into a network protected by a 128-bit WEP key, using two laptops. They created a random password by swiping a hand over the keyboard, and then cracked it in just three minutes – prompting the agent giving the talk to say in a surprised tone, 'Usually it takes five to ten minutes.'[7]

By October 2005, TJX had got the message. Its chief information officer Paul Butka signed off on a plan to convert the WEP systems in the organization's 1,200 stores to WPA.

But because older base stations couldn't run the WPA algorithm, it would take until January 2007 to get the pilot project using WPA implemented. Meanwhile TJX had another, arguably more urgent, timetable: to meet the requirements of PCI-DSS version 1.1, which would become mandatory for any organization storing credit card data, by September 2006. That also mandated the use of WPA, not WEP. (The 1.0 version, from December 2004, didn't specify what version of wireless encryption to use.) In addition, sales were picking up. The wireless systems seemed to be helping sales. Upgrading them would be costly and disruptive, and PCI compliance looked more urgent, especially given the scolding TJX had been given; the PCI had given it a little more time to become compliant, but failing to do so would mean fines. Butka didn't want that; TJX's e-commerce storefronts were being closed that month after heading towards operating losses of $15 million, which was money the margin-pressed business wouldn't have available for other projects. PCI versus WEP became a matter of priorities.[8]

# Failure to upgrade

On 23 November 2005, Butka emailed his IT staff, suggesting a delay to the upgrade from WEP to WPA because, although he recognized WPA was 'best practice', most of the stores couldn't run it yet. It would save money from that year's IT budget, though before taking that step he did want the staff to agree that the risks of not upgrading 'are small or negligible'.[9]

Most agreed. Some didn't, though. One responded on the same day, pointing out that even though the PCI had given TJX some extra time to comply, using WEP meant 'we are still vulnerable' – and also, strictly speaking, non-compliant with PCI. It 'potentially exacerbates any findings should a breach be revealed', the staffer warned.

Not only was TJX still using a system that it knew was insecure, it was also storing the most valuable data for a commercial hacker – credit cards' 'Track 2' data, which if copied can be used to make an entirely new fake card. TJX was only complying with 3 of the 12 'control objectives' of PCI-DSS, and its executives were aware of this, as internal memos presented in court later showed. Among the nine where it was not in compliance were those covering encryption of card details, access controls and firewalls. An external auditor for PCI-DSS scolded TJX once again in September 2006 for the poor security in its systems – citing its use of WEP, as well as the continuing lack of software patching for ageing systems, and the absence of firewalls to create perimeters within the system itself. 'These are the simplest of best practices,' Keith Gosselin, then IT Officer at the Biddeford Savings Bank in Maine, told *Tech Target* in November 2007. 'As a CIO, CEO or CFO, why would you not want your company to meet these requirements?'[10] He was also puzzled how a company as large and rich as TJX could have failed at them.

But failed it had. And there was even worse news to come. While Butka and his staff argued in November 2005 over the urgency of upgrading from WEP, its flaws had already allowed their systems to be infiltrated for almost six months – and the intrusion would go on for more than a year.

# Going public

Early in October 2006, the fraud department at Discover called its counterpart at TJX and pointed to a dramatic increase in fraudulent transactions on cards previously used at the company's outlets: they were being used to buy large-denomination gift cards from the discount chains Walmart and Sam's Club, which were then sold for cash (typically at below face value), providing an untraceable money laundering method. Florida police, alerted to the problem – in which a group of 10 people drove around the state buying the cards – also told TJX about their concerns in November 2006. Someone was clearly using stolen credit card details, and a lot of them: the losses to Walmart and banks was put at around $8 million. This was a system-level intrusion.

TJX's problem was that it didn't know who was behind the intrusion, nor what they had done, or how they had got in. Some of the picture began to emerge from the few network logs, and computer forensic examinations by IBM and General Dynamics, who were called in on 18 December to help figure it out. Three days later, TJX's lawyers called the US Department of Justice to explain the problem: there seemed to be intruders in its system, and it couldn't be sure what they had taken or why. The Secret Service asked them to not announce anything; the hackers might still be in the system. On Boxing Day, TJX told the banks and credit card companies about the intrusion. By 27 December, nine days after the discovery of the intrusion, they'd figured out that the hackers had taken customer data – though they still weren't quite sure how much.

Now, they had to go public. In a message on the TJX site on 17 January 2007, more than six months before Yastremskiy would be arrested in Turkey, Ben Cammarata, the chairman and acting CEO, announced the hack. In the typically tortured language of executives seeking to spread blame as widely and thinly as possible, he said that 'I can tell you that we were extremely disappointed when we determined that we have suffered an unauthorized intrusion into our computer systems that process and store information related to customer transactions.'[11] It's not quite clear who he was disappointed by, and the passive tense of 'suffered an unauthorized intrusion' makes it sound like a bout of influenza rather than a hacking attack which any large organization storing millions of credit card and customer details should have been concerned to prevent. (The linked press release on the site was titled 'The TJX Companies Inc Victimized By Computer Systems Intrusion; Provides Information To Help Protect Customers'.[12] The passivity of the language is striking, as though a multi-billion-dollar company were being unfairly targeted.)

The scale of the problem only became clear in an attached FAQ (frequently asked questions) popup.[13] This noted that a 'limited' number of credit and debit card details had been stolen; it didn't specify that the number was 'limited' to millions. Then it added that that was for transactions made during 2003, and for about seven months during 2006 in its stores in the US, Puerto Rico and Canada. 'We do not currently believe that personal identification numbers (PINs) were compromised,' it noted. That's not as reassuring as it might sound, since in the US at that time hardly any store transaction would use a PIN. Instead, it was completely common to validate a card transaction with nothing more sophisticated than a signature, which was rarely checked and could anyway be easily forged.

Was it safe to continue shopping in TJX stores? 'We believe customers should feel safe shopping in our stores,' the FAQ hedged, adding that it had now adopted a plan which its computer security experts had confirmed would keep safe in-store credit and debit card transactions. It didn't say whether those experts were the same ones who had been in charge during the hack.

A formal filing in March that year was more forthcoming: full details had been stolen, including Track 2 data, for about 45.7 million cards.[14]

Inside TJX, there was still confusion about what had happened. In May 2007 one source 'familiar with the investigation' told *InformationWeek* that the problem had occurred at in-store computer kiosks which let people apply for jobs in the group.[15] These were connected to the main network, inside its firewall. The suggestion was that the hackers had plugged a USB drive into one of the computers on the kiosk. The alternative theory, quoted by other sources 'close to the investigation', was that the Wi-Fi network had been hacked, by people sitting in a store's parking lot.

TJX's computer security came under withering scrutiny – and was found largely wanting. Even in August 2007, months after the announcement of the hack (and a month after Yastremskiy was arrested) a then-employee (and part-time hacker) was scathing about the lack of network security. 'My mother could pick better passwords,' he wrote on a hacker discussion board in August 2007.[16] Before the breach, he said, there had been times when passwords were written on Post-It notes, or sometimes were just blank, or the same as the username. Even now, he wasn't impressed. (The company tracked him down via his IP address, and fired him, after getting him to write down what he thought the weaknesses in security were, and threatening to sue him if he discussed it further. He had been a university student working part-time at the store.)

The hackers' identities were still unknown in September 2007 when the Canadian Privacy Commissioner published a scathing report into TJX's practices.[17] The incident showed how keeping too much sensitive information, or keeping it too long, was a liability which created 'an unnecessary security burden'.

It was especially blunt about the collection of driver's licence numbers which TJX used on merchandise returned without receipts to see if people were returning excessive inventory – which could indicate fraud: 'A driver's license is proof that an individual is licensed to operate a motor vehicle; it is not an identifier for conducting analysis of shopping-return habits...' A driver's licence number could be vitally useful to identity thieves, and is almost impossible to change, the report noted. (A simple but safe way to have retained that data would be to hash the number using a scrambling algorithm to create a unique string, and store that. For any future return with a driver's licence, its number could be hashed and then compared against the stored list to check for a match. Both would be equally quick to generate and check.)

# A world of suspects

At that point, in autumn 2007, the government's investigators were as puzzled as anyone. The Yastremskiy arrest hadn't been tied to any specific events in the US. The perpetrators of the TJX hack seemed to be a giant mystery. 'At that point we had quite literally the entire world as possible suspects,' Stephen Heymann, an assistant attorney for the state of Massachusetts, told the *New York Times* later.[18]

What wasn't a mystery was that they had got in via the wireless network's woeful security. Yet in that, TJX wasn't unusual in the retailing industry. George Ou, writing at *ZDNet* in May 2007, said that he had worked as a security consultant for big retailers in 2004 and 2005, and had realized that poor wireless network security meant 'this was a time bomb waiting to go off'. But, he added, businesses wouldn't fix it, 'through a combination of ignorance and denial'. One of his clients, he said, had taken the trouble to buy new WPA-capable systems but been told only to implement WEP 'because that was the "standard" their corporate headquarters used'.[19]

Yet even after the TJX hack and its method had been widely publicized, security still didn't seem to be a big concern for retailers. In November 2007, AirDefense, a maker of wireless security systems, did some 'wardriving' – literally driving around with laptops to seek out Wi-Fi networks in retail outlets – and found that a quarter of 4,748 access points it surveyed had no encryption at all; another quarter were using WEP.[20] That left just under half using WPA (Wireless Protected Access) or the essentially uncrackable WPA2. AirDefense also questioned the priorities in play: 'Most retailers seem to maintain stronger physical security than wireless security, as 95 per cent of retailers had some form of physical security system in place such as an RFID security alarm,' it observed. 'Nearly 70 per cent had security cameras installed and roughly 10 per cent employed guards at exit doors.'

The gang behind the hack, of course, had never had to worry about RFID tags, security cameras or door guards. The access came to them over the air.

# Ganging up with computers

In 1998, a year after WEP became a future standard, 17-year-old Albert Gonzalez was using the computer at his school in Miami to hack into an Indian government website. Born in 1981, he had been using computers since he was eight years old, and bought his own at the age of 12 with his own money. When it was infected by a virus, he was at first indignant, and then fascinated, and soon did what he would do again and again: form a gang to find out how far he could go on other people's computers. At 14, he had used the nascent internet to hack into NASA. That had earned him his first brush with the government, when the FBI came to see him, and told him to behave. It hadn't worried him. He was caught for the school exploit, and this time warned to 'stay away' from computers for the next six months. A former teacher later told the NY Daily News that 'he could do a lot of stuff that other kids couldn't do. He was kind of a computer-type kid with glasses, but not lacking friends. They were the same kind of kids, but they listened to him.'[21] The teacher added that for Gonzalez to find himself in trouble 'is not new to Albert. I'll leave it at that.'

Gonzalez did not come from a bad background; his parents were refugees from Cuba and his father ran a landscaping business. But he found computers, and hacking, and the money to be made from it, too alluring for his own good. Even at school, he was using his ability to hack sites to steal credit card details and buy goods with them. He read software manuals to figure out how to get free connectivity; then he'd put 'sniffer' programs onto the network to grab username/password combinations. Even so, Gonzalez wasn't great at programming. But he knew where to find people who were, and how to deploy their programs, and them, to best effect. His skills thus lay more in high-level understanding of the gestalt of a network, and the understanding of people and their motivations. He also knew the sort of hacking he preferred: in July 1999, in a pseudonymous interview with ZDNet under the handle 'soupnazi', he said he didn't like defacing websites.[22] To do that was 'showing the admins ... that go to the site that we own them. They wouldn't even know we were in [the systems], if we didn't deface [them].' He said he had told other members of his hacking crew that 'I'd rather have root' – the highest possible administrator-level control.

After leaving high school, he moved in 2000 to Manhattan and then to New Jersey, where he was hired to a company's security team – after explaining to them how he had broken into their computer systems.

But in July 2003, Gonzalez was in trouble again. This time, it was a lot more serious than hacking a government website.

One evening in New Jersey, a New York police detective reflected to himself that the young man standing by the cash machine just before midnight looked somehow suspicious. (The costume wig and nose ring didn't dispel that feeling.) Within a few minutes his suspicions would be confirmed by the mismatch between the man's clothing and the fact that he was extracting hundreds – soon thousands – of dollars from the machine, using card after card after card pulled from his back pocket. It was Gonzalez, who had started using the ATM just before midnight so that he could double his takings: he'd extract the daily maximum per card just before the end of the day, and then again as the clock ticked over.

The detective arrested him, and following the arrest the police team found data for millions of cards on Gonzalez's computer. The young man explained to them patiently how he had done it. He had become a lynchpin on Shadowcrew, an online forum where criminals would trade databases of stolen card data, information about how to make fake cards, and how to scam people. It was a one-stop shop for online crime. Like the greedy emptying of bank accounts, this was another aspect of Gonzalez's personality: he was working both as a security consultant and a credit card thief.

Once arrested, Gonzalez didn't have many choices. 'I was 22 years old and scared,' he later told the *New York Times*.[18] 'When you have a Secret Service agent in your apartment telling you you'll go away for 20 years, you'll do anything.' He was also a low-level drug addict, underweight from taking cocaine, ecstasy and ketamine. But one agent who dealt with him recounted that he was also 'disarming' and 'a master of social engineering and deception'.[18] The Secret Service paid his living costs while he came off the drugs and faced up to his choices: jail, or cooperation. He helped them indict a number of Shadowcrew users – at one point, by setting up a VPN, or virtual private network (which hides traffic from the rest of the internet, apart from its endpoints) for the 2,000-odd site members to access the site. The VPN was controlled by the Secret

Service's New Jersey office, which could thus see all the traffic and IP addresses of those accessing it.

Some of those arrested in the Shadowcrew bust realized that Gonzalez must have betrayed them. In October 2004, the Secret Service told him to relocate to Miami for his own protection. Meanwhile it also kept a copy of everything that had been on his laptop in New Jersey. One particular detail – an email address he was using, soupnazi@efnet.ru – would turn out to be crucial. (EFNet was the hacker forum where in his teens he met many of those who would later become his associates.)

Once in Miami, Gonzalez helped in another investigation, and was put onto the Secret Service payroll of 'informants', receiving $1,200 per month. He gave speeches at some of their seminars and conferences. In the Secret Service's eyes, Gonzalez was a triple win. They had not only caught a criminal, but also reformed him at minimal cost; his monthly stipend was far less than the cost of keeping him in prison. And they could use him to catch others: he would go to the chatrooms where carders gathered and set them up for busts.

The truth was less encouraging. Gonzalez and another hacker, Christopher Scott, had in 2003 figured out how to hack into the Wi-Fi network of another retail chain, BJ's Wholesale Club, and grab Track 2 data. Now they were after bigger targets. Once more, Gonzalez was playing both sides and looking to sate his greed.

## Miami vice

On arriving in Miami, Gonzalez befriended a number of other hackers – particularly a duo called Patrick Toey and Stephen Watt. They formed a loose gang. Gonzalez encouraged Scott and Toey to hack into the Wi-Fi network of a store called OfficeMax, from which they captured card data and PINs. But the latter were encrypted, so they called on Gonzalez to find someone who could crack them. Gonzalez did, and became the leader of the team, which now embarked on wardriving to find vulnerable Wi-Fi systems at retailers.

On 12 July 2005, Scott drove to the car park of one of TJX's Marshall's stores in Miami. It was a Tuesday, and the shops were open as usual. He sat in his car with a laptop hooked up to a telescopic radio antenna which looked a little like an empty tin of Pringles to amplify the weak Wi-Fi signal emerging through the glass doors. He waited while a program on his PC cycled through the possibilities until it had cracked the password.

Having broken into the Wi-Fi, he was able to traverse the network, capture the login details for administrators, and then traverse the network to the main servers for the entire company in Framingham.

There, the retail processing for the entire company was carried out, and the data warehouses were being filled, transaction by transaction, with a mixture of unencrypted and encrypted data from all over the continent. It was an Aladdin's cave for data thieves.

Scott hacked into one of the servers, and installed a 'sniffer' program which would inspect every passing internet packet travelling over the network for interesting details – a 16-digit sequence indicating a credit card number, or the word 'password' which would indicate a login detail. Called 'blablabla', it had been written for Gonzalez by Stephen Watt, a hacker and software engineer who was then working for Morgan Stanley on a $70,000 salary. The sniffer program sat silently on the server for months.

In September 2005, a month before Butka emailed staff about putting off the WEP upgrade, Scott logged back in and pulled out the data which the programs had been quietly collecting for three months.

But hackers tend to dislike slog. What the gang really wanted was both a 'sniffer' program that wouldn't be detectable, and a guaranteed way to siphon the data. After all, TJX might wake up to the dangers of WEP and change the security, which would lock them out. So on Sunday, 14 May 2006, Scott hacked into the TJX retail transaction servers again – and this time installed a VPN connection between them and another server which Gonzalez had hacked. Yastremskiy, at Gonzalez's request, provided the undetectable sniffer, which was installed later that week. By logging into Gonzalez's server and then into the VPN, the crew could pull the

Track 2 data from the sniffer program on the TJX servers, acquiring millions of credit card details used by trusting shoppers. In all, 80 gigabytes of data were transferred to Gonzalez's server in California. Scott then deleted some log files and altered others to cover his tracks.

It was audacious. But it went unnoticed. TJX didn't have protections in place to notice unauthorized access to its Wi-Fi network (which could have been done by device authentication); or to spot unauthorized logins to the central server; or close enough controls on what programs were installed; or sufficient logs of the activity on the network. A VPN encrypts its communications, so a cursory glance wouldn't reveal what was being transmitted. The wardriving gang, and Yastremskiy, to whom they were selling the card data, retrieved captured data again and again. It was Gonzalez's ideal setup: nobody knew they were in, and they had root. The last day they pulled a dataset was 18 December 2006 – which was when TJX's IT security team discovered the sniffer program and the VPN.

Eighteen months earlier, in April 2005, on the other side of the United States from Gonzalez's crew, the San Diego office of the US Secret Service had opened an online undercover operation called 'Carder Kaos'. The aim was to find and arrest 'top tier suspects participating in financial crimes committed through the internet'.[1] It led eventually to that July 2007 arrest in Turkey of Yastremskiy. His interrogation, and his computer, pointed to two people who had been instrumental in breaking into networks and selling him credit card numbers. Online, they called themselves 'Johnnyhell' and 'Segvec'. They'd sold Yastremskiy credit card details – 'dumps' – by the million. Comparing what was in their dump with the places where those cards had been legitimately used soon narrowed down their source. The 'Johnnyhell' handle was traced back (via data from yet another hack, of the Dave & Buster's restaurant chain) to a man called Alexander Suvorov; he was arrested in Germany in March 2008, as he was getting ready to go to Bali.

For the prosecutors trying to figure out who was behind the IRC logs – which Yastremskiy had kept meticulously – it was an exhausting period. At the time Kim Peretti was the Department of Justice's senior lawyer in the Computer Crime and Intellectual Property division, based in Washington, DC. She had worked with Gonzalez on the operation which took down Shadowcrew, but had no inkling he was involved in this one. All she could see was that more and more companies were coming to her, complaining that their transaction servers had been broken into. She trawled through the chat logs from Yastremskiy's computer, trying to understand who she was dealing with. Peretti recalled:

> It was thousands and thousands of pages of transcripts of chat logs and most of it appeared to be gibberish or just chat that had no specific meaning. Maybe they were talking about a disco, or some legitimate conversation about their activities or workouts, or the drugs they were using. And then mixed into all of that, almost before they were ready to sign off, they'd throw in a smoking gun and you'd see a [hacked organization's] name and then a question about it, soliciting help.[23]

A lot of the chat logs were effectively real-time discussions in which hacking help would be sought and provided – each a 'smoking gun' for Peretti and the team.

Another arrest was soon made in Spain, this time of an Estonian who had also been involved with Yastremskiy's detail-selling business. On his laptop they found an email for the registration with an instant-messaging client that had been used to converse with Yastremskiy: soupnazi@efnet.ru.

The agents on the case realized its significance at once. 'Oh my God!' exclaimed Peretti.[18]

# Tying up the threads

On 7 May 2008, two months after Suvorov had vanished from the online world, and 10 months after Yastremskiy's disappearance, the Secret Service arrested Gonzalez for hacking into the corporate network of a restaurant chain called Dave & Buster's and planting a version of Watt's 'blablabla' program on the point-of-sale systems to capture credit and debit card details.

There had been one problem with that version of 'blablabla': whenever the point-of-sale systems shut down, so did the program – and it wouldn't restart with the rest of the systems. So Gonzalez's team had to drive down to the store, hack into the Wi-Fi, restart the sniffer program, siphon off the collected data, and head out.

If you keep going to a restaurant car park but never buy anything, and you're known to the Secret Service, eventually someone will join the dots.

In August 2008, Gonzalez was charged with the TJX hack, and the Dave & Buster's hack. In January 2009 Heartland Payment Systems, a card processing company, detected a huge intrusion, and realized that more than 130 million credit card details had been stolen. Gonzalez had helped enable the theft.

Gonzalez had called his wardriving scheme 'Get Rich Or Die Tryin''. Neither happened. In January 2009 Yastremskiy, the Ukrainian whose arrest had set the dominoes falling, received a 30-year sentence from a Turkish court. Suvorov pleaded guilty in May 2009, and was sentenced to seven years' jail; he was released in April 2014. In March 2010, Gonzalez took what he thought was a plea bargain, expecting the Secret Service to quash the charges; instead to his surprise he was sentenced to two 20-year prison terms, to be served concurrently – at that time, the longest ever for identity theft or cybercrime. The TJX hack became the first major disclosed commercial hack, and remains one of the biggest ever.

But Gonzalez hadn't done badly on the riches. The indictment against him noted that he had $1.65 million in cash (about $1.1 million of it buried in bags in a backyard), a condominium in Miami (though its boarded-up windows belied its inhabitant's wealth), a new BMW 330i, a machine for counting cash, and three different PCs.[24] Scott had about $400,000, a Rolex watch and nine PCs.[25] Toey had just $9,500, three Sony Vaio computers, an iPod nano and an XBox 360.[26]

In September 2008, TJX's vice-chairman reflected that if the US had implemented chip-and-PIN (also known as EMV) for payments, the intrusion could have been avoided.[27] EMV, which had already been implemented by the UK and many European countries by 2006, validates the card and its associated PIN at the terminal, and then encrypts the card details before transmission for authentication. The US didn't make it compulsory for retailers (at pain of paying any fraud costs) until the end of 2016, and even then, American Express gave fuel stations until October 2020 to implement full EMV. Chip-and-PIN might have helped reduce card theft, but the US has been in no hurry to implement it.

Guesses at the potential total cost of the TJX breach ranged widely. In August 2008, MacDonnell Ulsch at the services provider Jefferson Wells told CIO.com that if you assumed it would cost $300 per card detail stolen for 41 million cards, you'd have $12.3 billion in costs – and that was before legal settlements and civil litigation costs.[28]

The reality turned out to be a lot less. In June 2009, just under four years after Scott had pulled into the car park of a Marshall's outlet and aimed his telescopic Wi-Fi antenna at its doors, TJX paid $9.75 million to 41 US states to settle the investigation into the data breach. TJX's chief financial officer at the time said the settlement would let both sides take 'leadership roles in exploring new technologies and approaches to solving the systemic problems in the US card payment industry' but also that the company firmly believed it 'did not violate any consumer protection or data security laws'.[29] The Federal Trade Commission found it in breach of privacy laws, and obliged it to 'establish and maintain a comprehensive security program' to protect the data it collected from customers.[30] According to securities filings over the years, the total direct cost of the breach to TJX was around $256 million.

# The expertise gap

I asked Walker, who is now a research professor in computer science at Oregon State University, what his reaction had been on hearing that the TJX hack was due to WEP cracking. Did he feel vindicated? Concerned? Or had he become inured to such hacks over the years? 'Yes, a good way to put it would be I became inured,' he responded. 'When it is so easy to break into a protocol, I always expect that criminals will do so.'[31]

The problem, he suggested, lies in the distance between the ease of designing a system, and the difficulty of designing a cryptographically secure system:

> There is still a very huge gap in expertise. Most engineers are never exposed to crypto during university, and as a result, do the best they can with their very limited knowledge. Standard engineering practice is to adapt whatever software libraries can be found, including crypto, to some pre-existing design. However, crypto algorithms are incredibly optimized algorithms and so too fragile to accommodate this practice. I tell people that applied crypto is really about redesigning a system to make the crypto library's assumptions true, because the usual practice of doing the opposite [redesigning the cryptographic method to suit the rest of the system] does not work.

In other words, the encryption method used for WEP was never going to be suitable; its designers had tried to force an algorithm to do something it never could – provide protection even while transmitting all the details needed to crack it every hour at most.

The credit card business did take note of the TK Maxx hack – but you wouldn't call its action hurried. In March 2008, the Payment Card Industry Security Standards Council announced that companies would be barred from using WEP for accepting or processing credit card payments – though not until July 2010. By that time, WEP's irredeemable flaws had been known for almost 10 years, and cracking it would be the work of moments, even against the longest possible keys.

Paul Butka, who had been promoted to Global Application Development Director inside TJX in 2008, left the company in November 2009. At the end of 2017 he was working at Bob's Discount Furniture, a Connecticut-based retailer, as its chief information officer. Asked in 2012 what he had learned from the data breach, he said, 'I've learned an awful lot about the payment card industry's data security standards.'[32]

Most of the people whose card details had been stolen received no cash settlement. Instead, they received a voucher to come and shop at one of the TJX stores – the same places from which their card details had originally been lifted.

Would that tempt them back? In February 2007, a survey by Javelin Research found three-quarters of debit card holders saying they wouldn't keep shopping at a store that had had a data breach.[15] But memories, and resolutions, turned out to be short-lived. By August 2007, eight months after the publicity about the hack, a survey by Gartner found that only 22 per cent of TJX customers indicated they were less likely to shop there. 'Most TJX customers clearly care more about discounts than about card security,' said Avivah Litan, for Gartner. 'They know banks will usually cover potential losses.'

Gonzalez, meanwhile, is in a minimum security prison in Mississippi, along with 2,100 other inmates. His release date is presently set for 29 October 2025, when he will be 44 years old.

# References

1 Verizon 2010 data breach investigations report, *Verizon*. Available from: www.verizonenterprise.com/resources/reports/rp_2010-data-breach-report_en_xg.pdf

2 Personal email

3 'Unsafe at any key size: an analysis of the WEP encapsulation'. Available from: https://web.archive.org/web/20030801000000*/http://grouper.ieee.org/groups/802/11/Documents/DocumentHolder/0-362.zip

4 Delio, M (2001) Wireless networks in big trouble, *Wired*, 20 August. Available from: www.wired.com/2001/08/wireless-networks-in-big-trouble/

5 AirSnort project page, 24 March 2002. Available from: https://web.archive.org/web/20020324032834/http://airsnort.shmoo.com

6 Wi-Fi protected access security sees strong adoption, *Wi-Fi Alliance*, 3 February 2004. Available from: www.wi-fi.org/news-events/newsroom/wi-fi-protected-access-security-sees-strong-adoption

7 Cheung, H (2005) The Feds can own your WLAN too, *SmallNetBuilder*, 31 March. Available from: https://web.archive.org/web/20090919074334/https://www.smallnetbuilder.com/index.php?option=com_content&task=view&id=24251&Itemid=100

**8** TJX gets out of e-commerce business, *Boston Business Journal*, 6 October 2005. Available from: www.bizjournals.com/boston/stories/2005/10/03/daily62.html

**9** Chickowski, E (2008) TJX: anatomy of a massive breach, *Baseline*, 30 January. Available from: www.baselinemag.com/c/a/Security/TJX-Anatomy-of-a-Massive-Breach

**10** Brenner, B (2007) Don't blame PCI DSS for TJX troubles, IT pros say, *Tech Target*, 5 November. Available from: http://searchsecurity.techtarget.com/news/1280854/Dont-blame-PCI-DSS-for-TJX-troubles-IT-pros-say

**11** Letter from TJX's chairman and acting CEO, *TJX.com*, 20 January 2007. Available from: https://web.archive.org/web/20070120175027/http://www.tjx.com/tjx_message.html

**12** The TJX Companies Inc victimized by computer systems intrusion: provides information to help protect customers, *TJX.com*, 17 January 2007. Available from: https://web.archive.org/web/20070128041906/http://www.tjx.com:80/TJX_press_release_Jan_17_ 07.pdf

**13** Frequently asked questions, *TJX.com*, 25 January 2007. Available from: https://web.archive.org/web/20070125215954/http://www.tjx.com:80/tjx_faq.html

**14** The TJX Companies Inc Form 10-K for the fiscal year ended January 27 2007, *SEC.gov*. Available from: www.sec.gov/Archives/edgar/data/109198/000095013507001906/b64407tje10vk.htm

**15** Greenemeier, L (2007) The TJX effect, *Information Week*, 11 August. Available from: https://web.archive.org/web/20110409104559/http://www.informationweek.com/shared/printableArticle.jhtml?articleID=201400171

**16** Cryptic Mauler (2007) TJX still lacks security, *Sla.ckers forums*, 22 August. Available from: https://web.archive.org/web/20080514070457/http://sla.ckers.org/forum/read.php?13%2C15148%2Cpage=1

**17** Report of an investigation into the security, collection and retention of personal information, TJX Companies/Winners Merchant International LP, *Office of the Privacy Commissioner of Canada*, 24 September 2007. Available from: www.priv.gc.ca/en/opc-actions-and-decisions/investigations/investigations-into-businesses/2007/tjx_rep_070925/

**18** Verini, J (2010) The great cyberheist, *New York Times*, 10 November. Available from: www.nytimes.com/2010/11/14/magazine/ 14Hacker-t.html

**19** Ou, G (2007) TJX's failure to secure Wi-Fi could cost $1B, *ZDNet. com*, 7 May. Available from: www.zdnet.com/article/tjxs-failure-to-secure-wi-fi-could-cost-1b/

**20** AirDefense's comprehensive survey of 3,000 retail stores finds many wireless data security vulnerabilities as holiday shopping season nears, *AirDefense.com*, 15 November 2007. Available from: https:// web.archive.org/web/20120503233357/http://www.airdefense.net/ newsandpress/11_15_07.php

**21** Meek, JG and Siemaszko, C (2009) 'Soupnazi' hacker went from nerdy past to life of sex, guns and drugs, *NY Daily News*, 18 August. Available from: www.nydailynews.com/news/world/soupnazi-hacker-albert-gonzalez-nerdy-life-sex-guns-drugs-article-1.394977

**22** ZDNet staff (1999) Does the media cause hacking? (part 2), *ZDNet. com*, 6 July. Available from: www.zdnet.com/article/does-the-media-cause-hacking-part-2/

**23** Personal conversation with Peretti

**24** US District Court of Massachusetts 08 CR 10.2.2.3 PBS, *justice. gov*, 5 August 2008. Available from: https://web.archive.org/ web/20091202110019/http://www.justice.gov/usao/ma/Press%20 Office%20-%20Press%20Release%20Files/IDTheft/Gonzalez,%20 Albert%20-%20Indictment%20080508.pdf

**25** US District Court of Massachusetts 08 CR 10.2.2.4 DPW, *justice. gov*, 5 August 2008. Available from: https://web.archive.org/ web/20110302200019/http://www.justice.gov/usao/ma/Press%20 Office%20-%20Press%20Release%20Files/IDTheft/Scott,%20 Christopher%20-%20Information%20080808.pdf

**26** US District Court of Massachusetts 08 CR 10.2.2.5 WGY, *justice. gov*, 5 August 2008. Available from: https://web.archive.org/ web/20110302200018/http://www.justice.gov/usao/ma/Press%20 Office%20-%20Press%20Release%20Files/IDTheft/Toey,%20 Damon%20Patrick%20-%20Information%20080508.pdf

**27** Fitzgerald, K (2013) 1+1 = $1 trillion in card payments: the gold rush for micro and small business, *Banking Technology*, 17 July. Available from: http://paybefore.com/pay-news/tjx-exec-chip-and-pin-could-have-prevented-breach-sept-5-2008/

**28** McAlearney, S (2008) TJX data breach: ignore cost lessons and weep, *CIO.com*, 7 August. Available from: www.cio.com/article/2434423/risk-management/tjx-data-breach--ignore-cost-lessons-and-weep.html

**29** Hennigan, WJ (2009) TJX reaches settlement on data breach, *Los Angeles Times*, 23 June. Available from: http://latimesblogs.latimes.com/money_co/2009/06/tjx-reaches-settlement-on-data-breach.html

**30** Agency announces settlement of separate actions against retailer TJX, and data brokers Reed Elsevier and Seisint for failing to provide adequate security for consumers data, *Federal Trade Commission*, 27 March 2008. Available from: www.ftc.gov/news-events/press-releases/2008/03/agency-announces-settlement-separate-actions-against-retailer-tjx

**31** Personal communication

**32** Davis, C (2012) Q&A with Paul Butka, president of Sophelle, *Worcester Business Journal*, 25 March. Available from: www.wbjournal.com/article/20110606/PRINTEDITION/306069979/qa-with-paul-butka-president-of-sophelle

## LESSONS FROM THE TJX HACK

- Before adopting new technologies, investigate their security thoroughly. TJX bought into Wi-Fi early on because it brought business benefits, but the standard being used for wireless security was compromised from the start – and that fact had been publicized.

- If you discover a security flaw in your systems, don't put off closing it in favour of other spending. The scale of the internet means that someone will find it sooner or later.

- Set up monitoring systems inside your perimeter. Question new connections.

- Don't put off compliance with financial security requirements. If others do it better and sooner than you, you will be a target.

- The first sign of a data breach is usually the trading of customer and financial data on 'dark forums'. You don't have to spend time there, but it's useful to know people who do and can warn you about potential breaches.

- Getting hacked is almost a fact of corporate life, but it is the reaction of the company that will determine how customers in future react to you.

- Don't underestimate the determination of hackers to get at financial details. In their eyes, big companies that deal with customer financial details are basically banks with worse security.

# 'It is time to pay'

## Ransomware

*I gave talks about it, and I said hackers – they do the hacking*
*just to get some glory, get some bragging rights, you know?*
*Well, imagine when it becomes a tool for a new industry.*
MOTI YUNG

Even in a crowded field, Joseph Popp was a very peculiar hacker. Having studied biology at Harvard, he studied hamadryas baboons in Africa for 15 years and opened a butterfly sanctuary in New York. In 2000 he self-published a book called *Popular Evolution* which insisted that humanity's only reason for existing was 'maximizing reproductive success'.

All this from a man who had once taken to wearing a cardboard box on his head while awaiting trial in the UK for his hacking exploits in 1989.

Popp's hacking wasn't the usual sort, which takes content that its owners want to keep confidential, and makes it available to the wrong people, or just everyone. He had stumbled upon an idea that would in future change hacking forever. His idea was to take the content the victim normally has access to, and deny that access until they paid a ransom.

Popp carried out this surprising attack in December 1989, when the small number of PCs in commercial use mostly ran the precursor to Windows, called MS-DOS, and had no internet connectivity; that was reserved for university mainframes. Without the internet to spread his malware, he instead posted 20,000 floppy disks labelled 'AIDS Information – Introductory Diskettes' to attendees from that year's World Health Organization's AIDS conference. It later turned out that Popp had had a mental collapse after being turned down for a WHO job; as ever, revenge is a common reason for hacking. But Popp had taken some care in the extent of his vengeance. None of his disks were sent to US residents. Possibly he was mindful that in September 1988 a US court had handed down a sentence of seven years' probation to Donald Burelson, who set up a logic bomb which wiped 168,000 payroll records from his employer, a Texas insurance company, after he was fired.[1]

Popp's disks didn't hide their intent. The leaflet packed with them noted that 'These program mechanisms will adversely affect other program applications on microcomputers ... you will owe compensation and possible damages to PC Cyborg Corporation; and your microcomputer will stop functioning normally.'[2] But even in 1989 the instinct to ignore licence details and get on with using things was too strong to ignore. Those unwise enough to put the disks into their PCs were greeted by a harmless-looking program installation screen which said it was 'designed to provide up-to-date information about you and the fatal disease AIDS... The health information provided to you by this program could save your life.' It asked a few questions and then calculated the user's risk of AIDS infection.[3]

A few days later, the program would pop up a dialog screen of white text on dark red saying, 'It is time to pay for your software lease from PC Cyborg Corporation,' which it said would cost $109 for '365 user applications' – a year's use.

Those who ignored it, which was essentially everyone, were met by a large ASCII message from the then-anonymous author saying:

> I have been elected to inform you that throughout your process of collecting and executing files, you have accdiently [sic] ¶HÜ¢KΣΔ yourself over: again, that's PHUCKED yourself over. No, it cannot be; YES, it CAN be, a √îrûs has infected your system. Now what do you have to say about that? HAHAHAHA. Have ¶HÜÑ with this one and rememeber [sic], there is NO cure for AIDS [the last word in gigantic ASCII capitals].[4]

Then nothing happened. At least, not immediately. However, after the computer had been restarted 90 times, the virus would go to work, encrypting and hiding (by renaming) directories and files on the system. Those affected were told to turn on their printer, which printed a page telling them to send $189 to the 'PC Cyborg Corporation', at a PO Box in Panama. (Popp would later claim this was to fund AIDS research.)

Unfortunately for Popp, his coding was as errant as his spelling. Though the encryption was robust, the keys used to carry it out were stored in a file on the machine, and were all the same. The nascent antivirus industry turned its attention to the problem and was able to help almost everyone – though not all: one Italian organization reckoned it had lost 10 years' work. Popp was questioned in Schiphol Airport for odd behaviour (he scribbled 'DR POPP HAS BEEN POISONED' on a fellow passenger's suitcase), and subsequently arrested by the FBI at his home in Willowick, Ohio, indicted and extradited to the UK. That was where the box-wearing began, and he was eventually adjudged unfit for trial.

Popp faded into obscurity. But the idea of ransomware had been unleashed on the world. Hacking would never be the same again.

## Loving the alien

One day in 1995, Moti Yung was in his office at the Department of Computer Science at Columbia University in New York when Adam Young, one of his master's thesis students, stuck his head round the door. He wanted to talk about cryptography and computer viruses – two topics which at the time seemed rather far apart. Cryptography is the science and mathematics of codes and codebreaking; computer viruses were unauthorized programs which could run on a machine and even spread over a network. Not that there were that many networks to spread over. The internet was still a new idea to most; Microsoft's Windows 95 would introduce native internet connectivity, but configuring it was difficult, and connectivity anyway was typically over dialup modems limited to 56 kilobits per second – 2 per cent as fast as a 3Mbps broadband line, and with none of the content or services that make the modern web attractive.

So marrying computer viruses and cryptography seemed like an abstract idea. Then again, as Yung explained to me, it already had a precedent:

> There was the AIDS virus [which Popp had written]. And given that this was well-publicized in the malware research community, the concern was that the bad guys are going to correct its faults [such as the decryption key being stored on the machine] and in order to prevent this happening without the community being fully ready for it, we ought to publish it.[5]

Weren't they concerned that publication might give criminals ideas to work with? Yung explained:

> The thought was like this. We have to publicize it in a respectable academic paper form, the kind of area that is available typically to academicians, and not something that the usual virus writer reads. This would popularize it in the, let's say, antivirus community, and other people working on the good side will get the idea that this is possibly coming, and they will start working towards countermeasures.

Online encryption relies on public-key cryptography, which in turn relies on the difficulty of factoring a large number generated by multiplying two large prime numbers together. Such a number can only be generated by those two numbers, and figuring out the factors gets harder and harder as the primes get bigger. (For a human-scale version, figure out which two numbers you have to multiply to get 323.)

Public-key systems in effect put the large number into the public domain, and keep its factors secret. The easiest way to think of it is that public-key systems create an infinity of digital padlocks which can only be unlocked by the private key (the factors of the long number) which is held by the creator. Without the digital key, the padlocks are effectively uncrackable even given years of computer time; with the key, it's the work of milliseconds.

If Popp could have found a way to use public-key cryptography to encrypt the files, and somehow held on to the private key, he could have made a lot of money.

The student and the doctor turned their focus to the essential weakness that Popp had demonstrated: how do you keep the keys for your encryption safe from hackers, and yet have them handy?

Their discussion broadened. They began talking about the creature from the film *Alien* which infects its host by laying an egg (the film's writers got the idea from parasitic wasps). What interested the duo was the creature's protection. If you tried to pull it off, it would strangle the host; if you tried to cut it off, its acidic blood would destroy anything it touched. What, they wondered, would be the digital and cryptographic analogue to that – a forced symbiotic relationship, where removing the virus is more damaging than leaving it alone? How do you make a cryptographic creature that you can't get rid of until it agrees to go? In ransomware terms, how do you generate the keys for encryption but keep them away from people who want to decrypt something with them? As Yung puts it, the question they came to was, 'How devastating could the most insidious malicious software attack be against a target?'

The obvious answer is to format the computer's hard drive. But that's a blunt attack which wouldn't persuade anyone to pay a ransom.

The discussion moved forwards: what if you left the data, but held it to ransom? 'We discovered the first secure data kidnapping attack,' Yung later explained in a paper for the CACM [Communications of the Association for Computing Machinery]. 'We called it cryptoviral extortion.'[6]

What they described is the mechanism used in today's ransomware. The hacker first creates a public–private key pair – infinite 'public' padlocks and a single 'private' key. Next, a virus infects the target machine, and gets ready to start encrypting files.

But it doesn't encrypt them with the public padlock – because if it did, anyone who later paid and unlocked their system could then unlock every other one attacked by the same virus. Instead, the malware first randomly generates a local key and uses that to encrypt files. Then it uses the hacker's original 'public' padlock to encrypt the local key. The victim is left with a computer filled with encrypted files, and a file that could unlock them all – except that is encrypted by the hacker's padlock. In effect, the key to unlock the files is itself in a locked safe, whose combination only the hacker knows.

If you want your data back, all you have to do is send your ransom and the encrypted local key to the hacker. Once the payment has gone through, the hacker unlocks the local key and sends it back. The files can then be decrypted. (Sometimes there is a deadline for payment, after which the file with the encrypted local key is wiped, rendering recovery impossible.) Status quo ante for the victim, minus some time and money. Payday for the ransomware author.

A couple of extra touches are all that's needed: get the computer to tell the victim where to send their payment; and set up the infrastructure to do this at scale without getting caught.

Presented in a paper at the 1996 IEEE Symposium titled 'Cryptovirology: extortion-based security threats and countermeasures', Yung and Young's work was seen as fanciful.[7] Yung recalled:

> It was seen as simultaneously innovative and somewhat vulgar. [Yet] we discovered that public key cryptography holds the power to break the symmetry between the view of an antivirus analyst and the view of the attacker … these methods weaponize cryptography as an attack tool as opposed to the previous uses that were defensive in nature.

They called the new attack 'cryptovirology'.

But for Yung and Young's idea to reach a global audience, and to be exploited by hackers, it needed some extra technologies. For the hacker, the hardest part of the process wasn't the cryptography, since viruses and encryption programs were both plentiful and easily available. The difficult bit was not getting caught. Both the communication and the payment might be traced. What was needed was anonymous communication – ideally, not involving email, nor any overseeing entity such as Amazon or Google – and anonymous payment.

A 'cryptocurrency' – digital currency, ideally untraceable – would be the best form of payment; and a method of hiding the identity of the website through which the payment was made even better. 'We even wrote that an electronic payments infrastructure with anonymous payments would be the right way to collect the ransom,' Yung says. 'We had started to envision all this, all this support technology that is actually needed around the basic attack.'

## Insecurity through obscurity

By 2004, the idea of ransomware had begun to attract interest among malware writers. But they still faced the difficulty of how to get paid: payments made through any banking system, including PayPal, could be traced, which would mean that any profit would be short-lived.

The ransomware industry began to grow. But technical flaws were common – so much so that one security researcher, Alexandre Gazet of Quarkslab, declared flatly in 2008 that ransomware as a means of 'mass extortion is probably doomed to failure' because the 'design is deficient' and large-scale operation would draw too much attention to the malware's author.[8]

Then in October that year, a research paper called 'Bitcoin: A Peer-to-Peer Electronic Cash System' was published on a cryptography mailing list. It outlined how one could create a cryptocurrency – 'money' with no intrinsic value or physical existence, whose units would consist of the solutions to factorizations of large numbers, in which each transaction was also tied immutably to every previous one by a system known as the 'blockchain', running simultaneously on millions of computers worldwide. Each of those solutions, called a 'bitcoin', would reside in 'wallets' – essentially, files on a computer – and could be bought and sold online via exchanges which accepted normal fiat currencies such as dollars, yuan or pounds, and yielded bitcoins.

Bitcoin provided the second leg of untraceability for the ideal implementation of ransomware. Though one could trace the movement of bitcoins to individual wallets owned, say, by a hacker – because every transaction is recorded on the blockchain – it would be comparatively easy to launder money through an exchange, either by swapping money from one bitcoin wallet to another, or exchanging it for a fiat currency. Attempts to make it easier to trace transactions were matched by efforts such as DarkWallet, which would merge an innocent and a laundering transaction in order to make an audit trail impossible.[9] Bitcoin began to take off as a means of exchange in 2010.

In retrospect, observed the writer Alina Simone, in a look back in 2015 at the evolution of ransomware, Yung and Young's work 'basically did for ransomware what the Bessemer process did for steel' – turning it from a craft into an industry.[3]

# Dark places

In February 2016 Professor Alan Woodward of the University of Surrey's Department of Computer Science began wondering: what was driving the growth in the number of Tor hidden websites?

Although they are simply web servers running on computers, just like any address on the wider web, Tor sites are effectively hidden from the rest of the web. Tor – which stands for The Onion Router – was devised by the US military in the mid-1990s to allow spies in the field to make web connections without being surveilled, and let the military set up sites which could not be found by ordinary web browsing. That made it perfect for spies.

Rather than .com or .org, Tor sites have a .onion suffix, and can only be reached by using the Tor web browser (or a standard browser with the Tor extension). Tor is in effect a self-contained web of machines, with entry and exit points to the wider internet. Tor anonymizes browsing: when properly configured, you can connect to machines across the internet without anyone being able to trace or eavesdrop on the packets, which are wrapped in multiple layers of encryption like an onion as they traverse the network.

'Hidden' Tor sites reside on those machines. In theory, you can't use standard methods to discover which physical machine is running a .onion web server, and your access to it via the Tor network can't be traced either. (In reality, hacks that work against any web server's software will work on .onion ones both to unmask it and its users; the US's FBI has done this against sites hosting child abuse imagery.

And the exit nodes of the Tor network are the weakest point for spotting people accessing it.)

Beyond spies, the Tor network was ideal for those looking to sell illicit goods and services on the 'dark web' – and also perfect for malicious hackers who needed a place to store data such as encryption keys, or communicate with people who badly needed access to those keys.

What Woodward noticed was that the number of .onion sites, as recorded by a Tor organization website, had rocketed from around 40,000 at the start of 2016 to more than 110,000 by early February.[10]

The cause, it turned out, was ransomware. The new sites were being created by Locky, a strain of malware which added another step to anonymity. Not only were payments demanded in bitcoin; the payment demands were hosted on a .onion site. This presented a double obstacle for the technically challenged hit by Locky, who were catapulted unwillingly to the frontiers of technology.

Locky arrived as an email pretending to be an invoice formatted as a Word document. If you opened it and had enabled macros (a simple scripting language built in to Microsoft Office which simplifies many tasks), it would get to work encrypting your files. If you didn't have macros enabled, it would ask you to turn them on – and encrypt your files.[11]

Locky thus leaned on two old technologies: the concept of ransomware, and malicious Office macros. The latter's potential for harm had first been demonstrated by an anonymous Microsoft employee in July 1995 – coincidentally the same time Yung and Young were considering malicious cryptography. Although the 'Concept' macro virus didn't do anything harmful – it simply displayed a dialog box with the number '1', which could be dismissed with the box's default OK button – it would infect the global template for future documents. If those were shared with others, their global templates would be infected too.[12] Concept somehow got included in documents on a CD sent out by Microsoft as a compatibility test in August 1995; that then spread to users. Increasingly malicious variants appeared over the next four years, taking advantage of Microsoft making macro execution the default setting on Office, which meant that unless you specifically turned it off, it would run the macros in any document you opened.

The glaring security hole that this offered culminated in March 1999 in Melissa, a macro virus in a Word file attached to an email saying 'Important Message From [sender]', where [sender] was the name of someone who the receiver usually already knew; as it transpired, they were in the sender's Windows Address Book.[13]

'Here is that document you asked for... don't show anyone else :-)', read the email's text; the attachment was called list.doc. Its contents were a list of pornographic websites. While the receiver was reeling, the macro was emailing copies of the same email to the first 50 people in the user's Address Book; this raised the chance of being opened by the receiver. It also infected Word's 'Normal' template, so any new document would also be infected (so if you created a new document and sent it to someone who hadn't been hit by Melissa, they would be).

Melissa's 50-multiplier effect meant that it spread alarmingly fast – though it wasn't particularly harmful. It could have wiped data, for example. Microsoft finally took the hint and disabled macro execution in 2000. But Melissa had shown the power of social engineering – persuading people to do things by enticing or fooling them to do something they should have been wary of, in this case opening a document – and the combination became a potentially lethal one which returned again with ransomware.

Attachments soon became a principal method of spreading malware, either embedded in its entirety or as a small program which could then download the rest of its payload from the internet. (In general, if you're opening an email, you're online.)

But it wasn't the only one. 'Drive-by downloads' which took advantage of flaws in browsers and their plugins, particularly Microsoft's Internet Explorer and Adobe's Flash Player, also became an increasingly popular and effective method of getting malware onto machines. Being able to take over someone's Windows PC through malware delivered through email, or increasingly via the browser, turned into a huge commercial business in the early part of the 21st century. Computers had power and internet bandwidth to spare, given that most people used them just for email and browsing. If you could use that spare capacity to generate and send spam, or send 'ping floods' to overwhelm sites, you could make serious money. Building 'botnets' of millions of PCs became a cottage industry for hackers who would hire them out by the hour.

But first build your botnet. To do that, the malware writers targeted the programs which were most widely installed, most widely used, and had the most flaws. As the decade developed, that turned out to be Adobe's Flash Player, especially in the plugin form used in Internet Explorer. Together, those were on more than a billion PCs, in both homes and offices. 'The Adobe Flash Player runtime lets you effortlessly reach more than 1 billion connected desktops across browsers and operating systems with no additional software installation,' Adobe's page proudly boasted in July 2012.[14, 15] And it added that 'more than 400 million connected desktops update to the new version of Flash Player within six weeks of release'. That, obviously, would leave 600 million running an out-of-date version at the end of the six weeks (and for an unknown period afterwards) – and a six-week window for millions more.

# High severity, high anxiety

But how vulnerable was Flash as an avenue for malware? The answer: very. Having begun simply as a means to display graphics files, Flash Player had expanded far beyond its original remit, and not only encompassed video content and animated games, but had also gained its own scripting language to create Flash applications, as well as the ability to write, access and read files on the user's computer. Keeping up with the security challenges on any one of those would be a serious undertaking. Adobe was trying to do all at once, on a product whose roots meant that its security architecture was sorely lacking.

That becomes clear when you look at Flash's security record on the CVE (Common Vulnerabilities and Exposures) site, run by the US government-funded Mitre Corporation, which collates a list of known security vulnerabilities, with a description and assigned level of risk for each vulnerability ranging from 1, the lowest, to 10, the highest.

By the start of 2016, Flash Player alone had more than 700 public vulnerabilities listed. Malware authors had hammered at it, and Flash had yielded. While the number of 'high severity' flaws (in the 9–10 range, which could lead to the most harmful attacks such as running an attacker's code on the user's machine) had been fairly consistent at about 55 per year from 2010 to 2014, and so would on average require a weekly update, in 2015 the figure leapt to 294, and in 2016 to 224.[16]

Although many of those new flaws were found by 'white hat' researchers, particularly at Google, their publication and especially the fixes for them tended to help hackers discover them in retrospect: a knowledgeable comparison of the unfixed and fixed versions of a program yielded important clues about how to exploit it.

Meanwhile, keeping up with so many flaws was a full-time job for Adobe, and for its users. The all-flaws total of 329 in 2015 would have required an update on average almost every day, including weekends. However, publication on the CVE database tended to be lumped into fortnightly or monthly collections of dozens of flaws which had been notified and fixed in a new update. That, however, meant people might have been exposed to risks for long periods, even if they had updated religiously. Yet as Adobe itself conceded with the boast about a billion devices and 400 million updating within six weeks, most people didn't. Almost everyone running Flash Player had an outdated version, whether they meant to or not.

Many older organizations also tended to rely on Internet Explorer (IE): it came bundled with the PC, and Microsoft, the world's biggest software company, was in charge of updating it. Malware authors hammered on that too. Up to 2012, IE had at most 22 'serious' vulnerabilities; fortnightly patching would keep on top of it.[17] But in 2013 the count rocketed to 114, and then to 217 in 2014. It didn't particularly matter which version you were running; any of the six in widespread use had hundreds of flaws to be exploited.

For the average user, for whom every Flash Player and Internet Explorer patch usually required a full restart of their machine besides the time needed to install the code, just managing those two pieces of software would be a full-time job; and even then you'd be behind. Many organizations chose instead to rely on their anti-virus systems, and hope that they would detect the code pattern of an already-known piece of malware. This relied, of course, on not being the first person to be hit by that malware; otherwise the anti-virus company wouldn't tend to realize it was malware.

Infecting Windows PCs quickly became industrialized. When a browser arrived at an 'infected' page, a small piece of code would identify its version, and what versions of potentially vulnerable software (Flash Player, Internet Explorer, Silverlight, Java) were running on its machine. The appropriate piece of malware would then be delivered from a remote server. Once the victim's machine was exploited, what happened next depended on the malware: it might turn the machine into a bot under remote control, or it might encrypt its files. (Sometimes it would do both.)

Avoiding 'risky' pages became more difficult as the criminals took advantage of the growth in third-party advertising networks to serve up their links to millions of people browsing reputable news sites. Such 'malvertising' hit publications including the *New York Times*, the BBC and the *Guardian* – the latter, in December 2015, on a four-year-old article about cybercrime being 'out of control'.[18, 19]

The only way to stay ahead of that was not to use a Windows PC (because the hassle for malware authors of writing code for the Apple Macintosh's entirely different operating system, and its comparatively small user base, made it a less fruitful target) or to keep Flash Player and Internet Explorer updated all the time. Except you couldn't.

The upshot of this 'update exhaustion' was that in the first nine months of 2015, eight of the top 10 flaws targeted by exploit 'kits' were in Flash Player; the other two were in Internet Explorer and Microsoft's Silverlight (its competitor to Flash Player). In October 2015, the networking company Cisco said it had identified 147 proxy servers that were being used to serve ransomware which was gener-ating around $30 million annually by targeting up to 90,000 users per day – or 13.1 million people per month – of whom about 40 per cent would probably be infected. Of those, around 60 per cent would be ransomware payloads, demanding an average of $300; and about three in every 100 would pay up.[20] Cisco estimated that this was half of the global business for this particular exploit kit, called Angler; that would make it worth $60 million annually. Talos, a security group within Cisco, observed that at that time 'a user browsing the internet using Internet Explorer with only basic antivirus protection is highly vulnerable to an Angler infection.'

# A stitch in time

Papworth Hospital in Cambridgeshire is renowned in the UK as a leader in heart and lung treatment; it was the location for the UK's first successful heart transplant in 1979. It is a top performer in the UK's National Health Service, and in a typical year treats more than 24,400 in-patients and day cases, and more than 73,600 outpatients (whose treatment doesn't require a bed). That's an average of about 67 in-patients and more than 200 outpatients every day of every week, with 24-hour requirement for treatment.

In 2016 the hospital's IT budget, aiming to implement a new electronic patient record system, was around £600,000, with the added complication of a planned move to an entirely new site in 2018, which complicated the task of running the hundreds of PCs and network-connected medical systems used by the 1,700-odd staff. Spending was under pressure; as one board meeting noted, savings on software could be routed to pay for private ambulances. The six-strong IT staff had to handle more than 60 servers, and a backup store of around 18 terabytes – thousands of gigabytes – of data. For the past year they had been coping with the rollout of an electronic medical record system, and planning and executing a scheme to upgrade their systems from Windows XP to Windows 7.

All that was abruptly put at risk one Saturday night in summer 2016. At about 11.00 pm, a worker in one of the clinical groups clicked on a link on a website. That initiated a drive-by download: a piece of malware silently installed itself on the PC, and began to reach out across the network, to copy itself on more machines.

A little after midnight, it began encrypting the files on the servers – including those for the clinical analysis department, where they were needed to collate and examine blood and other test results from urgent cases.

The first the IT staff knew about it was a high-priority call to the helpdesk. 'The pathology on-call department called the IT on-call person to advise them that people couldn't access pathology results,' explains Jane Berezynskyj, then in charge of Papworth's IT team. Once the engineer realized what had happened, the first infected PC was disconnected from the network. That wasn't enough. Papworth at the time had 'some fairly ancient application architecture' using filesharing servers, as Berezynskyj later put it: 'a crypto attack went through our fileshares and encrypted the data'.

By 1.00 am there were three IT engineers working on the system, trying to determine how far the ransomware had spread and what damage it had done. By 6.00 am on the Sunday morning, the hospital had declared a 'major incident'. With Berezynskyj staying in touch via messaging and email, the team continued working until 9.00 pm on the Sunday.

Papworth turned out to have been, as Berezynskyj later said, 'very, very lucky'.[21] The ransomware's timing mechanism had delayed its inception to just after midnight – which meant that it began to encrypt files soon after the daily backup had been completed.

Even so the recovery took two days. 'It really matters clinically – it's clinical safety,' Berezynskyj explains:

> We actually recovered the data really quickly, but we needed to make
> sure that we had recovered it as it was, that there hadn't been any
> changes – so we needed clinical input, clinical checks, before we did
> a general release of that information. We recovered it quickly ... but
> then we just wanted to verify that it was all OK.

Verifying that there wasn't something lurking behind, either on the PCs or the servers, was the key problem.

Berezynskyj also acknowledges that it was fortunate that the hospital was hit on the weekend, when there are generally no scheduled operations.

She also reckons that the person who clicked the infected link never reported what happened. Perhaps if they had, the infection could have been stopped sooner. 'One of our key weaknesses is our people and user behaviour,' she remarked in a speech she gave in November that year.[21]

So were Papworth and its patients lucky? Or was there something more to it? 'It wasn't luck,' Berezynskyj says:

> We had already been going through an exercise for more than a year looking at how you strengthen information security, data security in its broadest sense. We'd hired somebody to be specifically responsible for cybersecurity. So we'd done a lot to improve the depth and diversity of our defences ... there was information available on the intranet about what to do, how to respond, what to look out for. The messaging in the organization was very much 'This isn't an "if", it's a "when".'

## Revert to saved

Even though being hit by ransomware is a scary experience, it has one flaw: it can only encrypt the files that it finds. In a world of backups, file 'snapshots' and cloud storage, it is becoming easier than ever to erase and reinstall system software, and then to roll back to the last stored set of data. Although some ransomware encrypts files and then stays silent (in the hope that the affected content will be backed up), it's rare to have just one backup. Photos are usually the largest, and most personally valued, files; fortunately, the growth in the use of smartphones and cloud storage for those photos means that it's harder than ever to lose what we truly value.

For bigger organizations, that holds truer than ever. Freedom of information requests show that many NHS hospitals were hit by ransomware attacks in 2015 and 2016. In every case, their response to the attack was to isolate the infected systems, wipe them and restore them from backup. Standard practice was not to store any data on the individual PCs themselves; everything was held on servers.

That doesn't mean though that a ransomware attack can't be devastating. On Wednesday, 3 May 2017, the board of Southport and Ormskirk Hospital in Lancashire met, and among other topics discussed its vulnerability to a 'cyber-attack'.[22] When one director asked whether backup data was stored offsite, they were told that the cost was 'prohibitive'. Though there was a plan in place to tighten security both of stored data and the PCs in use, it would take until December to implement. The directors urged the three teams working on it to agree an earlier date and report back at the scheduled meeting a month hence.

Nine days later, at 11.30 am on Friday 12 May, one of Southport's IT infrastructure specialists got a call from the Queenscourt Hospice: their machines were 'behaving strangely and had crashed'. Then another call came in: the caller couldn't log into the electronic patient record systems, called Medway. That had crashed too.

Something dramatic was happening. But the antivirus system hadn't flagged anything. The specialist then checked the trust's five servers – and was shocked to find their CPUs all running at 100 per cent, a sure sign of trouble. So he switched them off. The trust's IT systems went dark.[23]

Thousands of organizations worldwide had had the same experience: Windows computers would suddenly stop working, and then flash up a blood-red screen with a lot of writing. It was ransomware, encrypting their contents. The screen contained a demand to pay a ransom in bitcoin then worth about $300 per computer to one of three 'wallets' over the Tor network.

At Southport, the stressed team searched on Google for news, and realized they, like many others, had been hit by a ransomware attack. But it took until 8.00 pm to get guidance for a recovery plan from NHS Digital, the organization that coordinates strategy for NHS systems.

Late on that same Friday, the British security researcher Marcus Hutchins discovered a 'kill switch' accidentally left in the software. The code checked for the online presence of a random-looking domain name; if that existed, the program would quit without doing anything. By registering the domain while most of the US hadn't turned on their computers, he prevented the attack spreading wider and becoming catastrophic. Though it was active for less than a day, the ransomware, quickly dubbed 'Wannacry', infected more than 230,000 machines in over 150 countries. Security researchers tracked it by reports of the inbuilt worm, which tried to spread the infection, hitting firewalls in different countries.

Southport Hospital was among those worst hit. It had to cancel all but urgent and emergency surgery. X-rays couldn't be accessed. Outpatients couldn't be contacted. Internal communications didn't work. In common with almost every victim, it paid nothing to the ransomware authors. But it took six days to return services to normal.[24]

Another affected hospital was Bart's, in London. Although staff began turning off systems within seven minutes of the first report of an infection, more than 2,000 of the 12,110 PCs were infected, and two out of its 790 servers. As one of the largest trusts in England, it had to refuse ambulances at its three A&E (Accident and Emergency) units for six days. It took 12 days before the trust was confident that it was back to normal. A key part of the problem was that nearly 200 servers were on the older Windows 2003, and 2,000 PCs and many medical diagnostic systems such as imaging scanners were on Windows XP. Microsoft had stopped providing security patches and support for both in 2014, but Bart's didn't have the money to upgrade them; and some, such as the diagnostic systems, couldn't be upgraded.[25]

As the world considered the attack, there was plenty of blame to share around. The malware spread by exploiting a flaw in Windows dubbed 'EternalBlue', which had been published online by a hacking group called 'Shadowbrokers', whose affiliation remained unknown but was suspected of being aligned with Russia. They in turn had stolen it from the US's National Security Agency from an insufficiently secured site.

But Microsoft had fixed the flaw in all versions of Windows apart from XP with a free update two months earlier, in March; in theory, everyone should have been protected. In practice, though, large organizations are wary of applying security updates without testing them against their own systems, in case they disrupt essential services that rely on something that the update blocks. EternalBlue exploited a flaw in the widely used SMB protocol, used to communicate over networks. Lots of organizations rely on SMB; changing its behaviour could cause endless headaches. And usually, delaying the installation of a security update isn't immediately calamitous. EternalBlue turned out to be the exception. Microsoft even put out a patch for XP, despite having ended such updates in 2014.

So who was to blame for not preventing the attack? The most affected machines – 98 per cent of those hit – turned out to be running Windows 7, not the much older Windows XP, nor the newer Windows 10. The finger pointed to big organizations failing to take security updates seriously.

## Fix, sort, understand

Though 16 UK hospitals were shuttered by the Wannacry attack, Papworth – which had since moved to hourly backups – remained unaffected. The IT team worked long hours over the weekend, but it was precautionary rather than remedial. In fact, some hospitals which were hit by Wannacry sent their patients to Papworth.[26]

'I think Wannacry has had a positive effect,' Berezynskyj argues. 'And that is that heightened sense of awareness, heightened understanding of the operational impact of these sorts of events.' Of ransomware, she says:

> [P]robably if you look five years ago [to 2012], it probably wouldn't have been on anybody's board agenda. Two years ago, it probably was on board agendas but at that stage it was 'Yes, we know there's a risk, but that's for you IT guys to fix and sort.' I think where we are now is there's greater understanding that it's not just for the IT guys to fix and sort.

Hospitals, especially in the NHS, face two big complications which make IT security difficult: the large number of temporary staff, especially in essential functions such as nursing; and the reliance on old but effective (and expensive) medical equipment which will only interface with old operating systems that are insecure or unsupported. 'I talked to HR [the human resources department] on a regular basis about the induction of new people, but also how do you educate people who are working on a temporary basis,' Berezynskyj explains. 'Everybody needs to understand both the implications of their actions and the potential consequences.' Of the second problem, she thinks that Wannacry 'showed the supplier marketplace has a role to play … in keeping the NHS a safe place.'

While the cost of other ransomware stayed largely under the radar, because incidents were sporadic, Wannacry's breadth and abruptness hit many high-profile companies. The logistics company FedEx, the automotive companies Renault and Nissan, and the Spanish telecoms giant Telefonica were all affected. Thousands of Russian and Chinese systems were hit. Cyence, which models the costs of cyber incidents, put the worldwide cost at anywhere between $4 billion and $8 billion, because of the interruption to business and the cost of support.[27] If it had reached the US, the costs would surely have been significantly higher.

## Quieter than war

Speaking to me just after the Wannacry attacks, Yung had no regrets about the chain of events that those few weeks in 1995 had created:

> What we noticed in the first eight or nine years after publication [of the original cryptovirology paper] was that people thought about it as a theoretical exercise. Indeed, it is a kind of bridge between two communities, malware and crypto, and the idea was that the malware writing people are not going to employ crypto. Some people didn't even understand what damage can be done by viruses anyway; they didn't understand exactly the economic power of launching an attack where I would hold in my hand the means by which to reverse it.
>
> In this sense, we saw [cryptovirology] as a big power, a great power for an attacker who is there to gain economically. I think I gave talks about it, and I said hackers – they do the hacking just to get some glory, get some bragging right, you know? Well, imagine when it becomes a tool for a new industry.

Would it not have been better though to have held back from publication? Couldn't the blame for ransomware be laid at his and Young's door? Yung says they did hold back: 'around the year 2000, we realized that the response [to the concept being described] was kind of lukewarm from the anti-malware community, so we actually withheld some other attacks and we didn't write about them'. That is, they imagined paths of attack, but held back from describing them. Did that prevent them happening?

> Some of them were written by other people. Some we wrote only in a book, thinking that that's another hurdle for those on the bad side: they're not going to read a book of hundreds of pages just to extract some idea from it. Our book has some types of viruses that we envisioned that we never wrote a paper about, such as a virus that attacks, but you can't track what it's doing: it accesses all your system memory and you don't know what was stolen. We just wrote things like this in a book because we realized that these people at conferences and so on were dismissing our work, in a sense. They weren't taking it seriously because they didn't invent it, and they're the experts [in malware]. At that time I was doing a lot of work on theoretical and fundamental cryptographic problems, and they'd put my stuff into this drawer of 'abstract cryptography'.

What about a fake ransomware virus that is just malicious – which simply encrypts your files and throws the keys away? 'Then it's completely disruptive,' Yung said. 'Then, it's infowar. This doesn't have the incentive or economic value, because if you have nothing in your hand, then it just destroys.'

However, he didn't see this as a credible threat model:

> We thought that the economics is what would magnify it, would make it a weapon of choice. With hacking, outside the domain of information warfare – where you really just want to destroy – it gives you some fame in the underworld. But with this, it gives you something to sell. And typically where there is an economic incentive, there is industry; where there is no incentive, things don't evolve. We thought it would boom and boom until it got widely known.

Yung noted the speculation that Wannacry wasn't opportunist hackers; 'there is speculation that this is a state-run operation, and it may well be. Or it may be just a test.'

Within a few days of our conversation, the first reports began tentatively linking Wannacry to North Korea. Two respected online security firms, Symantec and Kaspersky, separately reported that they had found similarities in the computer program of Wannacry to the malware used to hack Sony Pictures in 2014, and a Bangladeshi bank in 2016.

'The level of sophistication is something that is not generally found in the criminal world,' Kaspersky said in a blogpost about the work by 'Lazarus Group', which had been blamed for the previous two attacks.[28] There was circumstantial detail too: the first infected computer appeared to have been in Asia; the virus writers seemed to be fluent in Chinese but not at all in English (the wording on the screen after the ransomware ran had been produced by translation software).

A month or so later, in June 2017, the UK government's computer security agency GCHQ quietly pitched in: the attack had indeed come from Lazarus Group, it told the BBC, and they were North Korean.[29] The US's Computer Emergency Readiness Team (US-CERT) had the same view, though it called them 'Hidden Cobra'. (It noted in passing that they frequently exploited flaws in Adobe's Flash Player to attack systems.)[30] And to round it off, in December 2017 Thomas Bossert, the US president's assistant for homeland security and counterterrorism, wrote in the *Wall Street Journal* that 'after careful investigation, the US today publicly attributes the massive "Wannacry" cyber attack to North Korea'. He called the attack 'indiscriminately reckless' but said the US would apply 'maximum pressure' to curb future attacks. How that will play out remains to be seen.[31]

It had taken nearly 30 years. But ransomware had finally evolved from one man's ineffective obsession into a cyberwarfare weapon which could paralyse gigantic companies and organizations.

# References

**1**  Cobb, S (2002) When the logic bombs, CheyCobb.com, 20 December. Available from: https://web.archive.org/web/20030627035629/www.cheycobb.com/logic_bombs.html

**2**  Scherstuhl, A (2009) Dr Popp, the first computer virus, and the purpose of human life: studies in crap gapes at popular evolution, *The Village Voice*, 16 April. Available from: www.villagevoice.com/2009/04/16/dr-popp-the-first-computer-virus-and-the-purpose-of-human-life-studies-in-crap-gapes-at-popular-evolution/

**3** Simone, A (2015) The strange history of ransomware, *Medium*, 26 March. Available from: https://medium.com/un-hackable/the-bizarre-pre-internet-history-of-ransomware-bb480a652b4b

**4** AIDS trojan disk, virus.wikia.com. Available from: http://virus.wikia.com/wiki/AIDS_trojan_disk

**5** Personal communication, 2017

**6** Yung, M and Young, AL (2017) Cryptovirology: the birth, neglect and explosion of ransomware, *Communications of the ACM*, **60** (7), July. Available from: https://cacm.acm.org/magazines/2017/7/218875-cryptovirology/fulltext

**7** Yung, M and Young, A (1996) Cryptovirology: extortion-based security threats and countermeasures, *Security and Privacy conference*, May. Available from: http://ieeexplore.ieee.org/document/502676/?reload=true

**8** Gazet, A (2008) Comparative analysis of various ransomware virii, *EICAR conference*, May. Available from: http://esec-lab.sogeti.com/static/publications/08-eicar-ransomware.pdf

**9** Greenberg, A (2014) 'Dark Wallet' is about to make bitcoin money laundering easier than ever, *Wired*, 29 April. Available from: www.wired.com/2014/04/dark-wallet/

**10** Woodward, A (2016) Is the Tor increase malware?, *Cyber Matters* blog, 19 February. Available from: www.profwoodward.org/2016/02/is-tor-increase-malware.html

**11** Abrams, L (2016) The Locky ransomware encrypts local files and unmapped network shares, *Bleeping Computer*, 16 February. Available from: www.bleepingcomputer.com/news/security/the-locky-ransomware-encrypts-local-files-and-unmapped-network-shares/

**12** 'Virus: W32/Concept', F-Secure threat description database. Available from: www.f-secure.com/v-descs/concept.shtml

**13** 'Virus: W32/Melissa', F-Secure threat description database. Available from: www.f-secure.com/v-descs/melissa.shtml

**14** Deliver breakthrough experiences across platforms and devices, *Adobe.com*. Available from: www.adobe.com/products/flashruntimes/statistics.html

**15** Adobe Flash runtimes/statistics, Adobe.com [captured by archive. org], 17 August 2012. Available from: https://web.archive.org/ web/20120817195931/http://www.adobe.com/products/flashrunt-imes/statistics.html

**16** CVSS scores for Adobe Flash Player between 2000-01-01 and 2017-10-10, CVEdetails.com. Available from: www.cvedetails.com/ cvss-score-charts.php?fromform=1&vendor_id=&product_id=6761 &startdate=2000-01-01&enddate=2017-10-10&groupbyyear=1

**17** CVSS scores for Microsoft Internet Explorer between 2000-01-01 and 2017-12-11, CVEdetails.com. Available from: www. cvedetails.com/cvss-score-charts.php?fromform=1&vendor_ id=&product_id=9900&startdate=2000-01-01&enddate=2017-12-11&groupbyyear=1

**18** Kashyap, R (2014) Why malvertising is cybercriminals' latest sweet spot, wired.com, November. Available from: www.wired.com/ insights/2014/11/malvertising-is-cybercriminals-latest-sweet-spot/

**19** Blue, V (2015) Guardian article on cybercrime serves up Angler Exploit Kit, ZDNet.com, 11 December. Available from: www.zdnet. com/article/guardian-article-on-cybercrime-serves-up-malvertising/

**20** Biasini, N (2015) Threat spotlight: Cisco Taloss thwarts access to massive international exploit kit generating $60m annually from ransomware alone, *Cisco blogs*, 6 October. Available from: http:// blogs.cisco.com/security/talos/angler-exposed

**21** Mathieson, SA (2016) World-leading heart hospital 'very, very lucky' to dodge ransomware hit, *The Register*, 4 November. Available from: www.theregister.co.uk/2016/11/04/papworth_ransomware_dodge/

**22** Agenda of the board of directors (inc minutes of 3 May 2017 meet-ing), Southport and Ormskirk Hospital, 7 June 2017. Available from: www.southportandormskirk.nhs.uk/downloads/Trust%20Board/ Agendas/2017/E%20-%20June%202017.pdf

**23** Agenda of the board of directors (inc minutes of 5 July 2017 meet-ing), Southport and Ormskirk Hospital, 27 July 2017. Available from: http://www.southportandormskirk.nhs.uk/downloads/ Trust%20Board/Agendas/2017/F%20-%20July%202017.pdf

**24** Agenda of the board of directors (inc minutes of 7 June 2017 meet-ing), Southport and Ormskirk Hospital, 5 July 2017. Available from:

www.southportandormskirk.nhs.uk/downloads/Trust%20Board/
Agendas/2017/G%20-%20July%202017.pdf

25 Twelve days in May: how Barts Health coped with the NHS cyberattack, [in response to FOI request at What Do They Know?], 12 June
2017. Available from: www.whatdotheyknow.com/request/411468/
response/1003711/attach/html/3/Cyber%20narrative%20final%20
060717.docx.html

26 Meeting of the board of directors, Papworth Hospital NHS
Foundation Trust, 22 May 2017. Available from: www.papworth-
hospital.nhs.uk/docs/papers/17-07-06/Papers/Item%201iii%20
Minutes%20170522%20Board%20Part%201%20Unconfirmed.pdf

27 Laux, J, *et al* (2017) Cyber event briefing: Wannacry ransomware attack, AonBenfield.com, 22 May. Available from: http://
thoughtleadership.aonbenfield.com/Documents/20170518-ab-cyber-
wannacry-briefing.pdf

28 'GReAT', 'Lazarus Under The Hood', Kaspersky Securelist
blog, 3 April 2017. Available from: https://securelist.com/
lazarus-under-the-hood/77908/

29 Corera, G (2017) NHS cyber-attack was 'launched from North
Korea', BBC News site, 16 June

30 Alert (TA17-164A) HIDDEN COBRA – North Korea's DDoS Botnet
Infrastructure, US-CERT, 13 June 2017

31 Bossert, TP (2017) It's official: North Korea is behind Wannacry, *Wall
Street Journal*, 18 December. Available from: www.wsj.com/articles/
its-official-north-korea-is-behind-wannacry-1513642537

**LESSONS** RANSOMWARE

⊾ Ransomware variants are multiplying at a remarkable rate. They offer attackers something close to the hacking equivalent of the perfect murder: near-untraceable payment for an attack which requires the minimum of their effort. They never have to deal with your data; but nevertheless they have something you badly want.

⊾ The first line of defence against ransomware is equipment. Outdated software on insecure equipment is an open door. (Mobile devices such as tablets offer much better protection.)

⊾ The second line of defence is user education: don't click suspicious links (and all links should be treated as suspicious) or open suspicious attachments (and they should all be treated as suspicious). Make sure new or temporary staff are trained in this; attach warnings to equipment if necessary.

⊾ The third line of defence is backups. Restoring systems from backup is the simple answer to an encrypted system. But you need to be sure that the initial cause of the problem has been removed – else you'll ruin the backup too.

⊾ Paying the ransom often looks attractive, but it's a roulette spin whether it will work, and it makes future ransomware attacks more attractive to its creator.

⊾ When people's lives rely on systems working, find alternatives which can't be compromised by ransomware. This may mean your suppliers have to adapt much faster than in the past to help you deal with a threat which has emerged in the past decade to become a serious liability.

⊾ Even commercial antivirus systems can't guarantee to stop every form of ransomware. Forms of attack are still evolving and newer attacks are likely to keep eluding them – though at least you can be safe from the past ones.

# Called to account

# 07

## TalkTalk

Chair: *What threat are three-year-old children, Mr Graham?*
Christopher Graham, Information Commissioner:
*The threat from three-year-old children must not be taken lightly.*

Oral evidence to Culture, Media and Sport Select Committee on
cybersecurity, 27 January 2016

In the 1990s, running an internet service provider (ISP) in the UK
was the new gold rush. Consumers and businesses were discovering that the terra incognita of the internet held many wonders, and
were willing to pay for the time and services it offered – particularly
email, web browsing, newsgroups and minimal webspace. Dialup
modems, first at 14.4 kilobits per second and then 56.6 kilobits per
second, were the only way to connect; you paid a monthly subscription and on top of that a per-minute cost for access to the internet,
while BT, controlling 90 per cent of phone lines, got a proportion
of the cost of your phone call to the ISP's modem.

Dozens of ISPs sprang up, all fighting to reach the scale where
they could begin to make serious money from the capital investment
in huge numbers of modems and phone lines for people to dial in
to, as well as the servers and wide data connection to the actual net.
Given the sunk costs in equipment, they had to make sure it was
used to its maximum – which meant attracting the largest number
of clients for the longest period once they were signed up.

Making a profit was tough, however, because of the competition,
investment cost, and BT's rigid pricing. The well-funded Freeserve,
founded in 1998 with money from the profitable Dixons consumer

electronics retail chain, shook up the market by ending the monthly subscription requirement, and instead letting people dial in to a cheap local-rate number; its revenues came from its split of the call cost. (BT complained it was getting too little of the call payment.) That helped kickstart the internet revolution in the UK: in the single year from 1999 to 2000 the proportion of households with internet access in the UK almost doubled, from 13 per cent to 25 per cent. By July 1999 Freeserve had 1.3 million subscribers, and floated on the London stock market, valued at around £1.4 billion. By September 2000, it had more than 2 million subscribers, more than BT or nearest rival AOL, which had 1.5 million. But it was bleeding money, having made a £17.8 million loss on revenue of £14.6 million in the quarter ending August 2000. The next big shift – and hope for profit – was always-on broadband.[1,2]

Broadband access for consumers began appearing in 2000, though it took until 2007 for half of UK homes to have it. During that period, there was a furious bout of consolidation as dozens of smaller consumer-focused ISPs were bought by a few larger ones seeking efficiencies. The monthly price charged to the consumer became a key differentiator, because bits are the most fungible of commodities, and speeds were limited by BT's hardware in the exchanges.

Fighting for primacy in this turmoil was TalkTalk, launched in 2003 as the rebranded face of a small broadband provider called Opal Telecom. TalkTalk was itself a subsidiary of Carphone Warehouse, a huge retail business which had thrived on the explosive growth of the mobile phone business: as the name suggested, it began by fitting them in cars, but soon expanded into offering stand-alone handsets. CPW, as it was known, sought the fast-growth, consumer-facing businesses.

TalkTalk's biggest move came in October 2006, just six months after it began offering broadband, when it bought AOL's UK ISP business for £370 million, acquiring 2.1 million customers, 600,000 on dialup and 1.5 million on broadband. (AOL broadband connections had passed dialup ones in June 2005.) To make the deal profitable, the company would have to make a profit of £176 from each customer it had bought. So a five-year payback would require keeping them all and making a profit of £35 each per year, for example.

By the end of 2006, five companies dominated the consumer ISP market. BT had 24 per cent; Virgin Media, the final buyer for the UK cable TV companies of the 1990s, which had each gone quietly bust from debt overload, had 26 per cent. TalkTalk had 17 per cent, Italian-owned Tiscali 10 per cent, and Orange – owned by France's Wanadoo, which in January 2001 had bought Freeserve – had 8 per cent, with 1 million customers. The other 15 per cent of consumers were served by about 200 tiny ISPs, some with annual turnovers of less than £1 million serving perhaps a few thousand customers. The largest and fastest-growing was Sky, which had bought EasyNet in 2005 for £211 million, and had 0.3 million customers.[3]

# Slowdowns and synergies

From 2007, the growth in internet users slowed abruptly, from the double-digit annual growth seen earlier in the decade to low single digits. The consolidation continued: in May 2009 TalkTalk bought Tiscali in a £236 million deal. By the end of the year, the big five had become four: BT, Virgin, TalkTalk and Sky, together holding 85 per cent of customers.

By 2010, TalkTalk was the second-biggest UK ISP, with 4.15 million broadband customers (giving it a 23 per cent market share) and another 1.1 million 'non-broadband' (that is, dialup) users, plus about 160,000 small business users. It was now large enough to be floated off as a separate company on the London Stock Exchange – a splendid payday for its parent business. In the first half of its 2009/10 financial year, it had generated revenues of £789 million, or about £138 per customer per year; on that, it had generated EBITDA (earnings before interest, tax, deductions and amortization) of £107 million, or just under £20 of profit per customer per year. Broadband customers spent the most, with average revenue per user (ARPU, a key industry metric) of just under £24 per quarter, or £96 per year; those 4.15 million broadband customers generated about 75 per cent of its revenues.

But even while TalkTalk seemed to be flourishing, there were problems. A stock market presentation in February 2010 ahead of its demerger from Carphone Warehouse noted that following its acquisition of Tiscali it needed to deliver 'acquisition synergies' – business shorthand for eliminating duplication, especially of jobs – and that its business ISP, Opal, still existed as a separate brand. 'Integration – "one company",' said the top line on one PowerPoint slide, noting that it had already achieved 'one London head office for TalkTalk, AOL & Tiscali'.[4]

That skimmed over the reality: there was a great deal of duplication, caused by the many acquisitions that had been carried out over the years. Before its acquisition by TalkTalk, Tiscali had been struggling with this, having bought two other small ISPs, Pipex and Nildram. While bits are fungible – an internet connection from one company is just like another – people's logins and especially email addresses and webspace aren't. Many of the old ISPs which had been snapped up had tempted people by offering multiple free email addresses on the ISP's domain as a quick way both to get people familiar with the internet and make it useful. They would also offer free webhosting in a subdomain of your choice: everyone could build their own website, a virtual extension of the home-owning democracy.

Strategically, offering email and webhosting also tied customers to the ISP. If you signed up with Freeserve, your email address from your first days online ended with '@freeserve.co.uk'. But if you moved to another ISP (perhaps because it was cheaper or offered a better service), there was no way to redirect those emails; they were only accessible by dialling in to a Freeserve modem, which meant you were paying Freeserve. Similarly, when ISPs were acquired, existing customers grated at the suggestion that for branding reasons they might lose their existing email address. (Webpages tended to be easier to copy between domains, though they still meant the loss of a specific subdomain.) Acquirers appeased those customers by routing emails sent to the old address to the ISP's new one. In some cases, it was simpler to let the old email destinations remain available via webpage logins, so they would quietly fade away as newer free offerings such as Microsoft's Hotmail, Yahoo, and then Google's Gmail took over the market.

TalkTalk struggled to integrate its own customer database (replete with AOL customers) with those of Tiscali, Pipex and Nildram. In the subsequent attempt to amalgamate and coordinate all the customer details and billing systems, people complained of receiving multiple bills, late bills, and demands for repayment of non-existent debts. Customer satisfaction plummeted. The problems continued into 2010, when people were still being wrongly billed after the takeover. In January 2011, TalkTalk was awarded the *Daily Mail*'s wooden spoon for worst customer service, worse even than the UK's tax office. That month, the company undertook a £12 million reorganization, which it said in its financial results was to 'integrate technology and IT capabilities and consolidate back office functions'.[5]

In March 2011 the UK telecoms regulator Ofcom ordered TalkTalk to pay 65,000 customers a total of £2.5 million in compensation, or about £38.50 each, for being billed despite having cancelled their broadband. In August 2011 Ofcom followed that up with a £3.1 million fine for 'a serious breach' of telecoms rules in TalkTalk's treatment of the customers whose cases had come up in the 10 months between January and November 2010. In all, the fines were equivalent to just over £86 per wronged customer, or about £1.36 of forgone profit for each of its 4.1 million users.[6]

Even so, TalkTalk's performance began improving. But Tiscali, the takeover which had caused problems for so many people, would turn out to have a sting in its tail.

## Outsourced, out of mind

As Ofcom was handing out the £3.1 million fine, TalkTalk was closing its Waterford call centre, a move that it reckoned would save about £15 million annually, and contracting Wipro, one of the biggest IT services companies in India, to handle a bigger chunk of its call centre work from its Kolkata offices. TalkTalk had used Wipro for some call centre operations since 2004, with a portal built in 2002 to give access to customer details. The outsourcing made sense as the Tiscali acquisition (and problems) faded into the past: customer service call volumes were down, and the £15 million saving was significant against annual operating costs of around £600 million. A year later, half-year profits were up by £9 million even though revenues were down by £16 million. Part of that was from better customer service, the company said in its half-year results published in November 2012: calls to the customer service centre were down 19 per cent year-on-year.[7]

Outsourcing is attractive to those looking at the bottom line. If the company employs someone to staff a call centre phone, it has to pay them whether they're dealing with a customer or not. Outsourcers charge by the time spent actually on calls – typically 85 per cent of the time. That's a 15 per cent saving at once. Choose the correct country, and staff costs – which typically make up about 60–70 per cent of the operating expenses in running a call centre – are much lower. Salaries in the Philippines, which has around 60 million English speakers, are between one-fifth and one-half those of comparable jobs in the US or UK. India and South Africa are also popular for remote locations. Rent VOIP (voice-over-internet) lines and you don't have to pay expensive overseas phone call charges, and you can serve people much more cheaply than if you were to keep the operation at home in the UK or US.[8]

The downsides, however, include annoyance for customers who may find the calls difficult to hear (cheap equipment and VOIP using low-bandwidth lines reduce audio quality significantly) and misunderstandings due to accents and vocabulary. The other significant downside is security. If your customer data is accessible in a location you don't control, by a company you don't own, how do you ensure its security?

In summer 2013, Keith Aldridge was called by what he thought was a customer service agent. He had just switched to TalkTalk's phone service, but had been having some problems with it. The person on the line quoted details of his account, and knew about the problems he had been having. Aldridge wasn't suspicious; the number he had been given when he switched was so new that he had only given it to two other family members. The caller told him he would receive a refund as an apology for the problems. He got Aldridge to download remote viewing software, called TeamViewer, which let him take control of the PC; then they got the details of his credit card, and took money from it while assuring him they would credit it. But the credit never came.[9]

Furious and concerned when he discovered he'd been conned, Aldridge contacted the chief executive's office at TalkTalk to express his concern: how had someone got details about him which only someone with access to TalkTalk's customer database would have?

To those who have watched the Indian call centre industry, the emergence of that scam was no surprise. In 2010, I began researching complaints from a number of people who said they had been called from India (based on the speakers' accents). The callers insisted that the person's computer was 'virus-infected' and 'causing network disruption'.

This built on true stories from earlier in the century, when spam traffic had ballooned from PCs running Windows XP infected by viruses that pumped out huge volumes of email using self-contained mail programs. The PC owner's mailbox and email would be unaffected, leaving them oblivious to the problems they were causing.

The telephone calls, though, were pure scams. The callers – teams of people in call centres working from a script – slogged diligently through phone books and other databases, and said they were calling from 'Microsoft' or 'your ISP'. They would demonstrate the 'virus infection' by asking people to open a Windows program called Event Viewer. To the uninitiated, the lines of reports scrolling past there looked like a mess of problems. (In fact, it was the machine effectively mumbling to itself as it went about its work; the 'warnings' reported in Event Viewer are unimportant.) Having thus horrified their target, the scammers would offer to 'fix' the problem for a one-off payment, or generously suggest a single payment and then a subscription to their 'support' service. The 'fix' involved getting remote access via programs such as TeamViewer, moving the mouse around on the screen a bit, and declaring the machine fixed. Sometimes they would install software – in some cases, entirely new (often pirated) copies of Windows at inflated prices. Sometimes they would install malware which captured keystrokes and bank login details.

The number of people hit by the scam easily numbered tens of thousands. The UK's Serious Organized Crime Agency and the US Federal Trade Commission struggled to clamp down on it. It was obvious that the scams were run out of call centres in Kolkata, where the skills for doing so – trained English-speaking call centre staff with some technical knowledge and the ability to improvise from a script – were in plentiful supply. The problem was identifying the source and getting the police there to act.

The TalkTalk scam, of which Aldridge is the earliest known example, was an extension of that. The question was, where had the caller got the TalkTalk-specific information about him?

In autumn 2014, more TalkTalk customers began getting calls from people whose accents, and low-quality VOIP phone lines, implied they were based in India. They claimed they were calling from TalkTalk. Suspicious customers – of whom there were plenty – were reassured when the callers were able to tell them their TalkTalk account number, along with their name, phone number and postal address. The last three might be in a phone book, but the account number could only have come from TalkTalk's systems.

Thus reassured, hundreds and hundreds of people fell for a banking scam. The caller told them (after getting them to download software that let them control their PC remotely) that their router or PC had been hit by a virus; they would see screens with red warning signs. Now came the new wrinkle. TalkTalk, the caller would explain, was going to pay them £250 (sometimes the sum was £200) to apologize for the inconvenience of having been hacked. They were directed to a page with a number of banks' icons, asked to choose their own, and then asked to pass on the six-digit security code the bank would send to their mobile phone to authorize the transaction. In one version of the scam, customers would find their bank account seemed to have a £5,000 credit – at which point the caller would apologize and ask them to send back the excess by a different system, which they would help them with.

In both variants, the transactions were in one direction only: out of the customers' accounts.

On 10 November 2014, TalkTalk alerted the Information Commissioner's Office (ICO), which handles data protection issues (and especially those relating to leaks of personal data held by companies) that it appeared to have a breach of personal data from its customer service centre. (It was required to do so by law.) The ICO began investigating the cause and extent. But TalkTalk didn't notify customers that it was worried about a breach until February 2015, emailing them all to warn that scammers might have their data.

Why the four-month gap? There is no obligation, as chief executive Dido Harding later told MPs, to inform people. Yet for months there had been stories in the national media of people who had been scammed.

But the trouble wasn't nearly over for Harding and TalkTalk. Trying to stem the leaks in the call centres was only one element where the company was vulnerable.

# Mapping the unknown

Because he was under 18 at the time of the offences, our next hacker must go under a pseudonym. We'll call him Ed. Living in the northern suburbs of Norwich, a stone's throw from the airport, he had started out in hacking by working out how to take over the social media accounts of people with 'desirable' usernames – usually short one-word ones – and then sell them on to cachet-seeking buyers. Such usernames would indicate that you had got on board a social network early, or had some sway; they occupied the same place for many teens that personalized car numberplates would for their parents, and could sell for hundreds of pounds – a nice bit of pocket money.

But Ed had bigger aims. Armed with SQL Map, a free (and legitimate) program which lets you discover vulnerabilities in website databases – though, its licence carefully disclaims, 'only with the owner's consent' – he began exploring. Manchester University, Cambridge University and Merit Badges, a company based in North Wales which offers martial arts badges, were his first targets, where he found databases ripe for picking.

Looking around further, he discovered that TalkTalk had seriously neglected the security on its site.

On the face of it, TalkTalk should have been aware of the risks. Hacking was high-profile stuff: in 2011, the pursuit by US and UK law enforcement of the LulzSec hackers, who had attacked the websites of the FBI and the UK's Serious Organized Crime squad, had occupied news headlines for months. Four years had passed.

But years of acquisitions and cost-cutting had meant that security had been overlooked in a few key places. Ed was also good at finding flaws. In June 2015 he made his first report to a 'bug bounty' site of a flaw in a website, belonging to an architects' partnership. In September and October, he reported another 100 in a range of sites in multiple countries. The flaws were mostly trivial.

Ed was also active in hacker forums, where knowledge is swapped. In one of those, he began discussing what he'd found. Brian Krebs, a former *Washington Post* journalist who now tracks hacking and site breaches full-time for his Krebs On Security site, observes:

> A lot of times, what happens is you get these young kids and they come on these forums, they're impressionable and looking for a mentor. They're very easy [for others] to use and just spit out. By the time they figure out what they're involved in, their usefulness has expired and whatever use they had has gone and their erstwhile friends have disappeared. This is fairly common.

At the start of October, Richard DeVere, who runs a company called Antisocial Engineering, got in touch with TalkTalk: he'd found that it was possible to use TalkTalk's longstanding offer of 15 megabytes of free webhosting on a talktalk.net domain (a hangover from those earliest days of the chase for customers) to claim subdomains such as 'fraudsupport.talktalk.net' – which, if decorated with suitable content, would be a good way to fool people into thinking they'd found an official page. TalkTalk didn't respond to his complaint. Annoyed, he wrote a blogpost published on 9 October which showed how the fake 'fraudsupport' page could look, which would be useful for scamming people. But he also noted that one could query what subdomains existed. He found about 1,500. 'These sites should cease,' he stated.[10]

Ed would later say he found the weakness in TalkTalk via Google. Richard isn't sure if Ed stumbled across that blogpost. But he finds the timing suspicious.

Between Thursday 15 October and Wednesday 21 October 2015, a hacker began prodding at three webpages that had originally been part of Tiscali. An SQL injection attack led to a database which held names, addresses, dates of birth, phone numbers, email addresses and financial information – including bank account details.

On the morning of Wednesday 21 October, the TalkTalk website crashed under a sustained DDOS attack. As luck would have it, the head of the computer security team was on holiday, in Turkey. That afternoon, Harding held an 'incident call' with the board, and the systems were taken offline. 'At that point I received a ransom demand in my personal inbox, which was very credible.' The hacker – or hackers? – wanted 465 bitcoins, then worth about US$126,550, or else he – they? – would start publishing customer data. There was also a posting on Pastebin, a site initially intended to let programmers exchange snippets of code. Over the years it has mutated into the outlet of choice for hackers to anonymously post data from hacks, and to boast, threaten and gloat about things they have or claim to have done. In some ways, if it isn't on Pastebin, it hasn't been hacked. If it is, it probably has been.

The content there included a sample which appeared to be TalkTalk customer details including email addresses and, more significantly, details of transactions they had carried out. It also had a worrying message: 'We Have Made Our Tracks Untraceable Through Onion Routing, Encrypted Chat Messages, Private Key Emails, Hacked Servers. We Will Teach our Children To Use The Web For Allah.. Your Hands Will Be Covered In Blood.. Judgement Day Is Soon'.[11]

Harding declared the event a major incident, triggering a formal internal response. TalkTalk had never run a business continuity exercise in which it mimicked a cyberattack; but it had a plan in place for extended downtime. For the next 18 hours the team tried to evaluate the extent of the hack – knowing that system logs can be altered to hide activity which may have ranged far and wide through a network. By the Thursday morning, they realized that there might have been a lot of customer data stolen, but that it would take some time to figure out what and how much. Harding decided that everyone needed to be warned, 'to help protect my customers'.[12]

In the afternoon, the police told her not to: it could tip off the criminals. Harding refused, though she noted that other companies might have just paid the ransom, or chosen to keep quiet about it. (In October 2016, the ride-sharing company Uber did exactly that when hackers demanded a ransom after collecting details of 57 million users; the company paid $100,000 for an assurance that the hackers had deleted it. The then chief executive Travis Kalanick was informed a month later; the news emerged a year later. Uber is being sued by multiple organizations, as there is no way to know whether the hackers kept their word.)[13]

Later on Thursday afternoon, TalkTalk announced it had come under 'a significant and sustained' cyberattack and that names, addresses, birth dates, email addresses, phone numbers, TalkTalk account information and credit or bank details might have been accessed.[14]

Harding faced a tightrope in her many media interviews. She couldn't downplay the importance of the hack. She didn't know for certain how it had been done, nor how many people had been affected, nor how badly. She wasn't sure if the stolen data had been encrypted. There was widespread astonishment at the latter, but it was the problem of dealing with a sprawling company with a huge legacy. (It later turned out that none of the data had been encrypted, but that the credit card details had been 'tokenized' with their middle six digits removed, making them useless for fraud.)

On the Friday morning, Adrian Culley, formerly a cybercrime expert at the Metropolitan Police in London, told the BBC's agenda-setting *Today* programme on Radio 4 this was more important than just a hack. 'It appears at face value to be related to Islamic cyber-terrorism,' he said. 'TalkTalk has million of customers but it is also part of the country's critical national infrastructure. This is a matter of national security.'[15]

National security! The nihilistic group Islamic State was much in the news at the time. But while it would have been flattering for TalkTalk to be elevated to the status of an electricity or water provider, the reality was more prosaic, suggested Peter Sommer, visiting professor at De Montfort University's cybersecurity centre. Appearing on the programme soon after Culley, he suggested that a terror claim meant little; more likely the aim was to extort the company or access customers' bank accounts. The BBC's security correspondent reported that 'government sources' were confident it was just normal cybercrime. GCHQ, which would have informed those sources, often has a very precise overview of exactly who is doing what.[16]

Ed's posts to the bug bounty site halted abruptly in November. He hadn't lost interest. But on 4 November, while TalkTalk's investigation of the extent of the hack was still ongoing, he'd been arrested and bailed by police in Norwich. Three others were arrested on the same day. The police subsequently filed charges under the Computer Misuse Act against him. Separately, Daniel Kelley, then 19, of Heol Dinbych, a little town in south Wales, was charged with computer misuse, blackmail, fraud and money laundering. Two friends, Matthew Hanley and Connor Allsopp, from Tamworth in Staffordshire, aged 22 and 20, were charged with a mixture of computer misuse and fraud offences. Though they had wiped or encrypted their computers, police found chat logs and social media messages where Hanley and Allsopp discussed trying to sell the personal data.[17]

Meanwhile, people were reporting that their credit card details had been used for fraudulent purchases: one woman told the *Daily Mirror* newspaper that £600 of purchases from the supermarket Tesco and the shoe chain Office had been made on her card. It was never confirmed whether her details had been stolen in the TalkTalk hack, or somewhere else. But it did demonstrate the febrile atmosphere around the breach.[18]

# The 4 per cent resolution

Harding led the investigation into the extent of the hack. It was expected to take a few days with an incident team working around the clock on a two-shift system. Instead it ended up taking 14 straight days to 6 November. The online systems for accessing information remained offline for three weeks.

By then TalkTalk had revised its estimate of the damage substantially downward from the potential 4 million customers. 'Only' 156,959 customers, 4 per cent of its customer base, might have had their personal details leaked. Of those, 15,656 could also have had their bank account numbers and sort codes, the minimum data needed to set up a debit from a UK account, stolen.[19]

The strangely precise figure pointed to the origins of the hack. It was an old Tiscali page. (TalkTalk did not disclose this in its statement, as it might have compromised the police investigation and any subsequent prosecution.)

'What the criminals succeeded in doing is effectively finding a needle in a haystack of haystacks,' Harding later told MPs.[12]

It wasn't quite that tough. They'd found a server which had previously been used for a marketing campaign, and had collected customer data. When the campaign was over, the technicians at the time chose the simplest means of making it vanish from the human internet: they removed its DNS entry.

The DNS – domain name server – is the phonebook for the internet; it's the system which renders a human-legible domain name such as 'google.com' into a computer-comprehensible IP address (such as 216.58.198.110). That tells the sending computer what destination to put on each data packet, and which every intermediate computer uses to figure out where next to send that packet.

When you add a server to the internet, it will have an IP address. But until it has a DNS entry, it won't have a human-readable address. It is the DNS system which makes the web comprehensible to humans; otherwise we would be trying to remember 12-digit numbers to navigate between sites. It would be like having to remember the phone numbers of everyone you might ever want to speak to – family, friends, work, banks, shops, schools. Or else we would rely entirely on bookmarks, and hypertext, since sites wouldn't have names, only numbers.

Normally, removing a server's DNS entry is sufficient to protect it. But in this case it wasn't. And the data on it was extremely valuable. DeVere thinks that TalkTalk had removed the DNS entry when he contacted it about the talktalk.net subdomains. That hadn't, however, taken the pages offline.

But it wasn't Ed who had exploited it. Channel 4 News reported on 5 November that a group of hackers had been on a Skype group call, and that one had shared a way into the TalkTalk database. The hacker who spoke to the journalist said that 'at least 25 people' knew how to break in.[20]

The person who spoke to Channel 4 News said it was just 'a few friends laughing about a company with bad security. It's fun for us.'

The arrests ended the fun.

Despite all that had happened, Harding was bullish in a presentation to analysts (and the stock market) on 11 November, just under a month after the hack. 'None of the sensitive personal information on its own can be used to steal from our customers,' the slide said.[21]

That doesn't mean though that the information couldn't contribute to theft. Given a name and email, or name and address, a criminal can quickly expand their knowledge about someone to encompass their home and work details; social media details often then point to more information about someone. Genealogy databases will point to a mother's maiden name; once you have that sort of information, a con artist can do a lot – perhaps most easily, by calling the person in question and bluffing that they are from TalkTalk itself and quoting back the bank details and other information.

TalkTalk, said Harding, was making a provision of between £30 million and £35 million against the financial impact of the cyberattack. That represented the cost of investigating the attack and remedying it, the opportunity cost of lost sales while the sales pages had been down, the cost of the free upgrades and free credit monitoring on offer, and the likely loss of customers disenchanted with the company's security.

On 15 December, Harding gave evidence to MPs on the Culture, Media and Sport Committee at the House of Commons. The first question asked was: who was responsible for cybersecurity in the company? Harding replied that she was; cybersecurity was 'a board-level issue' and that in a telecoms company it was part of everything, 'which is why I think of myself as directly responsible for it'. There hadn't been anyone at the board level directly responsible for cybersecurity. Nor had the technology team (which was) had anyone to report to directly on the board. (Though it did now: in November, Harding had come under pressure from the board and recruited the company's first chief information security officer from one of its consultants, PricewaterhouseCoopers.)

'Who is line-responsible that [preventing such an attack] happens within the company?' asked Jesse Norman, the chair, sounding a little frustrated as Harding insisted again that she was, and that the responsibility for keeping customer data safe was split across teams: a security team, but also a technology team, and an operations team. 'It is impossible in a telecoms company to say that security only sits with the director of security,' she said. And, she added, 'if it is a criminal attack, it is entirely possible that none of them are responsible for the attack. The question is, was the company?'

It sounded a little solipsistic; a company must be responsible for its flaws. Krebs, who often talks to companies about the need for security, says they often aren't awake to the scale of the threat caused both by the access to expertise that the internet affords, and their own growth. He says:

> Most organizations, once they get something in place and it works, they tend to leave it alone. The way that most companies grow makes them very exposed to these types of vulnerabilities in web applications and things, because generally they acquire another company along with their IT services, and then they somehow combine that into the existing organization's operations in some kludge way, but they rarely go through and try to identify existing vulnerabilities that they're incorporating into their network. There's a lot of that going on where these legacy systems just get incorporated into larger networks, and they never get addressed or never maintained.[22]

## Underestimating the danger

MPs later interviewed the Information Commissioner, Christopher Graham, who commented that he had been shown a YouTube video featuring a cybersecurity expert demonstrating to his three-year-old how to break into a website using SQL injection. The committee chair, Jesse Norman, asked: what exactly was the threat from three-year-olds?

'The threat from three-year-old children must not be taken lightly,' Graham replied. Simon Rice, the ICO's group manager, added, 'There are a lot of automated tools where essentially a three-year-old can press the button' – running software which would scan the site for vulnerabilities.[23]

The ICO's subsequent report in October 2016 on TalkTalk's failings was blunt. 'The attack was able to probe for the vulnerabilities and perform an SQL injection attack [using] SQLmap, and then exfiltrate' – extract – 'data'. There were no checks against such SQL attacks, the vulnerable pages used outdated software libraries, and the MySQL database was outdated too, allowing an attacker to bypass the access restrictions – a flaw for which a free fix had been available since 2012. The pages that had been attacked dated back years, to before TalkTalk had bought Tiscali in May 2009.[24]

The ICO fined TalkTalk £400,000 for 'security failings' that allowed a cyberattacker to access customer data 'with ease'. The fine related to the loss of the personal data – names, addresses, birth dates, phone numbers and email addresses – of 156,959 people; for 15,656 of them, bank account numbers and sort codes were also exposed.

At the time, the fine was the ICO's largest ever. It worked out to between £25.50 and £2.54 per affected customer, depending on what value one puts on the exposure of the bank information. If you put a £20 value on the bank detail exposure, each individual's data exposure is worth £0.55; if each individual's data exposure merits £2 of fines, the bank details are worth about £5.50. So the fines equated to somewhere between £7 and £20 per person affected.

The ICO explained to me that it has a system for determining fines which examines not just the size of a breach and its content, but also the extent to which a company has been culpable in allowing the breach. In brief, it's not just about what data is leaked; it's also about how easily the flaw was exploited. (Ed would later tell magistrates he was 'just showing off' to his friends.)

The ICO fine was in stark contrast with that levied by Ofcom in 2011, where 65,000 customers were paid compensation for poor service averaging close to £40 each, and the company itself was fined an average £50 per person for the same failing, or a total of £90 per person affected. Ofcom is able to fine companies up to 10 per cent of their relevant turnover. The ICO, until 2018, had a fixed fine scale, topping out at £500,000 – a figure set by Parliament.

Yet once customer data is stolen, it can't be recovered; the loss is permanent. The message seems to be that bad customer service merits serious fines but losing personal data, in a world where it is a currency, does not. Speaking to MPs about the limitations he faced, the ICO's Christopher Graham suggested that being able to fine based on turnover would be more powerful. In the meantime, he said, the more important damage from a hack like TalkTalk's was to the company's reputation.

Yet Harding had data suggesting otherwise. In the presentation to the stock market on 11 November 2015, when the attack's breadth had only just been figured out, she put up a page of four graphs, with the title 'early indicators are that the majority of customers support our approach'. The first graph showed direct debit cancellations peaking on 27 October, four days after the announcement, and then returning to their normal level. The second showed 'unsolicited requests to cease' – when people demand an end to their contract – peaking on the same day, and then moving back down to about the long-term line. 'Loyalty save rates', indicating whether attempts to persuade people to stick with TalkTalk had worked, had plummeted the day after the announcement, but worked back up to their usual level. (Curiously, none of the graphs labelled the Y-axis, making it impossible to evaluate the true magnitude of the changes.) The fourth showed the response to a specially commissioned ICM poll, which had asked whether people agreed with the statement 'I appreciate TalkTalk's honesty in the way they are dealing with this' on 30 October and then on 6 November. It showed approval rising over the week from 48 per cent to 54 per cent. 'Most customers think we have done the right thing,' said Harding's slide for the analysts.[20]

The next year, as it showed its results from the fourth financial quarter (covering the first three months of 2016), the company proudly announced its lowest-ever 'churn' (turnover of customers) of just 1.3 per cent, compared with the historically high 2.1 per cent the previous quarter, when the attack had been publicized.

Perhaps people had decided they really trusted TalkTalk more now; or possibly all those who had been looking for a reason to leave had found it with the cyberattack, leaving a huge pool of those who were satisfied and unlikely to churn away. The company reckoned that the breach had caused about 0.6 per cent of the 2.1 per cent churn, or 95,000 customers abandoning it. That was about two-thirds as many as had been affected by the breach. (There's no way to know if they were the same people.)

There was also the fact that TalkTalk had snared a lot of customers with its 'quad-play' offer – any combination of broadband, phone calls, TV and mobile. Between a third and a fifth of customers were using at least two of the products, which made moving away a more complex business than if they were just using its broadband.

# Trial and punishment

In November 2016, 'Ed' admitted seven hacking offences linked to the TalkTalk attack. His iPhone, MacBook Air, a hard drive and a USB stick were confiscated. In his mitigation, his defence lawyer Chris Brown said that the teenager had 'created a number of personas online. Personas that talked about his abilities as a hacker.' Then the community had challenged him to do something; 'the thrill was in the chase, not in damaging their website or causing loss. It was playing,' Brown said.[25]

The teenager confirmed he'd known his actions were illegal: 'I didn't really think of the consequences at the time,' he said. In December 2016 he was given a 12-month rehabilitation order. His account on the bounty site remained silent throughout 2017.

In April 2017, Hanley and Allsopp pleaded guilty at the Old Bailey in London to charges relating to the October 2015 hack: Hanley had hacked into the site and shared 'a customer's personal and financial details'. (Only one instance is required to fulfil the threshold of criminality.) Hanley also gave data to 'another man' – unnamed. Kelley pleaded guilty to the charges of computer misuse, blackmail and fraud. He had been on bail for a DDOS attack when he had committed the offences.[17]

TalkTalk eventually put the cost of the cyberattack at £42 million. It didn't put a price on the breach of its call centre data.

## Collect call

In January 2016, police in India arrested three Wipro employees, who were accused of stealing TalkTalk customer data and using it for the scams. TalkTalk said in a statement that 'we are pleased that our investigations have yielded results' and that 'we are also reviewing our relationship with Wipro'. It didn't mention that the relationship went back as far as 2004.[26]

But TalkTalk still didn't seem to be secure. In February 2016, the BBC's *Moneybox* programme interviewed two people who had had telephone engineers visit them on behalf of the company, and had told them to expect a phone call from BT Openreach (which maintains the infrastructure) or TalkTalk in the next couple of days. The calls came – and the callers were able to quote account numbers, addresses and even the names of the engineers who had visited the property. Then they used the reverse payment scam.

TalkTalk refused to refund the customers, insisting there had not been a breach of its customer data, and hinted that the breach was down to a third-party company for which the engineers were working. That seemed unsatisfactory: though strictly speaking the scam hadn't been carried out by a TalkTalk employee, the customers didn't get a choice about which company TalkTalk brought in to service their lines, and they had taken care to try to verify the identity of the caller. The gap in due diligence seemed to be TalkTalk's more than the customers'. With some customers, TalkTalk did offer 'compensation' payments, but losses tended to be larger, and TalkTalk did not admit liability.

But in summer 2016 TalkTalk did decide to end its contract with Wipro, and withdraw all its customer services from India, consolidating them in the Philippines, South Africa and the UK. The move would take until summer 2017 to complete.

The problem didn't go away in the meantime. In March 2017 the *Guardian* reported on the case of Jane Hatton, a TalkTalk customer who had received a new router in January – and two weeks later received a call from someone with an Indian accent who knew about its associated contract upgrade, the router serial number and its password. The scammer tried the reverse payment scam, which failed because Hatton's bank blocked it; as a sort of reprisal, he locked her out of her computer by changing the password, and demanded a ransom. Hatton disconnected and wiped the computer. There were more cases, all pointing to a data breach at a company doing work for TalkTalk.[27]

When Graham appeared before MPs in January 2016, the ICO was still working on its breach report for TalkTalk's 2014 events. Would it finish 'in this calendar year, do you think?' asked the chair, Jesse Norman. Graham declined to give a definite answer, pointing out that the international dimension of the investigation complicated it. His 30-odd case officers were anyway typically working on 25 to 30 cases simultaneously at any time, he said.

In August 2017, almost three years after being alerted, the ICO published its investigation into the September 2014 data breach report, and fined TalkTalk £100,000 because it had 'failed to look after its customers' data and risked it falling into the hands of scammers and fraudsters'. Specifically, it said that three Wipro accounts had been used to access the data of up to 21,000 customers, and that 40 Wipro staff had access to the data of between 25,000 and 50,000 TalkTalk customers. Those staff could log into the portal from any internet-capable device, including a PC, smartphone or tablet anywhere in the world; it didn't have to be a Wipro-authorized device, just one with the login details. Once in, staff could do searches on wildcards – so 'A*' would give every surname starting with A – and then export it; and they could view up to 500 records at a time.[28]

'TalkTalk had ample opportunity over a long period of time to implement appropriate measures, but it failed to do so,' the ICO noted in its notice of the fine. The portal had been up since 2002; the flaw had probably existed that long.

Yet, incredibly, the ICO also said that it couldn't find direct evidence of a link between the compromised data and the scam calls. This remarkable disclaimer thus implied that the coincident timing of the data breach and the scams was entirely accidental, which was hard to believe given people's experiences and the fine meted out. It looked more like a legal sidestep so that the ICO couldn't be called into court as a witness if victims sued TalkTalk. (TalkTalk has maintained that it is not responsible for the losses suffered by those who were scammed, because they voluntarily made the payments to people not authorized by the company.)

The fine was equivalent to between £2 and £5 per customer who could have been affected – far less than those who were scammed lost.

For those who were hit by the scam, the ICO's sidestep and its small fine were infuriating. Yet they also felt both powerless and intimidated in the face of the seemingly indifferent quangos – quasi-autonomous non-government organizations – that they felt should be protecting their interests. One I spoke to who was scammed was excoriating in their description of the ICO's careful avoidance of assigning liability – but declined, despite repeated entreaties, to be named or even to have the quote itself used. They were concerned their words might somehow be used by the ICO against anyone who did manage to organize a class action against it for failing to determine that the TalkTalk customer details had indeed come from TalkTalk. It was a stark reminder of the power dynamics in the game of hackers, hacked and victims: the hackers and victims lost out, but the hacked organization sailed on.

# References

**1**  Share of households with internet access in the United Kingdom from 1998 to 2017, *statista.com*, 2017. Available from: www.statista.com/statistics/275999/household-internet-penetration-in-great-britain/

**2**  Freeserve losses double, *BBC Business News*, 28 September 2000. Available from: http://news.bbc.co.uk/1/hi/business/945842.stm

3   *The communications market: broadband, research report*, Ofcom,
    2 April 2007. Available from: www.ofcom.org.uk/__data/assets/
    pdf_file/0021/16185/broadband_rpt.pdf

4   TalkTalk group investor presentation, *TalkTalk*, February 2010.
    Available from: www.talktalk.co.uk/media/files/corporate/pdf/
    demerger-final.pdf

5   TalkTalk Telecom Group PLC preliminary results for the 12 months to
    31 March 2011, *TalkTalk,* 19 May 2011. Available from: http://irpages2.
    equitystory.com/websites/rns_news/English/1100/news-tool---rns---eqs-
    group.html?article=4243679&showPDF2=1&company=talktalk

6   TalkTalk and Tiscali UK fined £3 million for breaching
    consumer rules, *Ofcom*, 18 August 2011. Available from: www.
    ofcom.org.uk/about-ofcom/latest/media/media-releases/2011/
    talktalk-and-tiscali-uk-fined-3-million-for-breaching-consumer-rules

7   UK based broadband and voice telephony services company TalkTalk
    selects Wipro BPO as strategic partner, *wipro.com*, 3 August 2011.
    Available from: www.wipro.com/newsroom/press-releases/archives/
    uk-based-broadband-and-voice-telephony-services-company-talktalk/

8   Bocklund, L and Hinton, B (2008) Cost structure and distribution
    in today's contact centers, *Strategic Contact*, March. Available from:
    www.strategiccontact.com/pdf/CC_Cost_WP.pdf

9   Brignall, M (2015) TalkTalk customer reported data breach as early
    as 2013, *Guardian*, 8 November. Available from: www.theguardian.
    com/business/2015/nov/08/talktalk-customer-reported-data-breach-
    as-early-as-2013

10  Devere, R (2015) Social engineering & TalkTalk, *The Antisocial
    Engineer*, 9 October. Available from: https://theantisocialengineer.
    com/2015/10/09/social-engineering-talktalk/

11  Myers, R (2015) Every TalkTalk user has been 'hacked by Jihadis'
    who warn Judgement Day is soon, *Daily Mirror*, 23 October.
    Available from: www.mirror.co.uk/news/uk-news/every-talktalk-
    user-been-hacked-6693792

12  Oral evidence: Cyber security: Protection of personal data online, HC
    587, *Culture, Media and Sport Committee*, 15 December 2015.
    Available from: http://data.parliament.uk/writtenevidence/
    committeeevidence.svc/evidencedocument/culture-media-and-
    sport-committee/cyber-security-protection-of-personal-data-online/
    oral/26312.html

**13** Newcomer, E (2017) Uber paid hackers to delete stolen data on 57 million people, *Bloomberg News*, 21 November. Available from: www.bloomberg.com/news/articles/2017-11-21/uber-concealed-cyberattack-that-exposed-57-million-people-s-data

**14** Website attack affecting our customers, *TalkTalk (via Archive. org)*, 22 October. Available from: https://web.archive.org/web/20151022211310/http://help2.talktalk.co.uk/oct22incident

**15** Withnall, A (2015) TalkTalk cyber attack: 'Russia-based Islamic jihadists' claim responsibility for hack, *Independent*, 23 October. Available from: www.independent.co.uk/news/uk/crime/talktalk-cyber-attack-russia-based-islamic-jihadists-claim-responsibility-for-hack-a6705366.html

**16** TalkTalk cyber-attack: Boss 'receives ransom email', *BBC News*, 23 October 2015. Available from: www.bbc.co.uk/news/uk-34615226

**17** Fiveash, K (2017) TalkTalk hack attack: two men plead guilty to customer data theft, *Ars Technica*, 27 April. Available from: https://arstechnica.com/tech-policy/2017/04/talktalk-hack-attack-two-men-plead-guilty-to-customer-data-theft/

**18** Sassoon, L (2015) TalkTalk hackers go on £600 spending spree with stolen card details as boss says it's too early to consider compensation, *Daily Mirror*, 24 October. Available from: www.mirror.co.uk/news/uk-news/talktalk-hackers-go-600-spending-6694321

**19** Cyber attack update – Friday November 06th 2015, *TalkTalk Group via Internet Archive*, 15 November 2015. Available from: https://web.archive.org/web/20151115010858/https://www.talktalkgroup.com/press/press-releases/2015/cyber-attack-update-november-06-2015.aspx

**20** White, G (2015) TalkTalk hack – new details emerge, *Channel 4 News*, 5 November. Available from: www.channel4.com/news/talktalk-hack-insiders-reveal-how-it-was-pulled-off

**21** FY16 interim results presentation, *TalkTalk Group*, 11 November 2015. Available from: www.talktalkgroup.com/articles/talktalkgroup/Presentations/2015/FY16-Interim-Results-Presentation

**22** Personal communication

**23** Oral evidence: cyber security: protection of personal data online HC 587, *Culture, Media and Sport Committee*, 27 January 2016. Available from: http://data.parliament.uk/writtenevidence/committeeevidence.svc/evidencedocument/culture-media-and-sport-committee/cyber-security-protection-of-personal-data-online/oral/28091.html

**24** TalkTalk gets record £400,000 fine for failing to prevent October 2015 attack, *Information Commissioner's Office*, 5 October 2016. Available from: https://ico.org.uk/about-the-ico/news-and-events/news-and-blogs/2016/10/talktalk-gets-record-400-000-fine-for-failing-to-prevent-october-2015-attack/

**25** Boy, 17, admits hacking offences linked to TalkTalk attack, *Sky News*, 15 November 2016. Available from: https://news.sky.com/story/boy-17-admits-hacking-offences-linked-to-talktalk-attack-10658405

**26** TalkTalk cracks down on scam calls, *TalkTalk Group*, 27 January 2016. Available from: www.talktalkgroup.com/articles/talktalkgroup/TalkTalk-Group--moved-articles-/2016/TalkTalk-cracks-down-on-scam-calls

**27** Brignall, M (2017) Has TalkTalk's security been breached yet again?, *Guardian*, 11 March. Available from: www.theguardian.com/money/2017/mar/11/talktalk-security-breached-again-scammers-india

**28** Personal data belonging to up to 21,000 TalkTalk customers could have been used for scams and fraud, *Information Commissioner's Office*, 10 August 2017. Available from: https://ico.org.uk/about-the-ico/news-and-events/news-and-blogs/2017/08/personal-data-belonging-to-up-to-21-000-talktalk-customers-could-have-been-used-for-scams-and-fraud/

## **LESSONS** FROM TALKTALK'S EXPERIENCES

- When you acquire a company, you acquire all of its problems and vulnerabilities too.

- Legacy systems can hide multiple flaws which have been overlooked for years; being acquired, or being in a position that means you're a target to be acquired, doesn't tend to make organizations raise their security game.

- If you outsource functions such as call centres, you should consider them potentially hostile threats to your organization's data security. Your most valuable data about your customers is accessible through them.

- From 2018, fines in Europe and the UK for allowing the leaking of personal data will increase dramatically, to as much as €20 million, or 4 per cent of global turnover, whichever is larger. That's a dramatic contrast to the situation that existed before, when fines were nugatory compared with the possible effects.

- Customer inertia tends to be high even in the event of a breach.

- Have a plan in place for the possibility that you suffer a big data breach.

- Have someone responsible for cybersecurity who reports at board level.

- Don't pay ransoms. There's no way to guarantee that the data won't have already leaked further, nor that the person you're dealing with is the original or only person with access to it.

- Don't underestimate the ease with which systems might be compromised, and the youth of those who might be involved. The young have free time and the curiosity to see where things lead.

# The internet of hacked things

08

## Mirai

*I don't think there are enough facts to definitively point a finger at me.*
PARAS JHA, when asked by security researcher Brian Krebs
whether he wrote and operated the Mirai botnet

On Friday 21 October 2016, the internet looked wrong to a lot of
people on the east coast of the US. Those getting up at 7.00 am on
the east coast found Twitter wouldn't load. Nor would Amazon,
nor Spotify. Nor Reddit. Netflix wasn't showing programmes. Was
this the long-heralded cyber war? Except, strangely, some other
sites loaded fine. Had someone pulled out a plug somewhere? Or
was it something else?

After a couple of hours it seemed to stop. Life continued as
normal as far as most people were aware – though in fact, at around
1.00 pm on the east coast, technicians at a company called Dyn
were struggling to cope with the same phenomenon they had seen
earlier, and which had caused the trouble: a tsunami of data aimed
at their servers, known in the business as a DDOS (distributed
denial of service) attack. They managed to divert it. Later that evening, it happened again; but they managed to fend it off then too.

The first data tsunami was on an unprecedented scale. Dyn estimated that it was being assailed by about 100,000 devices spread
around the world, which were generating traffic flows as large
as 1.2 terabits per second. A terabit is a thousand gigabits, or a
million megabits. A typical home connection is about 10 megabits
per second; this attack used enough bandwidth to serve a town. If
a website were a house, a DDOS would be akin to having millions

of people from all over the world running up to the doorbell, ringing it and then running away. Life inside the house would become impossible, and nobody would be able to send or deliver anything because the path would constantly be blocked. That was what happened to Dyn's servers.

That in turn blocked people from loading sites because Dyn runs domain name system (DNS) servers for a swathe of the east coast. DNS is a lookup service: if you type netflix.com into a browser window, your computer sends a query to a DNS server asking for the best internet protocol (IP) location to address the packet to. (It's like a telephone directory for the internet, except most people don't use telephone directories any more, whereas DNS is essential.)

In the face of the paralysing DDOS attack, anyone using Dyn DNS to access the internet would get nowhere. Without an IP address response, systems freeze up. And this was a very exceptional attack. In the first quarter of 2017, Verisign reported that the average DDOS attack had a bandwidth of 14.1 Gbps; only 10 per cent lasted longer than 30 minutes. The Dyn attack had been 85 times bigger, and gone on for hours, multiple times.

In the days following the attack, a number of groups claimed, or were blamed for, it: Wikileaks suggested 'supporters' of its somewhat nebulous aims were 'taking down the US internet'; the Jester (an American ex-military hacker who has previously attacked Russian and militant Islamic sites, as well as Wikileaks itself) suggested it was the Russian government; and a group calling themselves New World Hackers, previously notable only for defacing a few Russian websites, said they had been behind it, saying they had used 'our own special coded supercomputer botnets' to carry it out.[1]

In its own dissection of the source of the attack five days later, Dyn said this was unlike previous DDOS attacks. Those usually emanate from 'PC botnets' – collections of thousands of Windows PCs subverted by malware, and used by their unseen controllers to silently coordinate attacks on sites, unbeknownst to their owners.[2]

This DDOS was a botnet, all right, but powered by devices that most people wouldn't think of as computers. Some of them were digital video recorders. Some were routers. Some were CCTV cameras. All were part of what is usually called the 'Internet of

Things', usually just abbreviated to IoT: devices with computing power and internet connectivity but no obvious way to program them directly. There was already a name for this gigantic botnet which had infected so many devices: Mirai.

That wasn't a new name to Brian Krebs. He knew all about Mirai already – including why and how it had been turned into a wrecking ball on the internet. That would be so that its original creators could cover their tracks.

## Call me blogger

Most people might settle for calling Krebs a blogger about hacking and cybersecurity. But that would underplay the threat that those he writes about perceive from him, and the threat they sometimes pose to him. He has had an armed SWAT (Special Weapons Arms and Tactics) team turn up at his house and handcuff him. He has been sent heroin in the post in a failed attempt to incriminate him in drug dealing. Multiple threats have been made against him and his family.

He's used to it now, though it's been a long journey. In 2001, Krebs was a writer for *Newsbytes*, a technology newswire owned by the *Washington Post*, when a worm locked him out of his home computer. That piqued an interest in hackers, which became deeper and deeper. The next year he became a full-time staff writer for the *Post*'s website, and went on to write hundreds of stories at the paper, and more than a thousand posts for its *Security Fix* blog. In 2009, he left to strike out on his own as an independent security journalist and researcher. The economics of writing a blog about hackers didn't seem obvious at first; but it was a space with an obvious gap. Before him, the security business mostly consisted either of security consultants who would come into businesses and suck their teeth at obvious and expensive-to-fix failings, or journalists who skimmed the surface of the deep pool of criminality beneath the beneficent surface of the World Wide Web. Krebs combined a journalist's ability to investigate a story, and then write it up, with a researcher's understanding of what was happening. Now he is in demand as a speaker and consultant, and advertisers seek out his *Krebs on Security* site: 'I just try to develop stories that you can't find anywhere else and develop a loyal readership,' he says. 'If you do that consistently and well enough, then the advertisers come to you.' Businesses, including banks, will often come to him for help in identifying the source of leaks or hacks.[3]

But Krebs' investigations, detailed on his site, aren't so popular with the people engaged in the commercial side of hacking – breaking into sites, knocking them offline, gathering and selling credit card and other personal details online, creating gigantic 'botnets' of infected PCs. Krebs taught himself to read Russian, a popular language among commercial hackers, and detailed their exploits. He often reveals that companies have been hacked long before they make it public, and names those he believes responsible once confident in his sources. Sometimes the sources are other hackers. The saying 'no honour among thieves' has benefited him many times, with rivals sending him tips and help as they try to unmask each other. (They want to remove obstacles to growing their own businesses. What they overlook is that others will do the same to them.)

In return, exposed hackers have tried to harass him: one phoned the police and said there had been a shooting murder at Krebs' address, prompting the SWAT team. Another sent the heroin, but Krebs had been reading the hacker forum where the shipment number was posted – the sender had wanted Krebs' arrest to be a spectacle for others – and alerted the police and FBI. He has also endured multiple attempts to knock his site offline through 'distributed denial of service' (DDOS) attacks.

But the DDOS attack that hit his site on 20 September 2016 was in a different league. At a sustained 280 Gbps, peaking at 620 Gbps, it was unprecedentedly high. It wasn't hard to figure out why he had been targeted: the day before, Krebs had detailed the identities of two Israel-based hackers who he said were behind a DDOS-for-hire service called vDOS. Over four months in spring 2016, Krebs said, vDOS had launched 'more than 277 million seconds of attack time'. Over the previous two years, its owners had been paid at least $618,000 to target sites.[4]

But with vDOS offline, where had the attack on Krebs' site come from? It had to be an entirely different DDOS-for-hire service. But which one?

The answer turned out to be Mirai, as the botnet was quickly named. And its bots came from all over: an analysis by Imperva found that there were Mirai-infected devices in 164 countries, as far afield as Colombia, Montenegro, Tajikistan and Hawaii – though the biggest numbers of devices were in Vietnam and Brazil, together making up nearly a quarter of the IP addresses used in the attack.

The Internet of Things had turned nasty.

What was just as worrying was people's attitudes when they discovered they were contributing to the problem, as Mikko Hypponen, chief research officer of F-Secure, explained to me:

> When Mirai hit last October, we located some of the sources of the attack. Actually phoned them up and spoke with them. 'Hello, sir, it's Mikko Hypponen calling from F-Secure in Finland here. Our analytics says that you have a heat pump in your house – do you?' And they'd say, 'Yes, I do.' 'Oh, is it connected to the internet?' And they'd say, 'Yes, it is.' 'Well, it's causing a denial of service attack as part of a 100,000 machine botnet, and it's right now taking out the DNS servers, which are the routing servers for the internet.'[5]

Hypponen paused, partly for effect, and partly in amazement. 'And the typical reply would be – "Uh huh, cool." Seriously. They were like, "That's really neat."'

People hadn't known their heat pump or video camera could also function to knock out the internet. 'Then they'd say, "Well, it's working fine – it's a heat pump, it's cooling my house right now,"' Hypponen recalled. 'And I'd say, "OK, are you going to do something about it?" and they'd reply, "No – why would I? I don't care. I think it's cool."'

Against indifference, the gods and internet wizards alike struggle in vain.

To explain Mirai's origins, you had to look at the botnet which preceded it: Qbot (also known as Bashlite and LizardStresser). And to understand why Mirai followed Qbot, it helps to know about Bagle, MyDoom and NetSky, and Srizbi and Storm.

# War of the botnets

In 2003, hackers began to realize that there was money in DDOSing sites. Pick a site which relied on uptime – online gambling and retailers close to peak shopping holidays were favourites – and either threaten or demonstrate that you could take them offline, and you could make money. It was a simple form of blackmail.

Using botnets to send spam emails from infected PCs by the million or billion was also lucrative, as the fixed servers spammers had relied on were increasingly identified and blocked by email services, or shut down.

So hackers tried to build bigger and bigger botnets, relying on the inherent weaknesses in the millions of Windows PCs running XP, which shipped with its firewall software turned off and without inbuilt antivirus; that made them comparatively easy to subvert, by tempting people to run 'Trojan' programs that pretended to be useful but installed silent malware, or simply by exploiting flaws in Internet Explorer, Flash Player or Windows. Microsoft, led by Bill Gates, launched an initiative in January 2002 called 'Trustworthy Computing', which recognized that security in Windows and other Microsoft products had fallen short and revised the way that programs were written – so that security for the existing code became more important than just adding features. But it would take years for its improvements in safety to percolate through to the hundreds of millions of PCs already in use.[6]

By early 2004, two competing viruses, called MyDoom and Bagle, had infected hundreds of thousands of PCs. There was a brief war with a 'disinfectant' virus called NetSky, which would wipe the other two from machines where it was found. But MyDoom and Bagle prevailed; MyDoom became so big that when on 26 July that year it targeted Google, the search engine was knocked offline. Hackers with a commercial mind realized that in botnets, bigger was better.

In 2007, a worm called Srizbi emerged and demonstrated an interesting twist: it didn't just find unaffected PCs to infect, but would remove malware installed by a Storm, a rival botnet. Virus writers now had to make themselves proof not only against antivirus companies, but other existing and unwritten viruses. A furious, silent war raged across the installed base of vulnerable PCs, with millions changing hands. The computers' owners might wonder why their computer seemed to be running slowly, or seemed to crash or freeze more often than usual, or took longer than usual to boot up, and use antivirus to get rid of the problem. But the evidence was that overall, few noticed, and any malware installations lost to user discovery were more than made up for by new infections. In 2009 a team at the University of California studied a botnet created by malware called 'Torpig', and found that it controlled more than 180,000 PCs, and that over the course of 10 days it added another 49,000.[7]

The most effective way to kill off botnets was to cut off the head: discover the 'command and control' (C&C) server that was instructing them and take that offline, a process known as 'sinkholing'.

The C&C server would typically have been registered using stolen credit card details and a fake name, but the server's host would often listen to complaints from big companies such as Microsoft as they hunted down botnets, and take the C&C server offline.

But identifying the C&C server became increasingly difficult as by 2008 botmasters began using a technique called 'domain flux': the bots' programming included an algorithm which told them to change the web address where they looked for their C&C server every day. In response, the botnet killers began trying to predict which C&C server address would come up next (by installing the malware on a virtual machine with the clock set forward), and try to grab that domain.

The botnet creators responded by updating the botnet code so that each machine would check for a specific response from the C&C server: if it didn't get it, the bot would generate the next domain name from its algorithm and try that. Some botnets relied on checking huge numbers of C&C domains, making it expensive for would-be killers to try to get ahead of the flux: the Californian team noted that the Conficker worm, which had appeared in November 2008 and infected between 9 million and 15 million Windows PCs, had an algorithm that generated 50,000 domains per day, any of which could be the C&C server chosen by its owner. Even with domain registration costing just $5 for a year's hosting, sinkholing Conficker would mean an upfront cost of at least $91.3 million.

The arms race between botnet creators and their would-be destroyers became a high-speed, subterranean pursuit. It was one that the overwhelming majority of people using computers were never aware of. The botnets, meanwhile, could be hired out on a per-second, per-gigabit basis on underground forums to attack a site of choice. One such had been vDOS, at least until Krebs' detective work came to the notice of the police in Israel. (The malware could also be used to steal bank details and passwords from the PCs on which it ran; that was a profitable sideline too.) And so Krebs had been hit by Mirai – which had been built to take down Qbot.

# A mob built of blocks

According to Krebs, the authors of Qbot (also known as Bashlite) got their start around 2013 attacking servers running Minecraft, a block-building game you can play on your own, or on 'servers' where multiple people gather, and build (or destroy) virtual worlds. More than 100 million copies of the game have been sold; millions of people play it every month. Servers are especially popular with male teens willing to pay for access.

Krebs reckons that the owners of a big server with a thousand players connecting daily could earn around $50,000 per month from people renting disk storage and processing power to build their own Minecraft 'worlds', and buying in-game items and 'abilities'. Being offline would be expensive for a server owner if, say, they were DDOSed by a botnet. If you controlled a botnet and threatened to DDOS them, you could make some money.[8]

But in 2014, how did one build a botnet? The most vulnerable PCs were already controlled by botnet operators who defended their turf fiercely; the others were much harder to break into because of improved operating systems and antivirus. More generally, the PC installed base was shrinking as people shifted to mobile. Smartphones and tablets, meanwhile, were hard to infect: Google and Apple had learned the lessons of Windows, and created much more robust architectures for the mobile age. To date, nobody had created a botnet of smartphones, even though they were soon more numerous than PCs. That was because you couldn't log into them remotely and control them; creating a worm that would infect them and then infect others had stumped those who tried.

But even if smartphones were beyond reach, there was a new class of internet-connected devices which offered new pastures for hacking: the IoT devices being installed by the million around the world.

Rather than an internet driven by humans moving cursors around screens to click links and browse text, listen to audio or watch video, the Internet of Things creates a world of connected devices – sensors and actuators – which relay data about their state to each other and create a penumbra of information about the world around us, and perhaps even on or inside us, via internet-connected personal devices.

The idea of extending the internet to control and monitor devices is longstanding. In the 1990s when Bill Gates was chief executive of Microsoft and unaware of the promise and threat that the internet could be, one of his younger staff showed him the Trojan Room Coffee Pot – a camera connected to the internet pointed at a coffee flask in a Cambridge University laboratory. Some of the university staff were several flights of stairs away and didn't want a wasted journey to an empty jug, so every few seconds a video frame capture program would upload a picture to a shared server that they could check. In November 1993 the server was connected to the World Wide Web, and 'XCoffee' became the first webcam.

From there, the sky had become the limit. The IoT included millions of devices around the world. As other markets for hardware became commoditized, it also held out the promise of extra revenues and profit for companies selling electronic hardware. With profit margins eroded by the flourishing factory complexes in Shenzhen, in the Guangdong province of southern China, taking otherwise humdrum products and adding internet capability – a light bulb you control from the internet! a power socket you control from an app! a coffee machine you turn on via the internet! a door lock you control from your smartphone! – looked like a sure-fire way to bump up the price and, as long as you could manage the supply chain, your profit margin too. Adding a Wi-Fi chip to a CCTV camera adds perhaps $3 to the 'bill of materials' required to construct it, and while embedding the chip would add complexity to the manufacturing and software assurance process, the difference in price compared with a conventional CCTV camera with a standard video-out feed was considerable – perhaps three or four times larger.[9]

However, there's an important difference between a door lock you open with a physical key, and one that needs an internet connection. The latter runs software, and all software contains flaws. If, miraculously, the programs don't, the operating systems that run them surely do.

Those flaws mean the software will need updating, or else it will be vulnerable to anyone who figures them out, and for an internet-connected device that becomes an invitation to hackers. But for the manufacturers, checking and updating software is expensive, as is finding ways to roll out updates to customers who may be anywhere in the world. What's more, both processes eat into profit margins. But if they are not followed, the device becomes a time bomb: its compromise is certain. All that's unknown is when.

In that sense, though the Internet of Things is often used in domestic settings, it has a dangerous ability to turn feral.

## Your password is password

The problem is compounded by the temptation to take shortcuts in design, such as assigning the same default password to every device. (It is possible to give each device a unique password, but it's more expensive and requires strict quality assurance testing: any error in matching the inbuilt password and the product's documents would be colossally expensive, both financially – you'd have to recall them – and in terms of reputation.)

For example, until April 2015 a company called XiongMai Technologies in Shenzhen made thousands of devices which had a hard-coded username and password for the administrator account, and a remote access facility that was difficult to turn off (if the owner even knew it existed). The user could choose a strong, unguessable name and password, though many didn't; but the vulnerability of the administrator account, able to do anything, would remain.

The devices were tiny web servers, running software which could communicate with any web address, and had a camera or video recorder attached. As the literature promised, you could control it from anywhere on earth. So could a hacker, if they could discover a way in. The fact that an internet-connected video camera would have plenty of bandwidth which could be diverted for an attack was even more attractive. (XiongMai did not respond to my questions about why it didn't use unique passwords for each device it made.)

The insecurity of IoT devices had been a growing concern for some years. For example, the Taiwanese company Supermicro grew fivefold in just six years to top $2 billion in revenue, partly on the strength of its IPMI – Intelligent Platform Management Interface – boards. They let computer systems administrators manage multiple systems remotely, even to the point of being able to reboot them. The IPMI is like a virtual person who can walk through a control room or up and down racks of servers, flicking switches; it means you can manage a server room without physically being there, which has huge cost and time benefits for personnel who might live far from the actual location.

But even since 2013 there had been doubts about IPMIs' security, because they ran their own operating system, independent of the systems they controlled. (This is a logical necessity: a device that has crashed or whose power supply is electronically switched off can't control itself or monitor its temperature. An IPMI can do that for a rebooting or stalled system.)

Bruce Schneier, a long-time security analyst, called IPMI 'a perfect spying platform. You can't control it. You can't patch it.' A greater concern would be if someone figured out the remote password to log into an IPMI that controlled dozens, or hundreds, or even thousands of servers, they could get the servers to do what they wanted.[10]

Then someone figured out how to get those passwords, reliably.

In November 2013, after reading 'a couple of articles on the problems in IPMI', Zachary Wikholm of CARI.net, a cloud-hosting provider based in San Francisco, discovered that Supermicro had created a password file (called PSBlock) which was stored as plain text, rather than encrypted; even worse, it was accessible by anyone over the internet on port 49152. He told the company about the fault, expecting it would post a firmware update on its site. Nothing happened, and so in June 2014 he went public with the vulnerability, which was then widely covered by security news sites. 'At the time of this writing, there are 31,964 systems that have their passwords available on the open market,' Wikholm wrote on the company blog. Of those, he'd found that 3,296, just over 10 per cent, still used the machines' default passwords.[11]

'Is it our fault for trusting our vendors, or is it our vendors' fault for "being human"?' Wikholm wondered. He said that embedded platforms needed stronger security, though his blogpost seemed potentially to have compromised the security of anyone using the Supermicro systems he mentioned: he had explained how to find the password blocks, including which port, and which search engine to use to look for them. But, he pointed out, modern search engines such as one called Shodan, specifically set up to find IoT devices, meant there was no more anonymity for poorly secured products. 'Recent findings ... have proven everything is visible,' he pointed out.

So how did one protect oneself against vendors offering unen-crypted password files and any-comers access? His advice: 'keep informed and stay involved... and finally, keep your device firm-ware up to date.' But in the case of some devices, firmware updates have either stalled, or do not – or cannot – address key security holes; as Wikholm had written earlier in the post, describing his frustration with Supermicro's assurance that the weakness had been patched in a new update, 'flashing a system [accessing the memory physically to update it] is not always a possibility'.

Clearly, many failed to secure their systems. The same month as Wikholm published his blogpost, a 300 Gbps DDOS attack hit ProxyPipe, a company which rented DDOS protection for Minecraft servers from Verisign. Reporting on it later, Verisign said that the attack had come from a 100,000-strong botnet running on Super IPMI boards.[12]

The next month, Supermicro quietly published a firmware update blocking the gap. The stories about its plain-text password access didn't feature on its 'Supermicro in the news' webpage. Nor did it issue a press release about the firmware update.

The efforts to build bigger and more vicious IoT botnets to attack Minecraft servers intensified. Another version of Qbot appeared in late 2014, exploiting a significant flaw in some old, and very widespread, code that security researchers had disclosed publicly in September. Known as Shellshock, the flaw existed in the 'bash' command program in Unix (and so Linux, and so pretty much every web server): you could make the server run any command by adding certain commands to a stored file. Five related flaws were discovered within days. On examining the source code, it turned out that the underlying mistake had existed for 25 years, since September 1989, but nobody had spotted it. Or possibly someone had, and kept it to themselves; while amateur hackers like to boast of their discoveries, commercial and state hackers guard their discoveries jealously.[13]

Qbot exploited Shellshock ruthlessly. It would scan IP addresses and use it to try to log in using the default 'admin' (for 'administrator') username and trialling half a dozen or so different passwords. Once one worked, it would upload a small program to the server's memory which reported back to the C&C server to identify itself as part of the Qbot network, and began trying to find new devices to infect. As the botnet grew, the resources for infecting vulnerable devices did too.

The rapid rise of Qbot, and many other botnets which exploited Shellshock on IoT devices, raised a number of questions. Could anyone update millions of devices whose software might not be intended to be upgraded, and whose makers had never budgeted to do so? Did open source advocate Eric Raymond's claim for open source software that 'given enough eyeballs [looking at the code], all bugs are shallow' – in other words, the fact that unlike Microsoft's Windows or Apple's iOS, anyone could read all the source code for bash and try to improve it – really hold up? And given that the answers to the first two questions seemed to be 'no' and 'no', was it wise to publicly disclose fundamental flaws exploitable by anyone?[14]

Even though Qbot had great success, its creators decided after a few months that the police might be closing in. Unlike criminals in the physical world, where the key to evasion is to hide the evidence, and especially the weapon used to commit the crime, they did what hackers do to create deniability: early in 2015 they published their code anonymously, publishing it on a hacker forum where they could be sure that plenty of others would see and download it to examine it. That immediately meant that having a copy of the code on your PC was not in itself incriminating. Some of those who downloaded the code also tweaked it and started using it. Soon multiple, slightly different, versions of Qbot were infecting IoT devices, creating more botnets to hassle servers and sites. For there was another thing that DDOS botnet owners liked about IoT devices: they tended to be connected to the internet 24 hours a day, seven days a week. They didn't have to be computationally powerful; sending out an internet packet as part of a DDOS isn't difficult. You just want something that is available to do it all the time.

## Mirai in the sky

Mirai was Qbot's successor – and created very much in the spirit of NetSky to MyDoom, or Storm to Srizbi: to displace it. Krebs explains:

> What Mirai seemed to be built to do was to destroy Qbot and to be much more aggressive about spreading. It had about ten times as many default username and password pairs that it would try, and it was very good at making sure that systems infected with Mirai could not be infected with Qbot or anything else afterwards.

In other words, IoT botnets had evolved within a year to the point that had taken 10 years or so for PC botnets.

Krebs told me:

> The people who wrote [Mirai] seemed intent on taking down all of the other Qbot infections and botnets, of which there were dozens. They said as much on hacker forums: 'Watch your Qbot bot counts because

they're about to go to zero.' And when they released Mirai, that's exactly what happened: pretty much all the Qbot bots became Mirai bots, and these Qbot controllers were left in control of nothing.

Mirai wiped out Qbot by first brute-forcing its way onto the system, logging in using one of the default remote login usernames and passwords, and then finding any process that was using ports 22 or 23 (conventionally used for file transfer, and often left open) or 80 (for web traffic); those would be terminated, and the ports blocked, preventing Qbot from reinfecting it.

A few Qbot botnets survived because their code contained protection against that process or used different ports. Now the Mirai owners began to flex their muscles, Krebs says:

> Their strategy then was to go after the ISPs that were hosting the control servers for these Qbot botnets. They started by asking nicely, saying, 'Hey, you're hosting this controller that's running hundreds of thousands of hacked IoT systems under its thumb, you should do something about that.' And some of them did, they were like, 'Oh, I didn't know, thanks.' The ones that didn't listen to the takedown request got hit with Mirai. And a lot of them at *that* point said, 'OK, alright, fine, we'll take this stupid [Qbot] controller down, there you go, go away.'

With that done, Mirai had free rein, and could be hired out to attack sites. But the security industry was paying more attention to the threat of IoT devices, and noticed its growth.

Krebs reckons that Mirai's creators had two aims:

> It's hard to say which was more important for them: fame or fortune. They knew that this would cause a disruption in the cybercrime ecosystem, they knew it would inconvenience a lot of people who were competing with them for whatever it was – fame, control over a finite number of IoT systems. There was certainly, I think, an aspect of getting one over on their peers. And then also I think they had some designs to sell access to their botnet as a DDOS-for-hire service.

Certainly, Mirai was built for that. An analysis by Level 3 Communications in mid-September noted that it was a multi-part system. The bots would carry out attacks and also scan the net for new target devices to infect, whose IP addresses were sent to a 'report' server; that then ran 'loader' programs to try to hack into those target devices and instruct them to download the Mirai malware, creating a new bot. Meanwhile the person controlling the botnet used the Tor anonymization network – which can hide both the location of those contacting a server and of the server itself – to keep tabs on the 'report' server and the C&C server. Would-be clients could use a dashboard on one of those 'hidden' servers to nominate DDOS targets and pay for them.[15]

But Mirai didn't have it all its own way. As Level 3 also noted, it was up against other IoT botnets, including Qbot (which Level 3 called Bashlight), which had the same modus operandi – using default usernames and passwords – and a million devices under its control. Qbot attacked the C&C servers for roughly 24 hours in mid-September with gigabit-level attacks. The servers survived, though. (Often they relied on companies which provided hosting on DDOS-proof networks: these work by putting a proxy able to filter out malicious traffic between the original website and the attackers.)

By the end of summer 2016, Mirai was ready: a gigantic botnet with access to colossal bandwidth, running on devices where it would be difficult to check what code was running on them. On 20 September, Krebs was contacted by the owner of a 'DDOS protection service' who was evidently annoyed about being mentioned in a piece on Krebs' site that suggested his business wasn't completely above board – that perhaps, rather as with the Mafia, the offer of protection might come from the same person who caused the problem. Krebs ignored him. Six hours later, the Mirai attack walloped his site and knocked it offline.

At almost exactly the same time the French hosting company OVH was also hit by a Mirai botnet attack targeting Minecraft servers. Soon afterwards another data tsunami descended on ProxyPipe, a legitimate DDOS protection service for Minecraft servers, preventing it from hosting them. Customers began switching away; ProxyPipe estimated that it could have cost $400,000 to $500,000 in annual revenues. ProxyPipe's owner then sought out the ISP providing Mirai's C&C server with its connectivity. Though the main one, in Ukraine, ignored him, one of the larger ISPs which connected to it 'blackholed' the Ukrainian IP address – setting its systems to ignore any request to connect to it – so that the bots could no longer connect to their controller. The original Mirai was hobbled. But this would turn out to make the problem worse.

On Friday 30 September, 10 days after the huge attack on Krebs' site, Mirai's owner capitulated – or perhaps obfuscated. In a post on Hackforums, a site that is enormously popular with amateur and wannabe hackers, a longstanding user with the handle 'Anna-Senpai' declared he had 'an amazing release'.

He explained that Mirai (which by implication he owned) usually consisted of 380,000 bots, but that after the DDOS on Krebs' site some people had spotted the weaknesses in their devices that had allowed him to take them over. Now the botnet had shrunk to about 300,000 'and dropping'. So he was releasing the source code for the malware and also the client to control bots, along with instructions on how to build them into working programs, on a free file-hosting service. From there the programs were quickly copied onto Github, one of the world's largest code-sharing sites.

The decision by Mirai's creators to try to get out before they were caught, as Qbot's had tried to do before them, was atypical for the hacking world. 'People involved in this type of activity tend to get caught because whatever their other motivations may be, they tend to have very fragile and touchy egos, and they end up pointing a path back down to their doorstep because of the mistakes they make,' Krebs says.

Relying too much on a longstanding identity, or intertwined identities, is a pattern that gets repeated again and again, ending with the hacker's downfall. They reveal some minor detail about a machine, or about other files in a shared directory, or fail to log in from a VPN and instead use a home connection, or mention something about their history, or reuse a favourite online handle that is more easily tied to their real-world identity, or post a screenshot that includes a vital clue, or leave a comment in some code that matches another, or even reveal themselves in the choice of name for a product. Any can be the end of the thread which investigators begin pulling and follow back to its source. (Two of Qbot's alleged creators in the hacking crew 'Lizard Squad' were charged in October 2016 and pleaded guilty two months later. In their case, the thread that the FBI began pulling was a phone harassment-for-hire service – rather like a voice version of DDOS – that Lizard Squad briefly offered. That led to an investigation of their more lucrative sites – one of which was later hacked, revealing all their personal details.)[16, 17]

In the case of Mirai, the botnet's name itself contained clues about its authors: 'Mirai' is the name of a Japanese anime (cartoon) series, about a boy who discovers he has to fight a *Hunger Games*-style battle for survival. Hackers tend to use names that resonate for them, at least when they are naming their own creation, though usually it's the security companies which baptize a piece of malware based on its behaviour or some comment found in its code.

But Mirai's authors were atypical, Krebbs says:

> They seemed to be pretty careful about covering their tracks, and from what I can tell, they planned well in advance how they would execute this attack and how they would unleash this thing and what kind of obfuscation they would plan in advance to try to confuse people about their identities and nicknames. They actually tried to think this through without ever having done it before.

So what had happened to make the owner of a potentially lucrative botnet effectively abandon it? Krebs reckoned Mirai had followed the same arc as Qbot: 'There's some evidence they did that [for-hire DDOS] early on, but they eventually had to leak the source code and give up on that.'

The motivation for abandoning it was also the same as the Qbot authors, he says: 'the [FBI] investigators were very zealously pursuing this case and had a lot of help internationally. I think the folks who were responsible for creating it and unleashing it felt like it would be really bad if the FBI showed up and found them with the only copy of the source code.' So once again they took the hacker's way out of destroying the evidence: give it to everyone. The identity of the hacker, or hackers, behind Mirai was still unknown.

# Unleashing the monster

With the release of the Mirai code, it didn't immediately matter who had written the original code. Everyone now had a bigger problem: the means to create a gigantic IoT botnet was publicly available, so anyone could copy it and build their own. And lots of people did, with minor variations. (A Twitter account called 'MiraiAttacks' counted more than 300 different ones, based on subtle differences in how they worked.) When the gigantic data storm hit the US east coast in late October, nearly three weeks after the release of the source code, nobody could be quite sure whose botnet it was; the motive was never made clear. The network used appeared to be smaller than those used in Krebs' attack, but was more targeted. Researchers suspected that its colossal effect was more of a demonstration or even a mistake than an intentional attack: 'DDOS attacks are noisy and draw a lot of attention,' noted Marcus Hutchins, a British computer security researcher, analysing the attack. It had become 'the subject of worldwide media attention and multiple law enforcement investigation backed by multinational companies; nobody looking to make money wants that kind of attention,' he commented on his blog.[18]

At the time of writing, nobody has been publicly charged with the Mirai attack of 21 October 2016. BitSight Technologies, which looks at cyber risks, reckoned Dyn lost about 8 per cent of its customers as a result of the attack, based on a sample survey before and after it. (Dyn declined to comment on the study.)[19]

Nor has an attack of that size been repeated, though in early November 2016 a 500 Gbps attack using a Mirai botnet targeted a mobile telecoms company in Liberia. However, the company had a DDOS mitigation scheme in place already, and was quickly fully back online.[20]

In late November 2016, the internet service provider Deutsche Telekom in Germany blamed a widespread service outage on a 'botched attempt' to hijack broadband customers' routers. That was caused by tweaked Mirai code which incorporated a newly discovered vulnerability in the remote login system used by ISPs to update customers' routers. Deutsche Telekom issued software updates for three of the dozen or so routers that it resold from a manufacturer in Taiwan. In December 2016, nearly 2,400 routers belonging to customers of the UK ISP TalkTalk were silently hijacked and used to mount a DDOS on a UK-based bitcoin site; they were exploited by the same flaw as had been sought in Germany. (TalkTalk issued a fix which reset the routers.) No hacking group claimed responsibility, and the variability of the targets suggested these were different owners. Mirai had metastasized, as Anna-Senpai had surely intended.[21]

# Pulling the threads

Krebs, meanwhile, hadn't lost interest in finding those behind Mirai. Quite the opposite. He kept finding threads to pull on. He discovered the connection between Minecraft, Qbot and its usurper, Mirai. He dug through a maze of Minecraft server suppliers, and DDOS 'protection' companies, which oddly often seemed to offer their services just as a colossal DDOS attack was about to happen. That led Krebs to a DDOS protection company called ProTraf, and to Josiah White, then aged 19, who was one of only two employees listed for the company; the other was Paras Jha, its 'president', aged 20.[8]

Krebs approached White, and asked him whether the rumours in hacker forums suggesting he had written Qbot were true. White said he'd written some of the components – including the worm code which spread it from machine to machine – but hadn't intended it to be sold or traded. He'd only posted it under threat of doxxing and 'SWATing' by another hacker, he told Krebs.

Krebs next looked at Jha, and his LinkedIn profile with its description of the computer languages in which he claimed proficiency. 'I was haunted by the nagging feeling that I'd seen this rather unique combination of computer language skills somewhere else online,' Krebs noted. Then he realized it exactly matched those claimed by Anna-Senpai on Hackforums. Much more digging later, he found other traces left by Jha, including a now-deleted personal site (registered by his father) and long-abandoned usernames.

One was 'dreadiscool'; someone with that handle had elsewhere listed Japanese anime films they liked, including one called 'Mirai Nikki' – the same as the botnet name.

And, showing how the collective intelligence of the internet can track down those who don't want to be found, one of the people at ProxyPipe noticed resemblances between some code in Mirai and some previously posted publicly by 'dreadiscool'. The threads began to lengthen.

Krebs kept following his leads, and the crowdsourcing of the internet continued to offer them: a pointer to two more handles, one of which linked to a Facebook account saying its owner had started reading computer engineering at Rutgers University in New Jersey in 2015.

So had Jha.

Strangely, Rutgers University had suffered a number of DDOS attacks since the autumn of 2015; its anonymous attacker kept telling it to buy a DDOS protection service.

Krebs also heard from a former ProTraf employee, Ammar Zuberi, who told him that at the end of November 2016 Jha had shown him text messages from an FBI agent who was investigating Mirai. Jha suggested he had deflected the investigator and sent him on a 'wild goose chase'.

Certainly the FBI would want to know who controlled such a gigantic botnet. Hackforums has been under the watchful eye of the FBI (as well as Krebs) almost from its launch in 2010. Until the public release, finding the Mirai code on Jha's computer would have been almost enough to charge him. But with the code in the open, proving its source would be much harder.

(Zuberi, now at Penn State University, subsequently erased his presence on LinkedIn, though traces of his presence linger, such as his participation in an 'anti-Mirai local network utility', to which he contributed program code, on the DevPost site.)

In January 2017, Krebs collected his findings into a big blog-post about who he thought was behind the original Mirai code and botnet. He contacted Jha, pointing out the multiple interrelated handles, the remarkable coincidences of timing, and asked him if he'd been involved with Mirai. On 19 January 2017, Jha denied writing Mirai or attacking Rutgers. 'I don't think there are enough facts to definitively point a finger at me,' he told Krebs.

Following up Krebs' detective work, on 20 January 2017 the NewJersey.com news site reported that Jha had been contacted by the FBI multiple times. His father told the site: 'I know what he is capable of. Nothing of the sort of what has been described here has happened.' Jha's lawyer said he had not been charged, and that Krebs had made 'several leaps of logic', adding that the firm was looking forward to clearing Jha's name.[22]

On 13 December 2017, the US Justice Department unsealed two guilty pleas made earlier that month by the authors of Mirai. One was Josiah White. The other was Paras Jha.[23]

They acknowledged having created, used and released the Mirai source code; Jha also pleaded guilty to the Rutgers DDOS attacks.

As a sort of bonus, the duo (and another man, Dalton Norman) also pleaded guilty to another form of botnet exploit they had set up after giving up on Mirai: a fraud system comprising more than 100,000 infected IoT devices which would click on ads, just like a human but more reliably, and earn advertising revenue for the sites on which they appeared. The trio faced years in prison if given the maximum sentence. Evidently, Jha hadn't been as successful as he had thought at diverting the agent from the FBI.

## Future imperfect

Was Mirai the end? Krebs isn't optimistic about the future:

> The majority of the cheaper IoT things being churned out have all of the features turned on, all of the options turned on by default. You know, kind of the opposite of what you want in a secure product. And they don't do much in the way of walking you through securing the device. There's a lot of room to grow in terms of helping people use these devices securely.

He describes recently buying an expensive security camera, and researching which, if any, of its ports should be open to the internet.

He then found a guide from the maker on how to 'harden' it against hackers: 'it was 24 pages of PDF on all these things to turn off. And I'm, like, "Why don't you just turn them off to begin with and then have a guide on how to turn them on?" Oh no, that would be too hard, customers wouldn't like that.' He had previously pointed out how a camera made by Foscam, another Chinese company, by default ran 'peer-to-peer' (P2P) software from a company called ThroughTek; that software would try to create a network with any other Foscam camera on the internet. It was an open invitation to hackers: infect one Foscam camera, and it would try to infect all of them. There was a setting to disable the P2P connectivity – but it didn't actually turn it off. Only when enough furious customers had complained on Foscam's forums did the company develop a firmware patch which could turn the P2P function off, though it didn't do that by default. Having first been reported in November 2013, the P2P 'fix' arrived in July 2016.[24, 25]

So what was the point of the P2P function? Foscam told Krebs it was so that the cameras could find out where the (user's) server notionally in control of the camera was located, and tell the camera to create a virtual private network (VPN) connection between the two; if it couldn't, the camera data would be encrypted and forwarded from Foscam's server.

Even though there was no direct evidence of Foscam or its cameras having been hacked, you don't have to be exceptionally suspicious to feel that letting Foscam be the nexus for all the communications happening anywhere in the world with its cameras isn't a great security model. But most people would buy the camera and not even know what it was doing; only that they could log in to it from anywhere. And most people wouldn't know there was a firmware upgrade, or apply it. Firmware upgrades are notorious for going wrong, and 'bricking' devices: the firmware starts the low-level functions of a device when it powers on, and any error in transcribing the program or in its coding can prevent the device starting. But if it won't start, you can't correct the firmware. Thus many people, even if they're aware of a firmware upgrade being available, tend to pass unless it adds some substantial functionality or security. If it ain't broke, they won't try to fix it. But they probably don't realize quite how broken it is, and how impossible to fix.

Instances of weak security around IoT devices abound, once you begin looking for them. In February 2017, a British hacker figured out how to get 150,000 printers around the world to print ASCII art, saying (in part) that they were 'part of a flaming botnet', by exploiting a remote code execution bug on Xerox's web interface for internet-connected printers. 'People need to take their printer out of the public internet unless it's needed, to be honest,' the code's author told the website *Motherboard*. He had already made that point on the printout. The devices weren't actually part of a botnet; he just liked the idea of worrying people.[26]

He obfuscated his age, describing himself as 23 on his @lmaostack Twitter profile, and 'under 18' to reporters. (The former is more likely: in 2017 he was citing the hacking history of others from 10 years ago.) He said he had been trying to 'clean up the IoT mess' since early 2015, but that the arrival of Mirai had made people take notice of the problem.

Like Krebs, he wasn't optimistic about the future, pointing to the business model where one company would sell the device, but a different one would have made and coded it. Those behind the latter were often 'sketchy Chinese developers', he told *Motherboard*. 'No racism intended here. Their code is shocking and there are multiple backdoors in a load of internet-enabled devices.'

Yet it is possible to do IoT well. 'Have you been to Ikea lately?' Mikko Hypponen, chief research officer of Finnish security company F-Secure, said to me when I asked him about Mirai:

Next time you go, look for the lamp section, and the light bulbs called 'Trådfri', which of course is Swedish, like all the names. Trådfri means without cables. So they have a small base station and light bulbs. It's an IoT lighting system: you can turn them off from your phone. You actually control the bulbs.

So a friend of mine bought this a few months ago – he wasn't really looking for an IoT lamp – and he was chuckling to himself. 'I'm going to open this and see what's inside,' he said. 'It's going to be horrible, surely, Ikea IoT.' Which was exactly what I was thinking. And it's actually fairly impressive.

What Hypponen's friend found was a custom real-time operating system with every TCP port but one closed. On that port, the device only accepts traffic that has been digitally signed by Ikea. Nothing really to be fixed. 'I was surprised,' Hypponen said. 'Ikea is leading the way to secure IoT. Wow!'

Hypponen spoke to the company, and learned that it had recruited a number of world-class security researchers, including one who had previously headed security for Nokia's by-then defunct mobile phone business.

But why would Ikea, famous for selling low-priced household goods, go to the trouble, and particularly expense, of making a properly secure IoT product? Hypponen again:

> I have a theory. Ikea stuff is really cheap, which means the [profit] margins are very thin. If margins are very thin, the way you make as much money as Ikea makes, and it is very profitable, is that you have to sell shitloads of the product. Millions and millions of the same product, all over the world, and you sell them for five, ten, fifteen years, on massive manufacturing runs.
>
> If that's your business model – thin margin, massive long runs – then the *worst* thing that can happen to you is a recall. If there's any problem with the product later on in the future, and you have to recall them, that's going to eat all the profits you ever made, plus much, much more.
>
> So you make sure you'll never have to do a recall. And if that's your mindset, then when you build a platform for IoT – which I'm sure they're going to re-use in everything else, not just lamps – it makes sense to invest in the beginning and then reap the benefits because you don't have to do a recall ten years in the future. [He pauses.] It's impressive, and surprising.

As to Krebs' concerns about kids in their parents' basement, they remain well-founded. In September 2017 Ankit Anubhav of NewSky Security described how in August he'd come across a data dump site called 'Daddyhackingteam', which also had Skype contact details for its owner, who was trying to build a Mirai-powered botnet of CCTV cameras. Virus code that NewSky discovered not long afterwards linked back to the site, and included the names of 67 other botnets that it would try to disable on systems it infected. A lot of the code was copied.[27]

But the site owner had also posted, using the same Skype ID, seeking a job writing PHP and setting up sites. 'I'm online for 15–18 hours each day,' the note said, before continuing, 'I'm currently out of school for 2–3 weeks.'

Amazed, Anubhav got in touch, undercover, with the 'hacker', who explained that he was only 13 years old. But wasn't releasing code to build botnets illegal? The hacker was confident he would be fine, because of his age: he couldn't be prosecuted. 'It's literally child's play to set up a botnet by attacking IoT devices,' Anubahv concluded.

# Weathering the storm

'Mirai' was yet another weather system in the climate of the internet. Rather as with the real climate, the increased complexity and energy invested in the internet (which takes the form of more and more devices of varying capability and security being attached to the network) are leading to more devastating, and less predictable, events. The only prediction you can make is that it will be bad.

Indeed, slightly more than a year after Mirai brought chunks of the internet to its knees, Krebs found himself writing about another piece of IoT malware. This one was dubbed 'Reaper' (or sometimes IoTroop), and Checkpoint, an Israeli security company, reckoned it had infected more than a million organizations, exploiting nine different security vulnerabilities in devices from five companies including Linksys, D-Link and Netgear (best known to consumers for their routers). Like Mirai, Reaper was a worm, spreading on its own from machine to machine – where 'machine' could mean an internet-connected camera or a router.[28]

Who controlled the Reaper botnet? What would they use it for? Only its owners knew, and they weren't saying. Meanwhile, others waited for the moment when the internet would stop working and they would know a new attack, of unclear purpose and extent, was under way. Hypponen doesn't see much cause for optimism. 'Many people thought that Mirai, which was a massive incident, was the wakeup call we needed; that *now* people will think about IoT security.' But recalling his calls to unwitting owners whose devices were causing the problem, he says 'it wasn't. It wasn't the wakeup call. It might have been for the victims of the DDOS. But clearly, other people? They don't care. They are definitely not going to start spending money to fix that.'

Meanwhile, the research company Gartner forecast in November 2015 that there would be 6.4 billion IoT devices in use in 2016, and nearly 21 billion by 2020; and that the average price of devices would fall over the five-year period. It doesn't seem to think people are going to spend money to stop their heat pumps attacking DNS servers either.[29]

# References

**1** Kesel, A (2016) Exclusive interview: new world hackers responsible for historic U.S. internet outage, *WeAreChange.Org via Internet Archive*, 26 October. Available from: https://web.archive.org/web/20161029122115/http://wearechange.org/exclusive-interview-new-world-hackers-responsible-for-historic- u-s-internet-outage/

**2** Hilton, S (2016) Dyn analysis summary of Friday October 21 attack, dyn.com, 26 October. Available from: https://dyn.com/blog/dyn-analysis-summary-of-friday-october-21-attack/

**3** Personal communication

**4** Krebs, B (2016) Israeli online attack service 'vDOS' earned $600,000 in two years, *Krebs on Security*, 8 September. Available from: http://krebsonsecurity.com/2016/09/israeli-online-attack-service-vdos-earned-600000-in-two-years/

**5** Personal communication

**6** Gates, B (2002) Trustworthy computing, Microsoft executive email, 18 July. Available from: www.microsoft.com/mscorp/execmail/2002/07-18twc.mspx

**7** Stone-Gross, B, *et al* (2009) Your botnet is my botnet: analysis of a botnet takeover, University of California, 9 November. Available from: https://seclab.cs.ucsb.edu/media/uploads/papers/torpig.pdf

**8** Krebs, B (2017) Who is Anna-Senpai, the Mirai worm author?, Krebs on Security, 18 January. Available from: https://krebsonsecurity.com/2017/01/who-is-anna-senpai-the-mirai-worm-author/

**9** 2012 smartphone guide: components, key suppliers, and market share, *Nomura Research*, 8 May 2012. Available from: http://image.52rd.com/Files/File20126191144177237.pdf

**10** Schneier, B (2013) The eavesdropping system in your computer, *Schneier on Security*, 31 January. Available from: www.schneier.com/blog/archives/2013/01/the_eavesdroppi.html

**11** Wikholm, Z (2014) CARISIRT: yet another BMC vulnerability (and some added extras), *cari.net blog*, 19 June. Available from: http://blog.cari.net/carisirt-yet-another-bmc-vulnerability-and-some-added-extras/

**12** Dunn, JE (2014) Massive 300Gbps DDoS attack on media firm fuelled by unpatched server flaw, *ComputerWorld UK*, 18 August. Available from: www.computerworlduk.com/it-vendors/massive-300gbps-ddos-attack-on-media-firm-fuelled-by-unpatched-server-flaw-3536702/

**13** Chazelas, S (2014) When was shellshock introduced, *shells.bash.bugs newsgroup*, 10 October. Available from: http://thread.gmane.org/gmane.comp.shells.bash.bugs/22418

**14** Raymond, E (1997) The Cathedral and the Bazaar, catb.org, 21 May. Available from: www.catb.org/~esr/writings/cathedral-bazaar/cathedral-bazaar/ar01s04.html

**15** How the Grinch stole IoT, Level 3 Threat Research Labs, 14 October 2016. Available from: www.netformation.com/our-pov/how-the-grinch-stole-iot

**16** American and Dutch teenagers arrested on criminal charges for allegedly operating international cyber-attack-for-hire websites, US Department of Justice, 5 October 2016. Available from: www.justice.gov/usao-ndil/pr/american-and-dutch-teenagers-arrested-criminal-charges-allegedly-operating

**17** Meisner, J (2017) Hacker-for-hire pleads guilty to shutting down company websites, *Chicago Tribune*, 19 December. Available from:

www.chicagotribune.com/news/local/breaking/ct-met-hacker-guilty-cyber-attack-20171219-story.html

**18**  Hutchins, M (2016) Mapping Mirai: a botnet case study, *MalwareTech*, 3 October. Available from: www.malwaretech.com/2016/10/mapping-mirai-a-botnet-case-study.html

**19**  Roberts, P (2017) Exclusive: Mirai attack was costly for Dyn, data suggests, *The Security Ledger*, 3 February. Available from: https://securityledger.com/2017/02/mirai-attack-was-costly- for-dyn-data-suggests/

**20**  Krebs, B (2016) Did the Mirai botnet really take Liberia offline?, *Krebs on Security*, 4 November. Available from: https://krebsonsecurity.com/2016/11/did-the-mirai-botnet-really-take-liberia-offline/

**21**  Ashford, W (2016) More than 2,000 TalkTalk routers hijacked by Mirai botnet variant, *ComputerWeekly.com*, 8 December. Available from: www.computerweekly.com/news/450404326/More-than-2000-TalkTalk-routers-hijacked-by-Mirai-botnet-variant

**22**  Clark, A and Mueller, M (2017) FBI questions Rutgers student about massive cyber attack, *NJ.com*, 20 January. Available from: www.nj.com/news/index.ssf/2017/01/rutgers_student_questioned_cyber_attack.html

**23**  Justice Department announces charges and guilty pleas in three computer crime cases involving significant cyber attacks, US Department of Justice, 13 December 2017. Available from: www.justice.gov/usao-nj/pr/justice-department-announces-charges-and-guilty-pleas-three-computer-crime-cases

**24**  Krebs, B (2016) This is why people fear the 'Internet of Things', Krebs on Security, 18 February. Available from: https://krebsonsecurity.com/2016/02/this-is-why-people-fear-the-internet-of-things/

**25**  Foscam dialing out to suspect hosts, Foscam forums, 13 November 2015. Available from: http://foscam.us/forum/foscam-dialing-out-to-suspect-hosts-t17699.html

**26**  Moyer, C (2017) This teen hacked 150,000 printers to show how the Internet of Things is shit', Motherboard, 8 February. Available from: https://motherboard.vice.com/en_us/article/nzqayz/this-teen-hacked-150000-printers-to-show-how-the-internet-of-things-is-shit

**27**  Anubhav, A (2017) IoT hackers shift to the dark side, *NewSky Security blog*, 5 September. Available from: https://blog.newskysecurity.com/iot-hackers-shift-to-the-dark-side-cd3d0005a5e0

**28**  Krebs, B (2017) Reaper: calm before the IoT security storm?, *Krebs on Security*, 23 October. Available from: https://krebsonsecurity. com/2017/10/reaper-calm-before-the-iot-security-storm/

**29**  Gartner says 6.4 billion connected 'things' will be in use in 2016, up 30 percent from 2015, gartner.com, 10 November 2015. Available from: www.gartner.com/newsroom/id/3165317

## LESSONS FROM MIRAI

- The business model for the 'Internet of Things' (IoT) isn't a good one for security: the idea of having cheap devices which can easily connect to the internet doesn't always allow the financial margins required for writing secure software and updating it when flaws come to light.

- If you deploy IoT devices, assume that they're insecure from the start, and try to tighten their security. Never let them be directly accessible from the open internet.

- Monitor network traffic from devices before full deployment. Sometimes they may be contacting manufacturers' servers that you don't want them to.

- Demand security updates. Manufacturers can be shamed or hassled into acting but it can be a slow process.

- The biggest risk at present with IoT devices is 'botnets' – huge numbers of compromised devices acting in concert – but other, subtler threats could surface over time. Hacking forums and security researchers' blogs tend to be well ahead of formal security bulletins in pointing to the latest flaws and exploits.

- As IoT use grows, multiple experts have pointed to it as the biggest potential threat in the future because of the size of deployments, potential for hacking, difficulties of upgrading securely, the potential importance for infrastructure and the risks of relying on data from them which might itself be compromised or corrupted.

- The business benefits of IoT can be huge, through feedback from remote locations and systems. Those are important – but so is security.

# Hacking: The present, the future

09

*Data, it has been said, is the new oil but it is also the new asbestos... it is a risk, potentially toxic, to the company.*
CHRISTOPHER GRAHAM, oral evidence to Select Committee on Culture, Media and Sport, January 2016[1]

Millions of Americans got some bad news on 7 September 2017. Equifax, one of the largest credit scoring companies in the US, had been hacked; the personal details of roughly 143 million Americans had probably been stolen. A few days later, the company announced that it had discovered that the intrusion had occurred because it hadn't updated one of its web interfaces which relied on a software framework called Apache Struts.

This seemed odd. A serious flaw in Struts had been publicized by the US's Computer Emergency Response Team (CERT) on 6 March; three days later, noted Dan Goodin at Ars Technica, 'the bug was already under mass attack'. Equifax had been notified of the flaw at the time, and its IT team had been told to patch it within 48 hours, as required by the company's policies on software patches.[2]

Except it didn't, as its then chief executive Richard Smith admitted in his evidence to the US Congress, where he was quizzed in October 2017 about the company's failure to safeguard people's details. He explained that despite the company's 225-strong cyber-security team, the failure to protect against the hack had been the fault of one person. When CERT had sent out a warning on 8 March about the Struts vulnerability, a system scan was carried out to check for it; this didn't identify it. Then a week after the CERT warning, the IT department did the same, but still didn't find it.[3]

The hackers had, obviously. But though there was outrage aplenty to go around, nobody seemed to blame those who'd broken into the systems. Instead, as it emerged that three Equifax executives, including its chief financial officer, had sold a total of $1.8 million worth of shares three days after the breach had been discovered – though the company denied any of them had known of the news at the time of deciding to sell the shares – there were growls from politicians: 'If that [stock trading] happened, somebody needs to go to jail,' said Heidi Heitkamp, a Democrat senator in the US. 'How is that not insider trading?' The anger was all directed at the company and its executives.

Notably, the reporting around the incident implicitly assumed that being hacked if you didn't update your systems was as inevitable as getting wet if you didn't fix your rickety roof. Those behind the hack were almost certainly professionals seeking data they could trade for money or influence, but there was as little anger directed at their intent to commit or aid identity theft as there would be at a thunderstorm for causing a lightning strike. The hackers were just doing what hackers do: break into computer systems. The failure was Equifax's.

Zeynep Tufecki, an associate professor at the University of North Carolina who has been an active voice about the rights of users over corporations, expressed her frustration in a *New York Times* article. 'Most software failures and data breaches aren't inevitable; they are a result of neglect and underinvestment in product reliability and security,' she wrote.[4]

It's a message that has, I hope, become increasingly obvious throughout this book: flaws and exploits are known and identified and highlighted years or even decades before they are exploited. Lack of investment hamstrings attempts to secure systems and their perimeters; those in charge hope that they will be lucky today, and that their luck will hold out until tomorrow, when the cycle can start again. It is the hope of someone sitting in the thunderstorm that the lightning will strike elsewhere – and usually it does; the web is, after all, very big. Sometimes, as at Sony Pictures, the lightning strikes from a place and for a reason that seems objectively unlikely until examined in hindsight; other times, as with Mirai, the exploitation is entirely predictable based on the business model and indifference to security and updates that the principals display.

But there's another element which has become clear: users have little recourse against companies. The example of TalkTalk, the UK ISP, is illustrative. It was fined more than £5 million for poor customer service relating to 68,000 customers. But when the details of about 21,000 people were stolen from a badly configured customer service portal and used for fraud, it was fined £100,000; when the details of more than 150,000 people, including some of their bank details, were stolen from an overlooked server, it was fined £400,000. What can one conclude? That it's much worse to wrongly send bailiffs to people's houses than it is to open them up to scams and identity theft for the rest of their lives. In the US, which doesn't have data protection laws equivalent to the UK or the rest of Europe, the Federal Trade Commission has had to fight for the right to sue companies over data breaches. It's still unclear whether it has any statutory powers to do so.

This would be concerning enough if technology and its uses were standing still, if we could somehow stop the clock, so that Equifax and Uber and TalkTalk and all the other companies which have had data stolen or held to ransom or published against their will could fix all the machines, and get rid of Adobe Flash and its vulnerabilities, and close the SQL injection holes, and all the 30-year-old code could be audited for hidden little flaws like the ones that enabled Shellshock and thus the Qbot botnet.

But instead the problems are multiplying. The publication of the source code for Mirai means that there are many more ways people can create botnets, while the business model for the makers of IoT (Internet of Things) devices that will get recruited to those botnets hasn't shifted one iota; it's still more profitable for them to make products whose software and firmware might be riddled with security holes and perhaps fix them later, than to make something which is very hard to crack in the first place.

## Code and correction

One problem is that there is more and more code running more and more devices, yet code is not getting any safer. No way has yet been found to write error-free code at any length, and even if one can guarantee a program's correctness, there always exists the possibility of errors in the underlying software which runs the program. SQL injection works by exploiting the gap between the humans who design the systems expecting 'sensible' SQL queries as input, and the utterly literal way in which the database interprets the queries put to it. That is a human-generated gap, and will never go away.

Indeed, there is a thriving industry trying to find those gaps and to monetize them – either by selling them for others to use, or selling them back to the companies which created them. A growing number of secretive companies offer services to governments around the world, of whatever stripe, in the form of 'zero-day' exploits that can be used against targets. 'Zero days' aren't publicly known, and usually aren't known to the company whose software is vulnerable. They've become a market in themselves, and an excellent way for hackers to make money without actually breaking any laws. In January 2016, the FBI paid professional hackers nearly $1 million for a zero-day exploit which would let it break into the work iPhone of Syez Farook, who with his wife killed 14 people in a terrorist attack in San Bernardino, California, in December 2015. Similarly, an Israeli security company, which usually works with government agency clients, was paid an unknown amount for a zero-day exploit that could be used against iPhones, turning them into silent monitors. That surfaced in August 2016 as a link in a text message sent to Ahmed Mansoor, a human rights activist who has been targeted by the United Arab Emirates government. (Mansoor, suspicious, instead passed the message on to Citizen Lab at the University of Toronto, which suggested that the UAE government was probably the source of the message.)[5, 6]

Alternatively, you can sell the exploits back to companies such as Google, Twitter, Facebook, Microsoft, Reddit, Apple and Uber. They pay 'bug bounties' to people who notify them privately of exploits so that they can be fixed before they become more widely known; that idea was expanded in November 2013 when Microsoft and Facebook expanded their schemes to sponsor bug bounty payments for some of the software that underpins the internet, such as OpenSSL, PHP, Python and Apache. With payouts of as much as $5,000 per bug reported, semi-professional 'bug bounty hunt-ers' can earn useful sums from legal hacking. There's even a venture capital-backed company, Bugcrowd, which acts as a nexus for security researchers (as it prefers to call them) to offer the vulner-abilities they've found. Bugcrowd says that bounty hunters split into five types: knowledge seekers, hobbyists, full-timers, virtuosos and protectors. The same profile works well enough to describe hackers.[7]

For the companies, it's far cheaper to pay an individual in private and fix an issue to their own schedule than to have to clean up the mess if a vulnerability becomes public. The number of vulnerabili-ties being discovered through such means is growing all the time; but there's still no way of knowing how many remain below the surface.

The ever-growing use of the 'Internet of Things' (IoT) is the biggest concern among security professionals I spoke to. Graham Cluley, who has followed the computer virus business since the first ones appeared, put it like this:

> IoT is the big problem. We can barely secure our desktop computers, and now every vendor on the planet is trying to 'connect' their device to the net – as cheaply as possible, and with no thought of security (encryption and updating infrastructure, etc). Also they're trying to deliver a device which doesn't gobble up too much battery life or CPU cycles. When you consider IoT with medical implants, it gets even more serious. If ISP-supplied routers [such as TalkTalk's] are so vulnerable, what hope for the rest of the Internet of Things?[8]

Cluley has been talking to the oil and energy industries about the potential they face for attacks. Saudi Aramco, the world's biggest oil company and probably the world's most valuable company, was hit by a malware attack on 15 August 2012 which knocked out 30,000 PCs on its network – 75 per cent of its capability, though the exploration and production systems, which used sepa-rate networks, were unaffected. The computers were offline for 10 days. A previously (and subsequently) unknown group calling itself Cutting Sword of Justice claimed responsibility; the claim was credible because the group cited the number of machines affected before Saudi Aramco did.

The puzzle was that the malware the group used, called Shamoon, wiped the hard drives. 'Nowadays, destructive malware is rare,' observed a spokesperson at Kaspersky Lab. 'The main focus of cyber criminals is financial profit. Cases like the one here do not appear very often.' An error in the code had prevented it having worse effects, it later emerged. Speculation about the authors revolved around the malware's name (picked for the same name being used for a folder inside the malware; 'Shamoon' is about as common in the Arabic world as 'Simon' in the English-speaking West). Once installed on a machine or network, it would wipe machines and then report back – which indicates how the group knew the head-count of affected PCs. But as with the Sony Pictures hack, the use of destructive malware pointed to nation-state hackers, rather than financially motivated ones or amateurs. A few months later in October 2012, US intelligence officials publicly blamed Shamoon on Iranian state hackers, suggesting it was retaliation for the Stuxnet virus which had hobbled Iran's nuclear weapons programme two years earlier.[9, 10, 11]

The Aramco hack put the energy world on edge. On one hand, connectivity is good: it allows real-time reporting and monitoring of hugely complex systems where rapid reaction can save millions in costs or days of lost production.

On the other hand, it opens up the potential to have all your systems wiped.

Cluley explains:

> There is a real problem there because of the collision of two worlds. In the conventional IT security industry it's all about CIA – Confidentiality [of data], Integrity [of systems], Availability [of systems/service], in that order. With energy, though, the most important thing is availability. No one wants the power to go off. This leads to organizations never updating systems for fear that they will break them.

This leads to obvious cracks that could be exploited, he says, 'there has even been some proof-of-concept work done about "ransomware for water filtration plants"'.

# Controlling the surface

Not only is the code too complex; the future is heading towards us pell-mell, bringing new opportunities for hackers to exploit. We can even predict what areas those might be in, based on what we see today. Hackers nowadays have a multiplicity of weapons they can deploy: database injection, phishing, subverting the Internet of Things, buffer overflows, sandbox escapes, brute force login attacks, distributed denial of service, DNS poisoning, man-in-the-middle attacks ... as one starts enumerating the number and form that attacks might take, it becomes clear how much more complex the world has become since 1986, when the first PC viruses appeared which used code that ensured they would survive the machine being restarted. For both viruses and worms, theoretical papers on the possibility of such programs were written long before they appeared 'in the wild'. One of the first was by the 'father of computing', John von Neumann, in 1949; another was by Veith Risak in a 1972 German paper which described how you could write a virus that would work on a Siemens computer. (A worm is essentially a virus which replicates itself over a network.) Another important addition to theory, and thus practice, was Fred Cohen's work which in the 1980s demonstrated that it was impossible to write an algorithm that could detect every possible virus.

Cohen's elegant theoretical proof did not put off the computer security industry, which has gone from strength to strength on the basis of catching most viruses – and playing catch-up on the remainder. The antivirus business alone was worth an estimated $23.6 billion in 2016; there's no sign of it slowing down. Even the rise of smartphones, which have led to a notional increase in personal security because the user has less power relative to the operating system (and so can't easily authorize the sort of actions that let a virus loose), hasn't daunted the antivirus vendors' enthusiasm. They offer antivirus and security programs for the billion or so Android phones.[12]

As the examples of ransomware, Wi-Fi hacking, Mirai, SQL injection and phishing show, hacking flaws and techniques tend not to appear abruptly. Often the systems and their associated flaws have been with us for decades. In the case of the Shellshock code flaw exploited in 2014, the vulnerability had existed since August 1989 – that is, 25 years. In January 2018, the computing world was stunned by the announcement of two deep-seated vulnerabilities (dubbed 'Meltdown' and 'Spectre') which exploited processor design decisions made decades earlier.

So what might the hacks of two or three decades hence look like? Let's look at a few examples.

# Speaking in tongues

**Scenario one:** You're at home, with your front door powered by a 'smart lock' which you can control with an app on your smartphone: it even works with voice commands, so all you have to say is 'unlock the door' and it does so. As you browse on your laptop, you're shown a targeted ad on a social network, with some puppies running around. You like puppies. You turn up the volume to listen to it better – and hear your front door unlock.

How? The advert, targeted specifically at you, included a 'Dolphin attack': voice instructions encoded at an ultrasonic frequency that you can't hear, but which your phone detects perfectly. A team from China's Zhejiang University demonstrated how it could be done in a paper published in November 2017.[13]

The researchers showed that the method of ultrasonic 'speech' instructions could be used to dial phone numbers, open websites and generally make smart devices do what you'd expect them to, without you realizing they've been told to.

A slightly modified version of this scenario – using a different approach – runs thus. You're at home with your phone on your table, and an advert comes on the radio; it seems to be for a horror film, with distorted voices. Silently, your phone activates and opens a website which contains a zero-day exploit that subverts your phone.

In this case, the hack is enabled by the voice assistants in Apple or Android phones, which are able to distinguish commands when humans hear only distortion. A joint team from Georgetown University and the University of California showed in summer 2016 exactly how this could be done, offering a video demonstrating the effect with and without background noise. It's the sort of subversion that could be useful to a government targeting specific people, or just to hackers looking to cause trouble.

A less harmful version was used by Burger King in April 2017 in a 15-second TV advert in the US: a character in the ad leaned into the camera and said, 'Okay Google, what is the Whopper burger?' The 'Okay Google' phrase triggered Google Home devices and Android phones, which promptly told their owners in millions of American homes what Google's top factual result (the Wikipedia entry) was. Google tweaked its systems to block the request on that ad. But Burger King tweaked it back, using different voices, and once more Google devices responded. It was a real-time evolution of a hacking technique that has plenty of room to grow.[14, 15, 16]

# Driven to distraction

**Scenario two:** You're a passenger in a new self-driving car, which is approaching a stop sign at a busy intersection. Ahead, cars are zooming across the intersection at right angles to you. The car, following the rules of the road, will have to stop and wait its turn. You're expecting it to do so, as it has done at every other junction today and previously.

The car carries on through the stop sign, and you're seriously injured in the resulting crash. Why didn't the car stop? Because someone messed with the stop sign by putting a couple of stickers on it. They're unremarkable to human eyes, but to the machine learning system deciding the car's movements, they were so radical that it didn't recognize it as a stop sign any more. A team of researchers from the universities of California, Washington, Michigan and Stony Brook demonstrated in September 2017 that they could get a neural network which normally recognized stop signs to misclassify it as an advisory speed limit sign. 'Our work does serve to high-light potential issues that future self-driving car algorithms might have to address,' the researchers wrote. Wasn't this helping hack-ers? 'No – on the contrary, we are helping manufacturers and users address potential problems before hackers can take advantage,' they commented.[17]

Such 'machine learning' (ML) systems are in their comparative infancy now, just as the personal computer business was in the 1980s. ML systems, often also called artificial intelligence (AI) systems, use 'neural networks' – interlinked computer logic systems which mimic the behaviour of neurons in the brain – to process inputs and gener-ate outputs. Train an ML system with a big set of photos of cats and dogs, and tell it that it is looking for the former and to reject the latter, and (depending on its computing power) the network will be able to tell you if the next picture you show it is a cat or not.

ML can be extraordinarily powerful. DeepMind, the British ML company bought in January 2014 by Google, developed an ML system called AlphaGo which by replaying professional games learned in a few months to play the Chinese board strategy game Go to a higher level than any deterministic program working to a set of programmed rules. Over the course of 18 months, AlphaGo beat the world's two top professionals, Lee Sedol of Korea and then China's Ke Jie. (For good measure, DeepMind then developed a new self-teaching ML system, AlphaGo Zero, which played Go against itself, and then beat AlphaGo 100 times in a row. Zero is the best Go player in the known universe.)

Because ML can tackle computing problems such as recogniz-ing photos and speech which have eluded solution for years, they are being adopted rapidly. But unlike a system reliant on obvious code and rules, you can't ask an ML system why it made a decision. There is no clear code branch that explains the decision to generate one output or another. Neural networks are essentially black boxes whose outputs we cannot predict, and which may surprise their human trainers.

A vivid example of that came when Lee Sedol was playing AlphaGo: in the second game, the computer played a move that amazed everyone watching, including the human opponent. 'That's a very strange move,' said one commentator, a Go professional. Another commented, 'I thought it was a mistake.' But Fan Hui, a European professional who had been defeated by AlphaGo during its training stages, saw it differently. 'It's not a human move,' he told *Wired*.[18]

In other words, we can't predict what will emerge from ML systems. That has naturally interested researchers in a broader question: if such systems are deployed in self-driving vehicles, and around our homes, and in our smartphones, how vulnerable are they to unexpected inputs, and what outputs could that produce?

ML systems generate their own internal explanations for the world that they are shown; we don't know how a system which identifies dogs and cats identifies them, any more than we understand how our own brains do. They're also entirely reliant on the data they're trained on – so that ML systems have displayed gender or racial bias, because of subtle pre-existing biases in their inputs. A study in April 2017 found that an AI system trained on common uses of words was more likely to associate 'female' and 'woman' with arts and humanities topics, and 'man' or 'male' with engineering and mathematical work, reflecting the biases in its learning data.[19]

An ML system that goes wrong, or gets hacked, is going to be a deep puzzle to fix. That might seem like a theoretical weakness. But the point about hacking is that weaknesses – whether in human behaviour, or systems – eventually surface and are exploited. Human behaviour, of course, is already difficult to adjust; thus designers try to get systems to replace human vicissitudes, but in turn tend to introduce new flaws to be exploited. ML systems might seem to offer no 'surface' for attack. But the greater the reliance we place on any system, the more likely we are to discover its new frailties.

## Not so smart now

**Scenario three:** You're in a city which has introduced 'smart meters' for electricity monitoring. They are internet-connected devices which monitor power usage inside the home, reporting back to the power utility as often as every half hour. For the utilities, installing them means they don't have to send expensive humans to remote locations to read meters every six months. It also lets the utilities offer variable tariffs, to switch those who default on contract payments to prepayment. *In extremis*, they can support rolling power cuts if there is a serious supply shortage.

For security, the meters communicate with the utilities using cryptographically signed communications: each end is able to check the other is who they say they are, based on the public key used to encrypt commands and responses.

It's late in the evening, in winter. Suddenly, the power goes off. You look out of the window of your high-rise flat: the entire city is dark, including the streetlights. Yet there's nothing obvious going on, and there were no warnings on the news. Your phone doesn't have any service either, because the cell towers rely on mains electricity – diesel backups aren't used in cities. It's starting to get cold.

Professor Ross Anderson of the computer science laboratory at Cambridge University is certain that smart meters amount to 'a significant new cyber-vulnerability'. In a 2010 paper with his colleague Shailendra Fuloria, they argue that any cyberattacker aiming to target a country would aim to knock out the electricity supply – 'the cyber equivalent of a nuclear strike'. In a sense, it's the opposite of a neutron bomb, which kills people but leaves buildings standing; a smart meter attack would disable the infrastructure, but (mostly) leave people unhurt.[20]

Without electricity, modern economies collapse, and might not recover. In 1996, the Irish Republican Army targeted six big electricity substations in London; had the attack succeeded it would have knocked out power to millions for months. The Iraq insurgency against US occupation forces in 2003 was partly fuelled by frustration among Iraqis at delays in restoring their power supply after the US invasion. What if, Anderson and Fuloria ask, an attacker is able to break into a smart meter system and send an order telling the meters to turn off the electricity, and then orders them to wipe or change their cryptographic keys? It would be like installing ransomware in every house's electric meter; and you might not even know if the meters could be reset. You'd have to replace them.[21]

Such a tactic would hardly be the choice of an amateur hacker. But a nation state might choose to do it as an alternative to a direct attack, with the advantage that cyberattacks don't leave missile trails back to their source.

Ransomware has already been deployed for a cyberattack, when Ukraine was badly affected by the NotPetya malware in June 2017. A piece of Ukrainian tax accounting software called MeDoc, used by around 90 per cent of the country's domestic companies, sent out an update which put ransomware on users' machines. It hit the country's national bank, public transport hubs and supermarkets.

NotPetya scared a lot of experts: it spread across internal networks in international companies, which meant that those with Ukrainian offices were affected too. Had the attack been aimed at a country with great connectedness, it could have caused 'catastrophic failure of all our systems and environments across the globe,' Dave Kennedy of the security company TrustedSec told the Associated Press. 'I mean it could have been absolutely terrifying.'[22]

All the signs were that NotPetya was a nation-state attack; and only one country, Russia, was at that time disputing Ukraine's borders. But unlike pictures of troops and missile launchers, there was no way to tie that attack to a country or group of people. You could imagine, though, that if Ukraine had been more advanced and reliant on smart electricity meters, it could have been even worse. But it was already bad enough: CyberReason put the total costs in lost revenue alone for all the companies which stated their losses at $1.2 billion by the end of 2017.[23]

As Anderson and Fuloria point out, the computer security infrastructure needed for smart meters has to be both simple enough to let any company enter the electricity market (to boost competition) while also secure enough to defeat attempts to break into them and simultaneously sufficiently future-proof that they can cope with needed software upgrades. Simple, secure, future-proof: it's the classic project management triangle, akin to 'good, cheap, fast; pick two'. Anderson disdainfully cast the idea as one dreamed up by the electricity meter industry: 'Why not replace old meters that cost £15 and last 50 years with new meters that cost £50 and lasted only 15?'[24]

Of course disrupting a country through its smart meters is just an idea in an academic paper at the moment. But so too was cryptographic ransomware with anonymous payment, once. Future nation-state attacks are likely to seek out connected infrastructure. Far easier to help your opponent's systems fail than to attack them directly. The cyber wars of the future might see a country surrender without a shot being fired; and the conquered country might be unsure even who to surrender to.

## Protect and survive

Bearing those scenarios in mind, how do we cope with the warfare of the future, where individuals and companies are under assault from amateurs, for-profit professionals and state actors?

From John Podesta's lack of two-factor authentication, to TalkTalk's sprawling collection of web systems, to TJX's reliance on an encryption standard that was flawed from the start, to the ability of ransomware to spread from an email, it's clear that there are two parallel sets of failings in the industry, especially around personal data. First, the costs arising from the risks and consequences of being hacked, which should be the responsibility of the providers – of email, of credit card storage for billing you – have instead been loaded onto the user. Why aren't you *obliged* to set up two-factor authorization on any webmail address (Google, Yahoo, Hotmail etc) that you've owned for more than a certain period? Why aren't companies *obliged* to announce when they discover they've been hacked? Why don't they have to make some sort of restitution to users who might have been affected?

Car makers, by contrast, seem to be in a constant lather of mandatory recalls and fixes. Certainly it matters that a runaway car can kill someone, while a runaway set of data – such as Equifax's – will only create hassle and annoyance for millions; there's no metric of suffering to give us an idea of their equivalence. Equifax, though, did show astonishing chutzpah by offering to freeze and/or monitor the credit of anyone who wanted – free for a year, paid after that. In other words, you'd end up paying Equifax for its having failed to protect your data. It was like the old joke about the child killing its parents and then pleading for clemency as an orphan. In response, two US senators introduced legislation in January 2018 with mandatory payments to customers if a credit reporting agency is hacked.

The second failing is in not avoiding such outcomes in the first place. As Tufecki says, neglect and underinvestment are the clearest pointers towards such run-of-the-mill hacks. This book has tried to show the combination of targeted attacks (HBGary, Sony Pictures, John Podesta) and random commercial attacks (ransomware, TJX, TalkTalk, Mirai). The hacks you hear about again and again on the news tend to be the random, commercial ones. By December 2017, they tended to be about hacks of bitcoin exchanges, where the notional value of the hack was in the millions because of the virtual currency's spiralling value. But it's notable that of the targeted ones described here, two were by state-sponsored actors, and the other by a federated group uninterested in monetary gain.

Yet if we live in an age of thunderstorms and lightning strikes, what are the best strategies for coping?

When I spoke to ex-hackers and security experts whose job is to protect against their successors, the message was consistent. You can't stop people trying to break in; you should probably accept that people will do. The answer is to look at what happens when someone has broken in to your system: how safe is it then? Can you control where an intruder goes? Can you watch as they try to traverse the network? Can you shut down access to them – in effect, to your own users?

Then there is the difficulty of protecting against everything. Sometimes, as with Sony, the lightning strikes out of a clear blue sky. Sometimes, as with HBGary, you might have an inkling that you're walking around in the rain holding a metal pole aloft. But nowadays, the tools available to the youngest would-be hackers are as powerful as those available to a trained nation-state hacker 15 years ago. TalkTalk's server flaw was discovered by a 16-year-old who said he was just trying to impress his friends. But would it have made any difference if it had been found by a terrorist organization? The threats are now pervasive and insistent.

For the average company, three hacking developments over the past five years seem to have made them rethink their approach to cybersecurity. The first is the rapid rise of ransomware, which turns the usual idea of hacking – someone else getting access to your data – on its head: now the problem is that you can't get at your data. That constitutes a serious risk to the business continuity of any organization, while for the malware's controllers it can be a comparatively easy way to make money, especially now that bitcoin enables almost untraceable payment.

The second is the growth in the use of embedded systems – the 'Internet of Things' (IoT). Both hackers and security experts I spoke to expressed concern about the risk that IoT systems pose, because of the breadth and hurried nature of their deployment, and the poor security model that they tend to embody. 'Fit and forget' is a good slogan for a product. But the internet doesn't forget that something is connected to it – and making such systems secure is harder than expected.

The third development is the emergence of countries such as North Korea and Iran as quiet, malicious players willing to disrupt and steal. That demonstrates that companies can't now ignore nation-state threats; everything is political, including trade and culture, and disruption of both has become both easier and more deniable as the internet has enabled a proxy war to be fought between countries.

Is there any good news? It may be too soon to answer. We know that we can't make every system secure, and that hackers' curiosity will never abate. But car crashes used to be far more lethal until manufacturers were forced by regulation to include safety features. Software is still a comparatively young industry, where it's easier to gain plaudits for making something than it is for making it secure.

Perhaps the data breaches we see in modern hacking are like the ozone hole: something which can be fixed by collective effort. The worry is that they are actually like climate change – and that everyone will wait for others to take affirmative action, while trying to make their own small positive impact.

# References

1 Q239, oral evidence: cyber security: protection of personal data online, Culture, Media and Sport Committee HC 587, 27 January 2016. Available from: http://data.parliament.uk/writtenevidence/committeeevidence.svc/evidencedocument/culture-media-and-sport-committee/cyber-security-protection-of-personal-data-online/oral/28091.html

2 Goodin, D (2017) Failure to patch two-month-old bug led to massive Equifax breach, Ars Technica, 14 September. Available from: https://arstechnica.com/information-technology/2017/09/massive-equifax-breach-caused-by-failure-to-patch-two-month-old-bug/

3 Prepared testimony of Richard F Smith, US House Committee on Energy and Commerce, 3 October 2017. Available from: http://docs.house.gov/meetings/IF/IF17/20171003/106455/HHRG-115-IF17-Wstate-SmithR-20171003.pdf

4 Tufecki, Z (2017) Equifax's maddening unaccountability, *New York Times*, 11 September. Available from: www.nytimes.com/2017/09/11/opinion/equifax-accountability-security.html

5 San Bernardino phone hack 'cost FBI more than $1m', BBC News, 22 April 2016. Available from: www.bbc.co.uk/news/technology-36110236

6 Marczak, B and Scott-Railton, J (2016) The million dollar dissident: NSO group's iPhone zero-days used against a UAE human rights defender, *The Citizen Lab*, 24 August. Available from: https://citizenlab.ca/2016/08/million-dollar-dissident-iphone-zero-day-nso-group-uae/

7 The internet bug bounty, *hackerone.com*, May 2014. Available from: www.hackerone.com/internet-bug-bounty

8 personal conversation

9 Mackenzie, H (2012) Shamoon malware and SCADA security – what are the impacts?, *Tofino Security*, 25 September. Available from: www.tofinosecurity.com/blog/shamoon-malware-and-scada-security---what-are-impacts

10 Perlroth, N (2012) In cyberattack on Saudi firm, U.S. sees Iran firing back, *New York Times*, 23 October. Available from: www.nytimes.com/2012/10/24/business/global/cyberattack-on-saudi-oil-firm-disquiets-us.html

**11** Riley, M and Engleman, E (2012) Code in Aramco cyber attack indicates lone perpetrator, *Unatech*, 25 October. Available from: www.unatech.com/2012/10/29/code-in-aramco-cyber-attack-indicates-lone-perpetrator/

**12** Gartner says worldwide security software market grew 3.7 percent in 2015, gartner.com, 14 July 2016. Available from: www.gartner.com/doc/3698417/market-share-security-software-worldwide

**13** Zhang, G, *et al* (2017) DolphinAttack: inaudible voice commands, *Zhejiang University*, 30 October. Available from: https://arxiv.org/pdf/1708.09537.pdf

**14** Carlini, N, *et al* (2016) Hidden voice commands, *Georgetown University*, June. Available from: www.hiddenvoicecommands.com

**15** Demo voicehack, *YouTube*, 25 June 2016. Available from: www.youtube.com/watch?v=HvZAZFztlO0&feature=youtu.be

**16** Snider, M (2017) Burger King just won't stop trolling Google Home, *USA Today*, 13 April. Available from: www.usatoday.com/story/tech/talkingtech/2017/04/13/burger-king-just-wont-stop-trolling-google-home/100410776/

**17** Evtimov, I, *et al* (2017) Robust physical-world attacks on deep learning models, IoT/CPS Security Research at the University of Michigan, 13 September. Available from: https://arxiv.org/pdf/1707.08945.pdf

**18** Metz, C (2016) The sadness and beauty of watching Google's AO play Go, *Wired*, 11 March. Available from: www.wired.com/2016/03/sadness-beauty-watching-googles-ai-play-go/

**19** Devlin, H (2017) AI programs exhibit racial and gender biases, research reveals, *Guardian*, 13 April. Available from: www.theguardian.com/technology/2017/apr/13/ai-programs-exhibit-racist-and-sexist-biases-research-reveals

**20** Anderson, R and Fuloria, S (2010) Who controls the off switch?, Cambridge University Computer Laboratory, 23 July. Available from: www.cl.cam.ac.uk/~rja14/Papers/meters-offswitch.pdf

**21** Bennetto, J (1997) How IRA plotted to switch off London, *Independent*, 11 April. Available from: www.independent.co.uk/news/how-ira-plotted-to-switch-off-london-1266533.html

**22** Bajak, F and Satter, R (2017) Companies still hobbled from fearsome cyberattack, Associated Press, 30 June. Available from:

www.apnews.com/ce7a8aca506742ab8e8873e7f9f229c2/
Companies-still-hobbled-from-fearsome-cyberattack

**23** O'Connor, F (2017) NotPetya still roils companies finances,
costing organisations $1.2 billion in revenue, *CyberReason
blog*, 9 November. Available from: www.cybereason.com/blog/
notpetya-costs-companies-1.2-billion-in-revenue

**24** Anderson, R (2017) No one's noticed, but the Tories are quietly
killing off the smart meter revolution, *Daily Telegraph*, 23 May.
Available from: www.telegraph.co.uk/money/consumer-affairs/
no-ones-noticed-tories-quietly-killing-smart-meter-revolution/

# INDEX